PAPAL CRUSADING POLICY

1244—1291

STUDIES IN THE HISTORY
OF
CHRISTIAN THOUGHT

EDITED BY

HEIKO A. OBERMAN, Tübingen

IN COOPERATION WITH

HENRY CHADWICK, Oxford
EDWARD A. DOWEY, Princeton, N.J.
JAROSLAV PELIKAN, New Haven, Conn.
BRIAN TIERNEY, Ithaca, N.Y.
E. DAVID WILLIS, San Anselmo, California

VOLUME XI

MAUREEN PURCELL

PAPAL CRUSADING POLICY

LEIDEN
E. J. BRILL
1975

PAPAL CRUSADING POLICY

The Chief Instruments of Papal Crusading Policy
and Crusade to the Holy Land
from the final loss of Jerusalem to the fall of Acre

1244-1291

BY

MAUREEN PURCELL

LEIDEN
E. J. BRILL
1975

ISBN 90 04 04317 9

PRINTED IN THE NETHERLANDS

CONTENTS

SECTION C

THE PAPACY AND MATERIAL AID TO *CRUCESIGNATI*

ACKNOWLEDGEMENTS

I wish to express my gratitude to Professor Dr. H. A. Oberman, Direktor, Institut für Reformationsgeschichte der Universität Tübingen, for including this work in the series of which he is the editor, namely, *Studies in the History of Christian Thought*.

I should also like to express my gratitude to the University of New England, N.S.W., Australia, for the grant of a scholarship which enabled me to carry out the research necessary to produce this book, and for a further grant to assist in its publication.

I wish to thank the editors of *The Journal of Religious History* for permission to incorporate material published in that Journal.

MAUREEN PURCELL

LIST OF ABBREVIATIONS

It has been found convenient to use the following abbreviations for works mentioned in footnotes. Full details of these books will be found in the Bibliography on the pages indicated.

St. Albert, *IV Sent.*   Albert, St., *Opera Omnia,Commentarii in IV Sententiarum*, p. 203.

Alexander of Hales,   Alexander of Hales, *Glossa in Quatuor Libros Senten-*
    Glossa IV Sent.   *tiarum Petri Lombardi*, p. 203.

Apparatus   Innocent IV, *In Quinque Libros Decretalium*, p. 205.

St. Bonaventure, *IV Sent.*   Bonaventure, St., *In Quartum Librum Sententiarum Magistri Petri Lombardi*, p. 204.

Bongars   *Gesta Dei per Francos*, p. 202.

C.P.L., I   *Calendar of Entries in the Papal Registers*, Vol. I, p. 202.

Cantilupe   Cantilupe, Thomas, *Registrum Thome de Cantilupo*, p. 204.

Constitutiones   "Constitutiones pro zelo fidei", in Finke, p. 204, and in Appendix A.

Correspondance   Alphonse of Poitiers, *Correspondance administrative*
    administrative   *d'Alfonse de Poitiers*, p. 203.

del Giudice   Charles of Anjou, *Codice diplomatico del regno di Carlo I e II d'Angio*, p. 204.

Giffard   Giffard, Walter, *The Register of Walter Giffard*, p. 204.

Hefele-Leclercq   Hefele-Leclercq, *Histoire des Conciles*, p. 209.

Hostiensis, *Summa Aurea*   Hostiensis, *Summa Aurea*, p. 205.

John Le Romeyn   Le Romeyn, John, *The Register of John Le Romeyn*, p. 205.

Joinville   Joinville, Jean de, *Histoire de Saint Louis*, p. 205.

Journal des visites   Rigaud, Eude, *Journal des visites pastorales d'Eude Rigaud*, p. 206.

Kaltenbrunner   *Actenstücke zur Geschichte des Deutschen Reiches*, p. 202.

Layettes   *Layettes du Trésor des Chartes*, p. 202.

Lunt, *Financial*   Lunt, W. E., *Financial Relations of the Papacy with*
    Relations   *England to 1327*, p. 209.

Lunt, *Papal Revenues*   Lunt, W. E., *Papal Revenues in the Middle Ages*, p. 209.

Mansi   *Sacrorum Conciliorum nova et amplissima collectio*, p. 203.

M.G.H. SS   *Monumenta Germaniae Historica, Scriptores*, p. 202.

Northern Registers   *Historical Papers and Letters from the Northern Registers*, p. 202.

Matthew Paris   Paris, Matthew, *Chronica majora*, p. 206.

Paulus   Paulus, N., *Geschichte des Ablasses im Mittelalter*, p. 210.

Peckham   Peckham, John, *Registrum Epistolarum Fratris Johannis Peckham*, p. 206.

Potthast   *Regesta pontificum Romanorum*, p. 203.

Quaest. Quod.   Aquinas, St. Thomas, *Quaestiones Quodlibetales*, p. 203.

Raynaldus   Raynaldus-Baronius, *Annales Ecclesiastici*, p. 206.

Regesta Regni   ed. Röhricht, p. 203.
    Hierosolymitani

Register   This is used for the series of papal registers in the

	Bibliothèque des Ecoles françaises d'Athènes et de Rome, each of which is in the Bibliography, part (ii), under the name of the pope concerned.
Riant, *Expéditions et pèlerinages*	*Expéditions et pèlerinages des Scandinaves en Terre Sainte au temps des croisades*, p. 210.
Ripoll	*Bullarium Ordinis FF. Praedicatorum*, p. 202.
Rymer	*Foedera, Conventiones, Literae*, etc., p. 202.
S.T.	Aquinas, St. Thomas, *Summa Theologiae*, p. 204.
Salimbene	Salimbene de Adam, *Chronica*, p. 206.
Sbaralea	*Bullarium Franciscanum Romanorum Pontificum*, p. 202.
Sternfeld	*Ludwigs des Heiligen Kreuzzug nach Tunis*, p. 211.
Theiner	*Vetera Monumenta hibernorum*, p. 203.
Wickwane	Wickwane, William, *The Register of William Wickwane*, p. 207.
William of Auxerre, *Summa Aurea*	William of Auxerre, *Summa Aurea in quattuor libros sententiarum*, p. 207.

SECTION A

INTRODUCTION

CHAPTER ONE

DEVELOPMENT OF THE IDEA OF CRUSADE

(a) General Introduction

Thirteenth century crusade presents the not uncommon problem of a movement caught between rapid advances in the competence and efficiency of its organisational forms, and an equally rapid decline in internal coherence. Like all forms of imperialism, crusade produced a frame of mind which outlasted the movement itself, and was incapable of recognising its own proper demise. In part this breakdown in coherence was the consequence of increasing concentration on the instruments of papal crusading policy as means to ends other than crusade to the Holy Land; in part it was the result of a dualism inherent in crusade from its inception. In either case the breakdown was at once intensified, and yet disguised, by the very efficiency of the machinery employed. To contemporaries it was by no means immediately apparent, for example, how far indulgence had come to supersede crusade as an instrument of wider papal policy, because ostensibly there remained an intimate link between the two. All plenary indulgences were still crusading indulgences, or at least indulgences "as for the Holy Land".

In effect, traditional crusade was no longer the inevitable, nor even the most usual, objective of its own organisational forms, and was in practice treated as an ever more remote alternative to both plenary indulgence and the redemption of crusading vows; it had thus become an anomaly. As a *vital* ideal crusade suffered an immense setback on the fields of Hattin, but though no longer vital, it survived until the fall of Acre when it rapidly became either merely an ideal stamping ground for political theorists, or a conveniently distractive appellation for the interested policies of cynical politicians. Even as the rallying cry of the sincere Christian reformer like Catherine of Siena it was a thoroughly subordinate means, and not an end in itself.[1] It is as if

---

[1] At the very outset of the Great Schism, Catherine of Siena tried to urge a crusade against the infidel for the purposes of converting them, and of regaining the Holy Places, but more especially to unite the dissident parties in the West; cf. her letter to John Hawkwood in E. Dupré Theseider, *Epistolario di Santa Caterina da Siena* (Fonti per la Storia d'Italia), Rome, 1940, i, No. 30. See also

Pius II, *crucesignatus*, dying on the shores of Ancona, deserted by princes and mercenaries alike, were a man trying in vain to find his way back into an heroic age.

The dualism inherent in crusade did not become wholly explicit until the thirteenth century, and even then, long established modes of thought precluded recognition of the fact. While the first crusaders would have considered that their corporate *raison d'être*, and ultimate aim, was to wage holy war on the infidel in order to recover the Holy Places, the papacy was activated by more basic Christian principles, at once of greater universal application and yet more closely related to Christian unity and current notions of papal supremacy. There was thus, even initially, a real stress between crusade seen in terms of the immediate Christian objective, and crusade accommodated to a longer, more complex view of the Christian economy of salvation. What followed from this initial duality was a not immediately perceptible dichotomy between the direct, and the indirect, developments in crusading thought and practice. Although not in every detail, nor in every single instance, twelfth century crusading ventures generally preserved an appearance of harmonising the divergent elements. This impression was heightened by the fact that crusades such as those against the Slavs were roughly simultaneous with and somehow, therefore, assimilated to ventures to the Holy Land, or were otherwise not considered equivalent in terms of indulgences and subsidies[2]. It was not until the thirteenth century that the two elements came to be separated in time, as in objective, without there being even then a clear sign from those most intimately concerned of their recognition of the need for a complete redefinition of crusade.

Awareness of the dichotomy does show itself momentarily from time to time in official documents where some pains were taken to

---

Nos 32, 33, 35, 39, 40, 41, 50, 52, 53, 54, 63, 68, 74, including letters to Queen Joanna of Naples, to Gregory XI, to Queen Elizabeth of Hungary, and a number of important fellow countrymen, such as the Signoria of Florence.

[2] In the twelfth century crusaders against the Slavs, with very few exceptions, were granted an indulgence of one year; cf. P. Riant, *Expéditions et pèlerinages des Scandinaves en Terre Sainte au temps des Croisades*, Paris, 1865, pp. 304 f. On the fluctuations in policy in the twelfth century concerning the granting of indulgences to crusades other than those to the Holy Land see N. Paulus, *Geschichte des Ablasses im Mittelalter vom Ursprunge bis zur Mitte des 14 Jahrhunderts*, 3 Vols in 2, Paderborn, 1922-23, especially i, Chapter V, and A. Gottlob, *Kreuzablass und Almosenablass*, Stuttgart, 1906, especially Chapters III-V. For an analysis of the geographical diversion of crusade see O. Volk, *Die Abendländische-Hierarchische Kreuzzugidee*, Halle, 1911.

link the divergent movements. The anti-Hohenstaufen crusade to Sicily, for example, was spoken of in terms of the importance of the Sicilian campaign to the Holy Land, a fact which makes Sicily eminently "cruciabilis".[3] On the whole, however, explanation and excuse were not forthcoming; either they were taken for granted, or were considered unnecessary, and by the mid-thirteenth century this almost total official blindness led to increasingly separate, and often inimical, crusading ventures. Less ambivalent attitudes are to be found in critics of papal politics such as Walther von der Vogelweide, pro-crusading reformers such as Humbert de Romans, and missionary zealots like William of Tripoli, all of whom suggested that the movement had lost its integrity, and needed urgently to be reformed, revitalised, or suppressed.

The above remarks are a commonplace in the history of the development of crusade. What remains a necessity is a close scrutiny of the detailed application of the major instruments of papal crusading policy, and their gradual absorption into other forms of activity, sufficiently tied to the notion of crusade at once to wrench asunder the traditional framework, and to preclude any effective revitalisation of that tradition. It is the intention of this work to enter into just such a detailed examination of the day to day use and abuse of the major instruments of papal crusading policy, and thus to estimate the extent to which crusade was destroyed by the organisational forms still being wielded in its name. The chief instruments so to come under review will be indulgences, redemption and commutation of crusading vows, and the grants to the *crucesignati*[4] of subsidies, privileges, protections and immunities; there will be some consideration given to the use of ecclesiastical sanctions as a means of ensuring the proper

---

[3] Cf. *Les Registres d'Innocent IV*, ed. E. Berger (Bibliothèque des Ecoles françaises d'Athènes et de Rome), 4 vols, Paris, 1884-1921, No. 6818. Clement was even more emphatic: "Cum promotio negotii terre sancte et Constantinopolitani imperii a negotio regni Sicilie pro majori parte dependere noscatur, nos attendentes quod facilior erit eorumdem terre ac imperii liberatio, si hujusmodi ejusdem regni negotium fuerit efficaciter, Deo favente, promotum . . ." See *Les Registres de Clément IV*, ed. E. Jordan (Bibliothèque des Ecoles françaises d'Athènes et de Rome), Paris, 1893-1945, No. 216.

[4] For the purposes of this discussion it seems both valid and necessary to distinguish between *crusader* as the word is used in everyday language, and *crucesignatus*. Whereas the term *crusader* is now generally applied to a man who actually took part in a crusade, *crucesignatus* was the term used in formal documents to describe someone who had taken the cross but who had not yet necessarily fulfilled his crusading vow.

functioning of these instruments and some attention will necessarily be paid to the relationship of the papacy to the various organising officials, with the crusade leaders both ecclesiastical and lay, and with the three great Military Orders.[5]

However, the personnel involved in the organisation and conduct of the crusades are more clearly symptomatic of the effects produced by the changing orientation of the instruments of crusading policy and as such they will serve rather as illustrations of the conclusions drawn from the examination of the more theoretically objective instruments. The period covered extends from the final loss of Jerusalem in 1244 to the ultimate disappearance of the mainland Crusader States with the fall of Acre in 1291, a half century as conclusive in its own way for the post-Hildebrandine papacy and for the Holy Roman Empire as it was for crusade. Of the twelve pontificates which this period roughly covers, not all are of equal importance for the purposes of this study, an inequality not always related to the length of the pontificate.

There is a sense in which it is true to affirm that the fall of Acre in 1291 was a concluding, rather than a conclusive, event in the destruction of the Syrian Crusader States; the precise timing of the fall is almost wholly irrelevant to any consideration of its causes. The remnants of the mainland Kingdom had been living on borrowed time for over a decade before the final *coup de grâce*. The delay was the result neither of any last effort at internal cohesion and strength on the part of the native Franks, which had made the Moslems hold off, nor of any efficacious crusading threat from the West; it depended almost entirely on fortuitous circumstances within Islam itself. By the twelve-eighties not only had crusade and its organisational forms been driven undeniably and irrevocably apart in the West, but so also had the Syrian Franks been driven far from any notion of corporate crusading purpose and existence. Not only had the forms of crusading policy in the West been divorced from any essential connection with the Holy Land, but the Eastern Crusader States had themselves become so absorbed in the exigencies of day to day survival as to have lost any sense of a *raison d'être* which transcended that of any other kingdom.

This study necessitates, then, an examination of the details of

---

[5] The last are, of course, a special case, and have already been the subject of detailed studies which, while not undertaken with quite the same aims as this, yet provide an abundance of relevant material.

papal crusading policy not only in relation to the West, but alongside, and in the light of, developments in the Frankish East itself, increasingly alienated as it was subjectively and objectively from crusade. Ricoldo de Monte Croce, writing his lament over the fall of Acre, found that the age-old mystical solution to the problem of the suffering servants of Christ produced no intellectual satisfaction on a severely practical level. Why, he asked, was no aid forthcoming, and his cry may be taken as expressing the bewilderment of a great many of his contemporaries.[6] Why, in fact, practical assistance was not available, is the basic query which underlies the whole discussion which follows in succeeding chapters.

How far did thirteenth century variants in the concept of crusade have their source and rationale in the ordinary historical development of the movement? As precise an answer as possible to this question is essential if one is to avoid the danger of a *simpliste* view, not altogether absent in certain historians from contemporary commentators onwards, that crusade was a holy war to, or on direct behalf of, the Holy Land and that anything else was a manipulation, or a borrowing, of the term.[7] Like all archetypes, the First Crusade suffered from being treated as an exact theoretical model, whereas practical allowances had to be made for sometimes violently altered circumstances, as in fact were produced by the impact of the First Crusade itself. There may still arise a certain amount of controversy about the relative importance of various background events in shaping the First Crusade, but that these events were influential is not in doubt.

---

[6] "Quapropter de tua plene benignitate confisus quero, peto, pulso, ut hostia michi divine misericordie patefiat et ecclesia, que in partibus orientalibus tanto patet contemptui apud infideles et sub persecutione Sarracenorum gravissime afflicta lacrimabiliter ingemiscit, divino citius auxilio roborata plenius consoletur. Pro responsione denique theorica gratias ago, practicam vero nichilominus affectuose atque indesinenter expeto"; from *Archives de l'Orient latin*, ed. R. Röhricht, Paris 1884, ii, Documents, p. 296.

[7] Contemporary opinions varied enormously as can be seen by referring to such a work as Palmer A. Throop, *Criticism of the Crusade*, Amsterdam, 1940, covering a restricted number of writers over a restricted period of time. For modern historians one may take as an example a definition of crusade given by P. Riant in *Archives de l'Orient latin*, Paris, 1881, i, 2. Crusade was "la guerre religieuse, proprement dite, provoquée par l'octroi solennel de privilèges ecclésiastiques, et *entreprise pour le recouvrement direct ou indirect des Lieux Saints*" (Italics mine). This sort of assumption about the nature of crusade determined, for example, the shape of such works as Sir Stephen Runciman, *A History of the Crusades*, 3 vols, Cambridge, 1951-54, and R. Grousset, *Histoire des Croisades et du Royaume franc de Jérusalem*, 3 vols, Paris, 1934-36.

Cluny's part in the Spanish *reconquista* may be subject to question, but not so the seminal influence of the anti-Islamic campaigns in Spain, and of the increasing boldness and prowess of the thrusting Italian fleets in the Mediterranean in the latter half of the eleventh century. Gregory VII's plan himself to lead an army to recover the Holy Places, was, like so many of that pontiff's plans, full of deep political intent; like them, too, it was seemingly abortive, though powerful of developments after Gregory's death. Victory over the Emperor of Germany, and over the anti-pope Clement III, permitted Urban II to revive Gregory's project. Urban's position was not secure enough, however, to allow him to revive the project *in toto*; he could not afford to lead the forces of Christendom in person. The venture was to be a triumphal expression of Western assent to the *fait accompli* of Hildebrandine papal supremacy. Western Christendom, thus united, could afford to turn its attention to the task of putting an end to the Greek schism, formally half a century old at the time of the Council of Clermont, but it was not so united that it could afford politically a reunion which would in any way call papal supremacy into question. Crusade thus constituted a carefully oblique approach to the settlement of the schism, an approach which skirted the central political and theological points of contention.

Granted the papacy's wish to find an expression worthy of the newly created sense of Christian unity, an expression which would at the same time deepen and intensify that unity; granted also the need to find a theologically, and politically, neutral cause for unifying co-operation with the Greeks, there still remains the question of the choice of holy war for the recovery of the Holy Places, already centuries in the possession of the infidel. The choice of a particular means was absolutely secondary to papal aims, but constituted the core and centre of the notion of crusade in action. The question of Christian attitudes to the use of war was an ancient controversy in the Church; from its inception the particular form of holy war which was crusade became the norm for the majority of Christians.[8] While

---

[8] Cf. M. Villey, *La croisade: Essai sur la formation d'une théorie juridique*, Paris, 1942, especially the Introduction (with Bibliography p. 21, note 1), and a shorter summary, "L'idée de la croisade chez les juristes du moyen-âge", in *Relazioni* del X Congresso internazionale di scienze storiche, Rome, 1955, Vol. III, *Storia del Medioevo*, Florence, 1955, pp. 565-594. For more general and exhaustive discussions of holy war as such see A. M. Vanderpol, *La doctrine scholastique du droit de guerre*, Paris, 1919, and R. H. W. Regout, *La doctrine de la guerre juste de St. Augustin à nos jours*, Paris, 1934.

circumstances did not demand otherwise the papacy acquiesced in this general view, but remained aware of the fact that crusade was merely one particular means of achieving a particular end, an end itself subordinate to more universal needs of Christendom. There is a striking and, in this context, not wholly negligible, analogy between the common notion of crusade and the scholastic formulation of the doctrine of the Incarnation in its relation to the Redemption. God's incarnation was condign, not necessary; redemption could have been achieved otherwise, but since God had chosen the mode of becoming man, it was impossible for the Christian to conceive any means of salvation more befitting the love of God, and the dignity of man.[9] In the same way it was impossible for most Christians during the high crusading period to conceive of any expression of the aspirations of Christendom more fitting than holy war in aid of Jerusalem, and all that it symbolised. As in their refined discussions of the mode of the redemption, scholastic theologians sometimes seem to lose sight of the end, so Christendom sometimes lost sight of the fact that crusade was essentially a means, not an end. Hence it also neglected to take into account the inherent dualism of crusade, or in any practical way to attempt to reconcile, or counteract, this duality.

In finally deciding why crusade was chosen, rather than any other kind of effort, one has obviously to look to the West for the immediately determinative factors. These are to be found, and, indeed, have been analysed at length, in the stage of feudal development in certain sections of the West, and in the social and economic problems to which that developing feudalism gave rise. There are already adequate discussions of this aspect of the beginnings of crusade in relation to demographic expansion, and the diversion of feudal military energies from finding expression within the confines of Christendom itself.[10] An ordinary imperialistic war, even against the pagans on the Eastern frontiers of Europe, would scarcely have served the purpose of symbolising a specifically Christian unity. On

---

[9] This is not to ignore the errors concerning the doctrine from Arius to Abelard and on through the ages. Even with the heresiarchs, the question was not of the fittingness, but of the nature of the incarnation, as similarly the question came to be of the nature of crusade.

[10] Crusade bibliographies provide ample reference for these discussions. The latest such bibliographies are those of A. S. Atiya, *The Crusade, historiography and bibliography*, Bloomington, Ind., 1962, J. A. Brundage, *The Crusades, A Documentary Survey*, Milwaukee, Wis., 1962, and H. E. Mayer, *Bibliographie zur Geschichte der Kreuzzüge*, Hanover, 1960.

the other hand, individual Christians had long since been taking considerable penitential risks to visit the Holy Places as pilgrims, for
their soul's salvation; instinctively Christians felt that these Holy
Places were peculiarly theirs, and longed for their repossession.
Whatever the linking of pilgrimage to the Holy Places with holy
war for the recovery of these Holy Places may have effected on a
spiritual level, psychologically it became one of the most creative
ideas in the history of mankind. From the point of view of human
motivation it provided an irresistible combination of spiritual and
temporal rewards, the one by the donation of the pope, the other by
his sanction. While the whole movement was initiated and loosely
directed by the papacy, participation was voluntary after the manner of
feudal volition—and the scope for personal gain was limited only by
the circumstances of the venture or by individual capacity to profit
by these circumstances. The question of material gain as an incentive
to the unarmed pilgrims who accompanied the first two crusades
in large numbers is not only impossible to judge, but relatively speaking, insignificant. Crusading history is essentially concerned with
the magnates, not with the lower orders, though it is unlikely the
latter should have been motivated solely by higher considerations.[11]

From the first, and archetypal, crusade, there emerged not only
a duality on the most profound level of ideology but, on the level of
practical action, an irreducible minimum requirement for conformity
to the concept of a true crusade. Allowing for the changes wrought
by the success of the First Crusade, and by the very nature of that
success, in the conduct of all subsequent ventures "overseas", it is
possible to separate and define these abiding characteristics. *Crusade
was a permanently possible expression of Christian faith and unity, sponsored*

---

[11] Gerhoh of Reichersberg's comment on the unarmed pilgrims accompanying
the Second Crusade is terse, and to the point: "Multitudo namque etiam rusti-
canorum ac servorum dominorum suorum relictis aratris ac servitiis ignorantibus
quoque nonnulli vel invitis dominis, parum aut nichil auri vel argenti habentes,
inconsulte expeditionem illam longissimam arripuerant, sperantes in tam sancto
negotio, sicut olim antiquo illi Israelitarum populo vel pluente desuper celo vel
undecumque celitus ac divinitus amministranda fore victualia. Sed longe aliud
quam sperabant evenit" (*De investigatione Antichristi*, Lib. I, § 59, printed in
Monumenta Germaniae Historica, Libelli de Lite, iii, pp. 374-375). The question lends
itself admirably to the theme of *The Pursuit of the Millenium* by N. Cohn, London,
1957, but one must accept this discussion with all the reserve one usually accords
such explorations of mass movements, more especially of mass psychological
phenomena. A more sober discussion is to be found in the works of P. Alphandéry,
particularly his posthumous publication, *La Chrétienté et l'idée de Croisade* (text
established by A. Dupront), 2 vols, Paris, 1954-59, *passim*.

*by the pope, organised by his officials, offering participants certain spiritual
and temporal advantages, and directed at the conduct of a holy war against
the enemies of the Church, whose specific crime consisted in their threat to the
unity of Christendom which unity was symbolised by the material possession
of Jerusalem. The spiritual nature of the crusader's intentions was made
explicit by a vow, and signified externally by his wearing the cross.*[12]

The continuity in this concept of crusade masked for the uncritical
the ultimately more powerful dualism, and the two distinct lines of
development to which this dualism gave rise. The continuous elements, because more readily observable, came to constitute the classic,
or traditional, notion of crusade; divergencies from the norm such as
conditional vows, for instance, because they seemed not to arise from
well-established precedents, appeared to the critical observer to be
even more basically divergent than in the last analysis they were.
Policy sometimes dictated a deliberate confusion of the two elements
before the thirteenth century, but most often the confusion arose from
a simple lack of awareness of any fundamental contradiction or
double thinking. The direct developments in the crusading movement,
namely those which may be said to conform in intention, if not always
in detailed application, with the restricted traditional notion of
crusade, may be summarised briefly. They do not require extended
discussion here because they have hitherto received far more attention than have the less direct developments.

(b) TRADITIONAL CRUSADE

The possession of the Holy Places led to the establishment of
protective Crusader States whose simple *raison d'être* that possession
constituted. Initially not regarded primarily as politically important
per se, the Crusader States had to rely on the West for military support
to offset their own inadequate numbers, and for the same reason
they had perforce to adopt a broader tolerance towards neighbouring Moslems than was understood in the West. Political independence in the Frankish East of necessity accorded ill with certain
elements in the traditional concept of crusade, and led to divergent
attitudes towards the object of crusade in East and West. The nature of
the victory won by the First Crusade dictated not only the geographical but also the political shape of the Latin Kingdom; subsequent
Western ventures tended at once to foster and frustrate political

---

[12] Compare this with the definition by Riant quoted on p. 7, note 7, above.

independence in the Crusader States. The demands of the Kingdom
of Jerusalem were urgently military, though there was a chronic
lack of settlers on all levels of society except that of the commercial
classes who were, in any case, far more interested in large profits
than in long term political security.[13] Because of the vital need for
increasing the military strength of the Frankish East, there were two
major developments in crusade—the evolution of the Military
Orders intended to constitute a permanent source of papally-control-
led, a-political soldiery, and the discouragement of unarmed pilgrims from hindering by their presence the military effectiveness of
crusades from the West.[14] While emphasis in the West was thus
placed more firmly on holy war than on pilgrimage, in the Frankish
East the stress was on the establishment of a viable feudal state capable of independent political action, and freed from the worse
implications of the siege mentality which its situation tended to
develop.

The major direct developments in crusading policy were concerned
with the more precise definition and specification of spiritual and
temporal advantages accruing to the persons of *crucesignati*. These
inevitably resulted from growing organisational skill, as much as
from the need to supply fresh inducements to take the cross, in the

---

[13] On the subject of colonisation in Frankish Syria and the problems which
it poses, cf. for example, E. Rey, *Les colonies franques de Syrie au XIIe et XIIIe
siècles*, Paris, 1883; C. Cahen, *La Syrie du nord à l'époque des Croisades et la principauté
franque d'Antioche*, Paris, 1940, especially Part II, Chapter V; and "Notes sur
l'histoire des croisades et de l'orient latin", Part II, in *Bulletin de la Faculté des
Lettres de Strasbourg*, No. 28-29, 1949-51, pp. 286-310; J. Prawer, "The Settlement
of the Latins in Jerusalem", *Speculum*, XXVII, 1952, pp. 490-503; "La noblesse
et le régime féodal du royaume latin de Jerusalem", *Le Moyen-Age*, LXV, 1959,
pp. 41-74, and "Etude préliminaire sur les sources et la composition du 'Livre
des Assises des Bourgeois' ", *Revue historique de droit français et étranger*, 4th series,
32nd year, 1954, No. 2, pp. 198-227, especially pp. 221-2. It is to be noted that
Hostiensis specifically excludes artisans and peasants from the commutation of
vows to go to the Holy Land because of their potential utility; cf. *Summa Aurea*,
Lyons, 1588, III, tit. De voto § 12 (Qualiter &).
[14] Unarmed pilgrims and poverty-stricken *crucesignati* were first banned from
accompanying a major military venture to Outremer by Frederick Barbarossa
who was possibly motivated by his experiences during the Second Crusade
when his uncle, Bishop Otto of Freising, was one of the few to escape the Turkish
annihilation of the band of German unarmed pilgrims. On this ban see the
Continuatio Sansblasiensis in *M.G.H. Scriptores*, Vol. XX, p. 319. "Quibus omnibus
imperator sequentis anni Maio tempus profectionis constituit, pauperioribus ad
minus trium marcarum expensam, ditioribus pro posse expensis preparari,
indicens; egentibus autem pondo trium marcarum sub anathemate profectionem
fecit interdici nolens exercitum vulgo minus idoneo pregravari".

face of diminishing opportunites for reward in the Crusader East.[15] Taken in themselves such developments did not offer a grave threat to the integrity of the notion of crusade; taken in conjunction with the indirect developments which constitute the main theme of this discussion, however, they can be seen to have contributed to the destruction of the notion from within by providing a semblance of adherence to traditional forms. This very semblance at once exposed the movement to the critic, and sharpened the point of his attack.

(c) JERUSALEM AS THE GOAL OF CRUSADE

The abiding symbolism of Jerusalem, adopted from Judaism, had exerted an incalculable influence on Christian thinking from the time of the early Fathers, and had been the source of the intense desire for repossession of the Holy Places as well as of the strong support for the crusading movement. This Christian thought, translated into cartographical terms, showed Jerusalem as the very physical centre of the earth, thus investing the wholly spiritualised and mystical notion of the New Jerusalem, with an exact geographical location.[16] The crusades helped to localise Jerusalem while at the same time lending it more profound spiritual significance. As an exact geographical location, and physical goal of crusade, Jerusalem was obviously a less flexible idea than Jerusalem, the symbolic goal of every Christian pilgrim to eternity. In part this fact accounts for the closer attention paid by critics to geographical diversions of crusade than to the more subtly destructive ideological and organisational ones. It would have been far easier to accommodate these aberrations to the traditional

---

[15] Without entering here into the controversy concerning the nature of money fiefs in the Latin Kingdom of Jerusalem, one can point to the fact that the extreme fluidity of the frontiers made the continued granting of land difficult, especially in the thirteenth century.

[16] The Hereford *Mappa Mundi*, which shows Jerusalem as the centre of the earth, is almost exactly contemporaneous with the period under discussion, being dated c. 1285. (On the subject of this map see the articles of G. R. Crone, (i) *The Hereford World Map*, London, 1948; (ii) *The World Map of Richard of Haldingham in Hereford Cathedral*, London, 1954; (iii) "New Light on the Hereford map", *Geographical Journal*, 131, 1965). Another such map with Jerusalem in the centre was that of Ebstorf, dated c. 1240. There is also an excellent early fourteenth century example to be found in the geographical excursus on the Holy Land appended by Marino Sanudo to his work on the recovery of the Holy Places; cf. *Gesta Dei per Francos*, ed. J. Bongars, 2 vols in 1, Hanover, 1611, ii, following p. 288. It is interesting to note that in the world map reproduced by Bongars, the centre is marked *Jerusalem* whereas in the Bodley manuscript Tanner 190 the centre is marked simply *Syria*, ff. 203v-204r.

norm had the shift in direction been merely geographical, but in all
other respects roughly equivalent to crusade to the Holy Land.
This simple change could have been generally absorbed into crusade
thinking, as it seems to have been by St. Bernard of Clairvaux, to
judge by his support for the diversion of many crusaders against the
Slavs. However, once the symbolic Jerusalem overshadowed the
geographical as a crusading goal, and made alliance with both
spiritual and temporal self-interest, then the diversion of crusade
from the Holy Land was open to wide interpretation. Geographical
diversion was primarily a symptom of a far more basic change in the
direction of crusade, and so the various extensions of the area of
crusade can be used to illustrate the lines of indirect development,
rather than being discussed in a separate section.

(d) SARACENS AS THE NORMATIVE ENEMY

(i) *The enemy in the East*

Perhaps the most fruitful of actual geographical diversions was
the notion of crusade as an expression of Christian unity. The First
Crusade had been directed against Saracens whose specific enmity
consisted in their unlawful possession of the Holy Places, and not in
their being an immediate threat to any actual Christian possessions.
This remark applies exclusively to Syrian Moslems, and not to the
Moors whose expulsion from the Iberian peninsula, already a long-
held desire, was only later absorbed into the history of crusade as a
fully acceptable alternative goal to the Holy Places.[17] Once the
Crusader States had been founded, crusade became a defence of the
frontiers of Christendom against the same Syrian Moslems, now a
direct threat. In this way crusade was turned into a defence of the
geographical unity of Christendom, while at the same time remaining
a possible expression of its mystical unity. It is obvious that, once the
transposition had been made from attacking an external enemy, to

---

[17] This delayed acceptance of Spain as a full alternative is witnessed by the
initial hesitations of the English crusaders in 1147 about giving their services to
King Alfonso-Henriques after they had been blown off course on to the Spanish
coast. Even the bishop of Oporto, the king's emissary, talked only in terms of a
'just cause' and of raising the Christian Church in Spain. The important thing,
he was careful to point out, was not to have been to Jerusalem, but to have led
a worthy life on the way. See Osbernus, *De expugnatione Lyxbonensi* printed in
the Introduction to Volume I of *Chronicles & Memorials of the Reign of Richard I*,
ed. W. Stubbs, Rolls Series, London, 1864, pp. cxlii-clxxxii. The bishop's sermon
appears pp. cxlvii-clii.

defence against an actually threatening one, this aspect of crusade was open to very liberal interpretation. A threat to the frontiers of the Christian world could legitimately be interpreted as the work of an enemy equivalent to the Saracens, of an enemy worthy of crusade. It is to be noted, however, that even in the thirteenth century, Saracens remained the normative enemy. In Outremer the situation was vastly complicated by the various waves of Far Eastern invaders, and, though the Syrian Franks quickly learned to distinguish between the numerous groups of Moslems, not even they had the expertise to assess the degree of threat exercised by the successive barbarian hordes. In the thirteenth century the Tartar invasions understandably confused the issue not only because of their widespread irruptions into the East and the West, but also because of the persistent rumours of their openness to Christian conversion. There is plenty of evidence to suggest that the general Western attitude, once the immediate threat had passed, was less intransigent than it remained towards the Saracens.[18] These external enemies might in fact roughly be divided into two groups, those who represented a relatively ephemeral threat such as was offered by the sporadic discontent of individual tribes of Slavs on the Eastern frontiers of Europe, and those whose threat was of a more permanent nature. In point of fact the distinctions were easily blurred. The relevance of this to the present discussion is clear—definition of an enemy against whom crusade could be preached, and directed, became ever more tenuous when related to those outside the frontiers of Christendom.

(ii) *The enemy on the frontier*

Even before the Second Crusade the pagan Slavs on the Eastern frontiers of Europe were subjected to a great deal of colonising aggression on the part of German Christian landholders who wished to extend their territories eastwards. St. Bernard's preaching had set the seal of official Christian approval on the idea of this conquest of the Slavs as crusade.[19] This situation pertained on the Eastern fron-

---

[18] First hand experience of the Mongols did not always lead to a tolerant view. John of Plano Carpine in fact sets out detailed ideas on how to wage a successful crusade against them, beating them with their own tricks of war; cf. A. Van den Wyngaert, *Sinica Franciscana*, I, Florence, 1929, Itinera et relationes fratrum minorum saeculi XIII et XIV, No. 1, Fr. Johannes de Plano Carpine, *Ystoria Mongalorum*, Cap. VII and VIII, pp. 84-101.

[19] It is significant that the term "Saracen" was being applied to undefined enemies of Christianity in Eastern Europe in the mid-twelfth century, about

tiers throughout the twelfth century, but was further complicated
by the Tartar invasions which not infrequently drove the Slavonic
tribes backwards, into Christian lands. This in turn provoked further
crusades, of which the campaigns of the kings of Dacia, Norway,
and Lithuania are typical examples.[20] It is easy to see how this state
of affairs effected a further transformation in the concept of crusade.
From being an *offensive* against an external enemy as an expression of
Christian unity, crusade became a *defence* of the unity of Christendom;
the next step was another shift in emphasis which made crusade
synonymous with the defence of Christian frontiers, where 'defence'
was often a euphemism for the conquest of pagans whose territorial
possessions constituted an obstacle to expansion by Christian landholders. At this point crusade and conversion met, though conversion
by conquest was by no means a new form of special pleading on
behalf of aggression. It is on the Eastern frontiers of Europe, and
at the hands of the Teutonic Order, that feudal military aggression,
disguised by all the trappings of genuine crusade, achieved its master-
piece in diversion from the norm of crusade.

(iii) *The enemy within*

It is arguable that the evolution of crusade in the direction of
defence against external enemies was in a direct line from the arche-
type, but the same can scarcely be said of the other group of
enemies with whom crusading ventures came to be more and more
concerned. These were potentially the most dangerous of all
enemies, those within Christendom itself, schismatics and heretics.
If, however, crusade were a defence of Christian unity, then it could
scarcely be a matter for criticism if it were directed against these two
quintessential enemies of that unity. According to the canonists, the
crime of schismatics lay precisely in their disunifying activities,
setting themselves as they did over and against the body of the Church.

---

the time when St. Bernard had been preaching his crusade against the Slavs.
See, for example, *Vincentii Pragensis Annales*, *M.G.H.*, SS., XVII, p. 664. "1146.
Anno dominice incarnationis 1149. Waladizlaus dux Polonie collecta maxima
multidudine tam Sarracenorum quam Rutenorum, Poznan fratris sui Bolezlai
civitatem obsidet; at Bolezlaus cum Meskone fratre suo iuniore, plus in Deo
quam in numero hominum spem ponens, tantam multitudinem eorum militia,
ferro aggreditur, et maxime Sarracenos et Rutenos cede crudeli prosternens,
civitatem ab obsidione liberat . . ."

[20] These campaigns, and their implications for a detailed study of the breakdown of crusading policy will be discussed below, pp. 88-91.

Though not initially heretics, schismatics were held to be unable to avoid falling into at least material heresy,[21] in which case they became doubly the enemies of unity. First in importance among the schismatics were the Greeks whose separation crusade ultimately served to confirm and strengthen, despite papal hopes to the contrary. No one reading such a document as *The Alexiad* could have any doubts about the intransigence of the Greeks, nor the shoddiness of the Western image as presented by the early crusaders. With the widening definition of enemies to be combatted by crusade, the Greeks could scarcely avoid inclusion on more than one score, both political and theological. Forcible reconversion of schismatics and heretics was allowed by canonists and theologians because only inside the fold was salvation possible for those once of the faithful. Violence used against such people was an act of charity, though it was strictly forbidden to coerce the pagans into the fold.[22] If one ignores the moral problems inherent in all holy war, one becomes aware that the specific ambivalence in the concept of crusade as it was applied to the Greeks, lay not so much in their being fellow Christians, for they were plainly errant, but in the heavily political overtones with which the struggle was endowed. The papacy was never in the forefront in reorientating crusade in the direction of Greece, and was never really adamant in its support for the Latin Empire of Constantinople; nevertheless it did acquiesce in putting the instruments of crusading policy at the service of that Empire. The link between Greek conquest and crusade was real for all that it now looks like mere rationalisation and political opportunism. The roots of the connection lie in the First Crusade, though the intention was then strictly pacific. By comparison with the Greeks, other minor groups of schismatics had very little influence indeed on the course of crusade development.

As permanent and grave a source of disunity within the Church were the various recurrent heresies. Among these may be distinguished two main categories of heretics who may loosely be termed lapsed Christians, and relapsed pagans. The latter were, of course, mainly to be found on the Eastern frontiers of Europe, where, despite canon-

---

[21] Cf. Hostiensis, *Summa Aurea*, V, tit. De Schismaticis § 1 (Dictum est supra) and § 2 (Quid sit schisma).

[22] Cf. Innocentii IIII Pont. Max., *In Quinque Libros Decretalium*, Venice, 1578, III, tit. De baptismo Cap. IIII § 1 (Majores eum). See also, St. Thomas Aquinas, *Summa Theologiae* (Cum textu ex recensione Leonina), ed. De Rubeis *et al.*, Rome, 1948, IIIa Q 68 a 10.

ists and theologians, conversion had advanced at sword-point,[23] and had embraced whole tribes, or ethnic groups. By a corollary, relapsing into paganism was a sign of resurgent 'nationalism', and was nearly always accompanied by a reasserted independence. There was very little evangelical zeal at the roots either of the initial conversion of these groups, or of the crusades which purported to seek their reconversion. These unfortunate peoples, often harried on both sides, were seen by their Christian, and covetous, neighbours, as being at once enemies threatening the frontiers of Christendom from without, obstacles to Christian expansion, and heretical enemies of Christian unity within the fold. Any one of these would have been sufficient pretext for a crusade. The situation was further confused by the political ambitions of neighbouring Christian magnates, including powerful ecclesiastics, and, in the thirteenth century, of the Teutonic Order. These Eastern European ventures were never at the centre of crusade development, chiefly because papal involvement was minimal, even when the usual instruments of policy were employed, but they represent a constant divergence from the tradition.

Much more dangerous to Christian unity were the relapsed heretics to be found in the very heart of Christendom, who propagated an alternative Christian doctrine, unlike the pagans who merely reverted to their pagan cults. Campaigns against heretics were epitomised by the Albigensian crusades which had a major influence on all subsequent thinking about crusades. Certainly the Catharist sects were a positive menace to Christian unity, and even more specifically, to papal supremacy. In the areas where heresy raged, it almost always assumed a political significance, sometimes unexpected in form since it must be remembered that Frederick II was especially severe in his anti-heretical legislation; anti-papal feeling among heretics did not always argue pro-imperial support. The two areas of special disunification were the South of France and Northern Italy. Considering the shifts in emphasis in the identifying features of crusading enemies, the preaching of the cross against these heretics was a logical, and even defensible, step.[24] Though not startlingly tangential in themselves,

---

[23] St. Bernard contributed to the acceptability of this mode of action. "We utterly forbid," he wrote to the faithful, "that for any reason whatsoever a truce should be made with these peoples, (i.e. the Slavs) either for the sake of money or for the sake of tribute, until such a time as, by God's help, they shall be either converted or wiped out." Letter 394 in *The Letters of St. Bernard of Clairvaux*, translated by Bruno Scott James, London, 1953.

[24] In support of this, one may cite the remark of Innocent III that the Catharists

these anti-heretical campaigns assumed a potential destructiveness with regard to crusade because of their political connotations,which exerted an enormous influence over the evolution of purely papal crusades in the course of the thirteenth century.

(iv) *Enemies of the papacy*

The whole post-Hildebrandine mentality of the papacy favoured an equation of the papal cause with that of the Church, by a very simple process of identifying the papacy with the ever more aggrandised *Roman* church; that is to say, the process was simple in itself, though by no means so in application or effect. As a result of this process the enemies of the papacy became enemies of the Church, because the two were identified. In fact, the papal crusades to which this gave rise epitomised the divergence of crusade from the traditional norm. Papal opponents were eminently "cruciabilis" because they were, basically, enemies of the Church; during the long struggle with the Hohenstaufen, enemy of the papacy and enemy of the Church were most strictly identified. Frederick II embodied many of the elements which made for the divergence of crusade; he was an inveterate excommunicate, considered a material heretic, suspect of being a formal heretic, an ally of notorious heretics and excommunicates, a friend and protector of Saracens in Italy and "overseas", and a threat to the papal states,[25] which were, by reason of the above identification, frontiers of the Church to be defended by crusade.

Again it was an easy step from the crusade in defence of the recognised papal states to crusade for possession of states over which the pope claimed suzerainty, as for example Sicily, which became the centre of crusading policy in the second half of the thirteenth century. This crusade was first declared for the recovery of Sicily into papal hands, then it was transformed into a crusade in support of the papal claimant to Sicily. It retained papal support even when that claimant, namely Charles of Anjou, openly flouted the papacy, and held ambitions which involved activities inimical to the good of the

---

were worse than the Saracens, quoted in Hefele-Leclercq, *Histoire des Conciles*, 100 vols, Paris, 1907 —, Vol. V, Part 2, p. 1270.

[25] These accusations were levelled by both Gregory IX; cf. A. Huillard-Bréholles, *Historia Diplomatica Friderici Secundi*, 12 parts in 7 vols, Paris, 1852-61, iii, pp. 23 *et seq.*; v, pp. 286-9 and 457-61, and by Innocent IV in his condemnation of the Emperor at the First Council of Lyons, 1245; cf. Matthew Paris, *Chronica Majora*, ed. H. R. Luard, 7 vols, Rolls Series, London, 1872-1883, iv, pp. 445-55.

Holy Land. Even more remote was the threat of crusade issued in
support of a papal ally in his purely domestic troubles, since his opponents were judged to have ruined papal policy in Sicily. This was,
of course, Henry III, a *crucesignatus* of recurrent commutation, and a
pious perverter of the instruments of crusading policy to his own
ends, whether these were financial or political. With all these divergent tendencies in thinking about the nature and object of crusade,
these two extreme cases show how far the original concept had been
changed, and yet how the remotest cases were not altogether divorced
from the tradition. Rather are they illustrations of the destructive
duality, at length out of hand.

At the very end of the thirteenth century, posterior even to the
fall of Acre, Boniface VIII pushed to its ultimate absurdity the use
of crusade as an instrument of narrowly papal, rather than universally
Christian, aims. This was the declaration of a full crusade against the
Colonne who were engaged in what was little more than a family feud
against the Pope. It was a far cry from the Council of Clermont to the
encyclical *Unam Sanctam*, but Boniface VIII, defining papal supremacy,
and using crusade against his personal enemies, is in the line of development which Urban II set in motion when he preached the First
Crusade, aiming thereby to give a practical proof of the victory of the
papacy over its imperial opponents. The other very striking extremity
of crusading evolution was, in fact, prior in time to the pontificate of
Boniface VIII, but may well be termed anti-crusade. Beginning as the
excommunicate Emperor Frederick II's defiance of the papal prohibition of his setting out "overseas", this anti-crusade embraced an
imperial declaration of crusade against the pope as an heretical enemy
of the Church,[26] and even as antichrist.[27] The Emperor assumed the
rôle of the saviour of Christendom,[28] and the defender of ortho-

---

[26] Cf. A. Huillard-Bréholles, *op. cit.*, Vol. V, Part 1, p. 311, where Gregory is
denounced as a wolf rather than a shepherd, a lover of schismatics, a protector
of heretics, an enemy of the faithful and so on. The Pope is later declared to be
no real Vicar of Christ (pp. 350-1). Frederick blamed Gregory and Innocent in a
letter to Richard of Cornwall (*Ibid.*, vi, 2, pp. 254-9), for the loss of Jerusalem
in 1244, and for all the calamities afflicting the Church.

[27] Typical of this form of imperial propaganda is the *De correctione ecclesiae
Epistola et Anonymi de Innocentio IV P. M. Antichristo libellus*, ed. E. Winkelmann,
Berlin, 1865. The *De correctione* is the work of the Dominican Arnold and the
number of references to the cross and the crucifixion are evidence of an intention
to counteract the crusading bent of the papal campaigns against the Emperor.

[28] See *De correctione*, p. 10. For a general examination of the rôle of Frederick
as saviour see E. Kantorowicz, *Frederick the Second*, 1194-1250 (translated E. O.

doxy,[29] against the destructive forces within the Church. The material organisation of Frederick's campaigns of necessity resembled that of papal crusade, but so also did the forms of propaganda, and the avowed object.

Clearly all these differing and divergent uses of crusade exerted powerful pressures on the internal development of the instruments of crusading policy, as well as on the notion of crusade. Though such internal developments might have been intrinsically logical, consistent, and acceptable when each instrument was taken in isolation, yet they frequently rendered each instrument incompatible with one or more of the others in general use within the traditional framework of crusading policy. Plenary indulgence, for instance, was a doctrinal development quite consistent with the notion of indulgence as such, and with the fittingness of a uniquely valuable spiritual reward for the Christian endeavour *par excellence* which was crusade. The logical doctrinal consequence from that point, however, was the availability of these spiritual riches to all the faithful; this was quite incompatible with the effort demanded by crusade. While indulgence itself thus developed beyond crusade, traditional ways of thought preserved a formal connection between the two. Only by sacrificing the notion of the unique value of crusading effort as a penitential work could plenary indulgence be extended to more of the faithful than actually went on crusade; traditionally only a connection with crusade could give plenary indulgence its efficacy. This impasse resulted in an internal lack of coherence that could not but lay both crusade and indulgence open to abuse. In turn the lack of internal coherence in indulgence as an instrument of crusading policy reacted upon, and influenced, the other instruments of crusading policy, reducing their consistency one with another.

It can now be seen that it is the intention of this study to examine the interaction of external pressure and internal development on the instruments of crusading policy in the thirteenth century, relating the findings of such an examination to the norms of traditional

---

Lorimer), London, 1957, especially pp. 495-516. Cf. also N. Cohn, *The Pursuit of the Millenium*, London, 1957, Chapter V.

[29] Frederick himself claimed his unimpeachable orthodoxy in a letter to Louis IX printed in *Acta imperii inedita saeculo XIII*, ed. E. Winkelmann, 2 vols, Innsbruck, 1880-1885, ii, No. 43. The *De correctione* listed twenty five forms of heresy rife in the church which Frederick's efforts would extirpate. Frederick's harsh legislation against heretics, itself acceptable to, and adopted by, the papacy, was part of his image as defender of orthodoxy.

crusade as set out in the definition given above.[30] It is a further
intention to explore the interaction of these two with the more
general historical development of alienation between the Frankish
East and the West. In this way there will be provided a clear indication of the exact nature of the breakdown in crusade in the thirteenth
century, hitherto accepted as a plain fact, but not analysed in the details
of papal policy.

---

[30] See pp. 10-11.

CHAPTER TWO

THIRTEENTH CENTURY CRUSADING DECREES

Since by reason of its nature this work ought to rely primarily on formal crusading documents, it seems important to set out at the beginning a discussion of the texts of the conciliar decrees concerning crusade issued by the Fourth Lateran Council and the First and Second Councils of Lyons.[1]

Each of these decrees was aimed at organising a crusade for the recovery of the Holy Places, though in vastly differing circumstances. The crusade planned by Innocent III was intended specifically to win back Jerusalem, lost to Saladin in 1187; that announced by Innocent IV was the result of the fall of Jerusalem to the Khwarismians in 1244, after it had been regained for Christendom by the efforts of Frederick II in 1229. Gregory X who had himself been a crusader to the Holy Land, was personally aware of the urgent need for swift and effective action if the Crusader States were to be saved at all. The Fourth Lateran Council was held at a time when the papacy's long struggle with the Empire was temporarily in abeyance; the First Council of Lyons was largely a papal challenge to an Emperor grown over-bold in his claims to supremacy.[2] The Second Council of Lyons came hard upon the apparently final victory over the Hohenstaufen in Sicily, in an atmosphere of hopeful negotiations with the Greeks, and the Tartars, when there seemed once more to be no major obstacle to a successful venture to Outremer.

The preamble to the decree of 1215 states simply the pope's great desire to liberate the Holy Land from the hands of the impious; that of 1245 refers at little more length to the recent calamity in the Holy Land, that is the fall of Jerusalem as the urgent reason for a crusade. The preamble to Gregory X's "Constitutiones pro zelo fidei" is far longer, dwelling at length on the miserable state of the Holy Land as

---

[1] The texts of the decrees will be found in Appendix A.

[2] The Council was clearly understood as such by contemporaries, and hence its relatively unrepresentative nature. The main business of the Council was fivefold according to Innocent IV's letter of convocation: crusade, the Greek schism, heresy, Tartar invasions and the contest of papacy and Empire, but was above all concerned with the deposition of Frederick II. See Matthew Paris, iv, pp. 410-412.

recently witnessed by the pope himself. It refers also to the second reason for calling the Council, that is reunion with the Greeks. This means that what we have is actually the preamble, not to the crusading decree as such, but to Gregory's speech outlining the chief work of the Council, the goals towards which the other work of the council would be directed.

It is easy enough, in recollecting the different circumstances in which each decree was formulated, and issued, to account for the different tones of the preambles to the decrees. There is a more confident tone in the arrangements of the decree of 1215 for a definite date and places of assembly, and for the promise of Innocent III's personal organisation and benediction of the departing forces. It is to be regretted that we possess only a (presumably) mutilated version of the decree of 1274 because it was probably in the course of guiding this decree through the Council that Gregory X announced more explicitly his intention of returning to the Holy Land at the head of the crusading army. We know that such was his intention since he set aside certain parts of the collection to be used for the expenses of his journey.[3]

Innocent IV, on the other hand, who merely promised an apostolic blessing to the departing crusaders, was in no position to consider either going himself on crusade, or even going in person to Aigues-Mortes to bless Louis IX's army when it set out in 1248. It is instructive, on this account, to consider the reason for the holding of the Councils of 1245 and 1274 in Lyons. Innocent IV had gone there in exile; though the pope had desired the safer confines of Louis IX's kingdom, the French king would not run the risk of taking sides openly against the Emperor. Lyons provided a safe compromise since it lay in territory disputed by French and German princes, at once unlikely to be attacked by Frederick, and within easy reach of French help. Gregory X, on the other hand, chose Lyons quite freely as a place of easy access for the conciliar fathers.[4]

The two earlier decrees provide for the spiritual exhortation of the Christian forces to lead godly lives in keeping with their state, in order to bring a blessing on the venture. Humble and contrite, they were to live temperately, and in amity with one another. The 1245

---

[3] *Les Registres de Grégoire X, 1272-1276*, ed. J. Guiraud, Paris, 1892-1960, No. 1041. In this letter Gregory laid claim to the contributions of the Cistercians and Premonstratensians.
[4] See the preamble to the *Constitutiones*, Appendix A, p. 196.

decree added more specific instructions for rich *crucesignati*, who, by curtailing their expenditure on luxurious living, would be in a position to subsidise poorer *crucesignati*, or to pay for mercenaries.[5] These provisions are absent from the 1274 decree.

The first financial provisions of the two earlier decrees omitted in that of 1274 were on behalf of clerics *crucesignati* who were to enjoy the full fruits of their benefices for three years as if they were resident, and were, if necessary, to be allowed to borrow money on the security of their benefices. This clause is isolated in the decrees from the other financial provisions, but it will be as well to survey the remaining ones at the same time. The hierarchy were to exhort the faithful, more especially the rulers and magnates, and the various powerful communes, that those who did not intend to set out should make provision for sending substitutes in their stead, for three years. This work was to be rewarded with a remission of sins, as also was the provision of ships. These clauses were included in a slightly compressed form in the 1274 decree. All three decrees precede the main financial provisions with an admonitory exhortation against the ingratitude offered by a refusal of help to Christ whose death on the cross is salvation for all.

The differing circumstances of the popes show themselves in the financial provisions as these applied to the pope himself. Innocent III was in a position to promise a very generous subsidy to the crusade, as well as making special provision for the transport and subsidisation of *crucesignati* from Rome and neighbouring districts; to this was added the ordinary ecclesiastical tenth for three years to which the pope was pledged along with the cardinals of the Roman Church. Innocent IV had inherited an impoverished papacy from Gregory IX, and was, besides, separated by exile from his proper revenues. It was inevitable that his appeals for money [6] should far outstrip his contributions. Financially the papacy was further ruined by the long involvement in the Sicilian affair, by the hard-headed bargaining of Charles of Anjou, and his carelessness of meeting even the obligations which remained after the terms of the contract had been agreed.[7]

---

[5] From the text it is difficult to tell whether the decree refers to *crucesignati* proper, or to mercenaries in the stricter meaning of the term.

[6] This is a subject on which numerous contemporaries expatiated, though not all at such length as Matthew Paris.

[7] The long negotiations, and their impact on the papacy, both financially and otherwise are discussed in great detail by E. Jordan in *Les origines de la domination angevine en Italie*, Paris, 1909, pp. 420-514. The letters of Clement IV are most revealing

Gregory X was in no better position than Innocent IV to do more than pledge himself to the payment of a tenth for six years. In Gregory's case this was exactly the same as was being demanded of the clergy, whereas in 1245 they were asked to pay a twentieth, that is, less than the pope and the cardinals.

Innocent IV's own state of desperate impecuniosity probably accounts for the more detailed and specific sumptuary "laws" [8] outlined in the decree of 1245. The significance of the clause making such sumptuary provisions lies in its promise of an indulgence, to be granted at the discretion of the preachers, for such a contribution. In the light of the grant of a plenary indulgence to all *crucesignati*, this further partial indulgence seems questionable, unless one assumes a view of plenary indulgences as effecting only a quasi-plenary remission of sins.[9] This would accord with ideas expressed in his *Apparatus* by Innocent IV,[10] his failure to mention Hugh of St. Cher's doctrine of the treasury of the Church, and his opinion that, though all remission of sin was a matter of God's liberality, there was also an element of justice involved in a crusading indulgence, because of the magnitude of the work undertaken. Thus it would seem ridiculous to offer a partial indulgence simultaneously with a plenary one, to the same people. In this regard Joinville gives interesting evidence of what seems to be the granting of an extra *plenary* indulgence to crusaders on the occasion of their gathering in procession at the seneschal's suggestion, and by the behest of the legate, to intercede for the safe arrival of Alphonse of Poitiers.[11] Judging from records, moreover, Louis IX was an inveterate collector of indulgences, over and above his plenary remissions, and his devoted pursuit of this spiritual insurance became something of a family hobby by the end of the century.[12]

---

of the financial distress of the papacy. See, for example, those to Charles of Anjou concerning the miserable state of the Holy See and the expedients necessary for raising money printed in *Codice diplomatico del regno di Carlo I e II d'Angio*, ed. G. del Giudice, 2 vols, Naples, 1863-69, i, Nos x and xx.

[8] These sumptuary provisions were clearly to be self-imposed, and were not therefore "laws" in the general sense.

[9] This whole subject will be discussed in the section of the theological background to indulgences.

[10] V, tit. De penitentiis et remissionibus Cap. IIII (Quod autem).

[11] J. de Joinville, *Histoire de Saint Louis*, texte original, ed. N. de Wailly, ninth edition, Paris, 1921, xxxviii, § 181.

[12] Cf. A. Tardif, *Privilèges accordés à la couronne de France par le Saint-Siège* (Documents inédits sur l'histoire de France), Paris, 1855, pp. 1-105. There are far more grants to Philip III and Philip IV than to Louis VIII and Louis IX.

The two earlier decrees specifically exempted certain religious from the crusading tax, as well as *crucesignati*, whereas Gregory X very carefully removed all possibility of an exemption on any pretext, not even excluding *crucesignati*, though one presumes from other evidence that this omission argues a *lacuna* in the text, or an assumption that the exemption of *crucesignati* went without saying. This decree also omits all mention of the special protections and privileges accorded to *crucesignati* in 1215 and 1245, including not only immunity from taxes, but a moratorium on debts, and protection against usurious extortions.

There are, however, far more specific and detailed provisions in the "Constitutiones pro zelo fidei" and these bear witness to Gregory X's determination to exploit every possible means of raising funds, as well as to his sense of the obligation of all the faithful to contribute to the saving of the Holy Land for Christendom. This sense of the need for corporate action involving all Christians, springing from Gregory's own essential holiness, accounts for the rather oddly assorted regulations concerned with financial contributions. It appears somewhat curious for the pope to have isolated fines for blasphemy for inclusion among the sources of funds, unless one realises that Gregory saw blasphemy as peculiarly injurious to the spiritual energies needed to carry crusade to success as a Christian venture.[13] Other financial provisions in the *Constitutiones* also spell this special sense of the need for corporate unity of action, as in the cancellation of all exemptions from the tenth. In addition Gregory revived a much earlier provision for the placing of a crusader chest in every church.[14] Instead of granting a specific indulgence for contributions placed in this chest by the faithful, Gregory X commanded that a public mass be sung once a week for the remission of sins of those offering alms in this way. One further measure, explicitly aimed at achieving corporate action by way of contribution, was the direction to all rulers to levy a tax of one penny of Tours, or one silver penny a year on every single person in their lands and territories. The

---

[13] Blasphemy was, of course, considered to be akin to atheism, as in the case of the man of whom the Psalmist speaks who said "There is no God". Gregory X, in fact, helps to define his own sense of the word by speaking in his preamble of the Holy Land as devastated 'per ... plasfemos et perfidos Sarracenos'. See below, p. 196.

[14] Innocent III, following the earlier example of Henry II of England had ordered crusader chests to be placed in churches in 1199. See W. E. Lunt, *Financial Relations of the Papacy with England to* 1327, Cambridge, Mass., 1939, p. 423.

smallness of the sum was expressly intended by Gregory to allow all to participate in the subsidy, and the merits accruing to contributors for the remission of sins.[15]

The Council of 1245 had made provision for the exhortation of the faithful to remember the Holy Land and its needs in their wills,[16] but this canon was not incorporated into the crusading decree itself as it was in that of 1274. A further concentration of attention on the needs of the Holy Land was Gregory X's decision that the tenth should be levied for six years, instead of the more usual three. In addition to this his decree displayed the improved organisation of papal finances by announcing the exact date of the inception of the levy, and making provision for semi-annual payments on Christmas Day, and the feast of John the Baptist. With a far better bureaucratic system at his disposal than either of the earlier popes, Gregory could also arrange for the division of Christendom into twenty six collectoral districts for the purposes of a more efficient collection.[17] In this way he laid down the basic outlines of what has been called the first really universal tax.[18]

In the decrees of 1245 and 1274 there are two notable omissions, namely the failure to make specific provision for commutation or deferment of crusading vows by those with major impediments, or for a minimum time of service by *crucesignati*. It is difficult to see the reason for the first omission unless one attributes it in Innocent IV's case to his possible view as a canonist that the redemption, commutation, and deferment of vows were implicit, and needed no specification. If one believes the substance of Matthew Paris' allegations [19] it is perhaps even more likely that the increased trade in redemption and commutations of crusading vows by 1245 made it impolitic to draw attention to the possibility of such actions within the decree itself. This last reason would be even more operative by 1274, by which time abuses were even more rife.

Less conjecture is possible about the reason for the second omission. Innocent III had required a *crucesignatus* to serve for at least a year before he was eligible for exemption from monetary exactions,

---

[15] Throop appears to have made a mistake in claiming that there was to be no remission of sins for this contribution. See his *Criticism of the Crusades*, p. 243; cf. *Constitutiones*, below, pp. 197-8.

[16] Canon 15.

[17] See p. 199, below.

[18] Cf. L. Gatto, *Il pontificato di Gregorio X*, 1271-1276, Rome, 1959, p. 87.

[19] See below, pp. 127-9.

but the decree of 1245 does not mention minimum service, nor does that of 1274. The idea of a mutually arranged period of military service was built into the feudal system and the later decrees may not have considered it necessary to specify a time which could, in fact, cut across the arrangements, and feudal customs, of the *crucesignati*. Both the earlier decrees insisted on a three year subsidy for *crucesignati* being sent as substitutes but this may well simply point to the discrepancy felt to exist between simple almsgiving and crusade as works of penance. There seems, in fact, no good reason for this omission from the later decrees; moreover, Gregory X raised the minimum service for officials to three years,[20] a fact which indicates an awareness of the need for regulation in this matter. Because of the unsatisfactory state of the unique text of the *Constitutiones* it is unwise to draw any conclusions which do not allow for *lacunae*.

All three decrees provide for stern measures to be taken against pirates who should hinder the passage of the *crucesignati*, and against merchants who should ignore the ban on trade with the enemy for the duration of the passage, thereby providing the Saracens with necessary ships, arms, and other materials of war for use against the Christian armies. Another common provision is that for the maintaining of peace at home while the crusade should be in progress.[21]

In connection with the maintenance of peace, the decrees of 1215 and 1245 reiterated the long standing ban on tournaments. The case has been argued for the original inclusion in the *Constitutiones* of the clause prohibiting tournaments,[22] and the form of the decree as it stands does indeed suggest that an earlier version may have been differently arranged, with more explicit provisions for crusading privileges and immunities. It is otherwise extremely difficult to account for the complete absence of any reference to privileges with regard to debts and usury, for example.

The final clauses of the three decrees deal with the grant of indulgences to those who take the cross, and to those who in other ways contribute to the success of the venture by the donations of money, ships, and advice. The decrees then end on a promise of prayers that those who piously undertake the work of crusade may thereby profit unto eternal salvation.

---

[20] See below, p. 61.
[21] The 1274 decree differs from the earlier ones in providing for a period of six years where the provisions of the others ran for four years.
[22] Cf. H. Finke, *Konsilienstudien zur Geschichte des 13 Jahrhunderts*, Münster, 1891, p. 14.

Since this section was aimed at an analysis of the chief differences in the thirteenth century conciliar decrees on crusade it has seemed unnecessary at this stage to discuss in full those points in which the decrees coincide. The above differences apart, therefore, it is clear that the three decrees coincide on the general lines of papal crusading policy, so that there was continuity at least in intention from the time of the Fourth Lateran Council. It is also clear what were considered the major instruments of that policy. These may be reduced to three principal categories:

(i)   Instruments concerned with organising and guaranteeing the spiritual advantages to *crucesignati*, namely crusading indulgences, and crusading vows with their commutation and redemption;

(ii) instruments concerned with the material advantages guaranteed to the *crucesignati*, namely the subsidies, privileges, protections and immunities granted to them;

(iii) instruments concerned with making good the promises of material advantages to *crucesignati*, and with removing such obstacles to the successful conduct of the venture as were presented by disturbance at home, trade with the enemy, and piratical attacks on transport ships, namely instruments of ecclesiastical censure, excommunication and interdict.

The personnel concerned with the implementation of crusading policies, with whom this study will be dealing to a lesser extent than with the instruments mentioned above, may for interest be divided also into four principal categories:

(a) those employed in the administration of the various instruments related to the spiritual advantages mentioned in (i) above, namely the crusading legate and his deputies;

(b) those employed in the administration of the instruments concerned with the material advantages mentioned in (ii), a group frequently synonymous with (a) as to personnel, but distinct as to function;

(c) those employed in the task of leading the actual venture, the papal legate, and the secular princes or magnates;

(d) the standing papal crusading militia, namely the Military Orders operating in the Crusader East.

These categories, whether of instruments, or of personnel, have been abstracted from an ideal situation in which crusade was intended to be, and actually was, the sole end of its own organisational forms as far as the papacy, papal officials and all *crucesignati* were concerned. Such an ideal never existed. The boundaries of spiritual and material advantages were frequently blurred because the same personnel were responsible for the administration of both. Papal policy overlapped with the organisation of crusade by lay leaders such as Louis IX or his brothers, Alphonse of Poitiers and Charles of Anjou. At times in the course of the discussion such imprecision of boundaries will lead to the inclusion of matter strictly extrinsic to papal policy, though not without influence on it. The aim of this discussion, however, will be to concentrate rather on the obviously papal policy, even when this entails a logical rather than a real line of demarcation; it will aim also to be concerned with the organisational forms of crusading policy rather than on the personnel involved. This course of action seems to be justified on two scores, the one because the instruments of policy are more open to the kind of investigation outlined in the general introduction, and the other because a proper examination and exposition of evidence related to the personnel would constitute a quite separate, and even more lengthy task.

SECTION B

SPIRITUAL ADVANTAGES OFFERED TO *CRUCESIGNATI*

INTRODUCTORY REMARKS

The two chief instruments of policy related to conferring on the *crucesignati* the spiritual reward proper to their state were indulgences and vows. This reward consisted specifically in the granting of plenary remissions of sin, and it depended on the crusading vow as the proximate cause of that grant. The vow constituted for the *crucesignatus* his bond of good faith, and his right to claim his reward. As an external symbol of that pledge and that right he wore the crusader cross.

The spiritual advantages thus offered to *crucesignati* did not differ basically from those offered to all Christians, namely salvation through the forgiveness of sins. It was precisely because of questions arising from considerations of the nature and manner of the forgiveness of sins that the instruments concerned with spiritual advantages offered to *crucesignati* became caught up in a far wider theological discussion which had begun in early Christian times, and continued with increasing momentum throughout the middle ages.[1] For this reason it has been considered necessary to begin this section with a chapter on the theological background of the doctrine of indulgences as it had developed by the mid-thirteenth century. Such a brief discussion will not pretend to cover all aspects of the history of that doctrine because much lies beyond the scope of this inquiry. It is, therefore, on the notion of plenary indulgences that the theological excursus will concentrate.

After this theological discussion there will be a detailed examination of the use of plenary indulgences in connection with crusade first to the Holy Land, and then for causes other than that of the Holy Land. This will be followed by a chapter on crusading vows which, by reason especially of papal use of commutations and redemptions, had serious implications for crusading indulgences, and crusading policy as a whole.

---

[1] In fact this constituted one of the basic questions underlying the theology of Protestant reformers, and much of their dissatisfaction arose from a rejection of a too complicated machinery of forgiveness interposed between God and man.

CHAPTER THREE

THEOLOGY OF CRUSADING INDULGENCES [1]

By far the most characteristically crusading of all the chief instruments of papal crusading policy in the thirteenth century was the plenary indulgence. So characteristic had this become that no plenary indulgence was granted apart from crusade. This does not imply that plenary indulgences were specifically crusading in origin; in fact they were not separate in origin from partial indulgences, but were merely the same idea carried to its farthest conclusion. That crusade provided a context for plenary indulgences indicates that it alone was seen as a suitably condign work of satisfaction for a plenary remission of sin, and that no other penitential work was so considered. Works dedicated to tracing the history and development of indulgences generally agree that plenary indulgences for crusade were theologically a peculiarly thirteenth century development. Earlier crusading indulgences had acknowledged themselves to be a full remission of *enjoined penance*, according to the formula used, or at least reported to have been used, by Urban II at the Council of Clermont[2] and not a "full remission of sin" as granted by the crusading decree of the Fourth Lateran Council in 1215.[3] The difference was purely one of emphasis in accord with the developments in scholastic theology of the sacrament of penance, but the plenary indulgence as granted by the Fourth Lateran Council was far more

---

[1] The standard historical work on indulgences is that of N. Paulus, *Geschichte des Ablasses im Mittelalter vom Ursprunge bis zur Mitte des 14 Jahrhunderts*, 3 vols in 2, Paderborn, 1922-23. The more recent works of B. Poschmann, however, make use of advances in theology, and the light these advances throw on the historical perspective of the question of penance. The most important of these works for the present discussion are *Der Ablass im Licht der Bussgeschichte*, Bonn, 1948, and *Busse und Letzte Ölung*, Freiburg, 1951. Important reviews of the last work are those of Karl Rahner in *Zeitschrift für Katholische Theologie*, 71, 1949, pp. 481-490, P. Galtier, "Les indulgences: origine et nature", in *Gregorianum*, 31, 1950, pp. 258-274, and F. Courtney, "New Explanations of Indulgences" in *Clergy Review*, 44, 1959, pp. 464-479. An older, more restricted, work is that of A. Gottlob, *Kreuzablass und Almosenablass*, Stuttgart, 1906.

[2] Cf. J. D. Mansi, *Sacrorum Conciliorum nova, et amplissima collectio*, 31 vols, Florence and Venice, 1759-98, xx, col. 816. The actual words quoted are: "iter pro omni paenitentiae reputetur".

[3] Cf. Mansi, xxii, col. 1067.

open to liberal interpretation and adaptation than was that of Clermont.

Indulgences were always peripheral to the important scholastic
discussion on the nature and effect of the sacrament of penance; at
the end of the thirteenth century they were still theoretically subordinate to the sacrament, though in practice they had become
increasingly detached from it.[4] This gradual movement away from the
sacrament eventually exposed indulgences to abuses of a magnitude
undreamed of by Abelard who had attacked not only the practice, but
even the notion of granting indulgences.[5] Peter Lombard, however,
had not considered indulgences of sufficient importance to warrant
discussion, and until the thirteenth century developments in the
doctrine of indulgences were almost wholly implicit in teaching on
the sacrament of penance. The practice had become so widespread,
on the other hand, as to warrant an admonitory rebuke at the Fourth
Lateran Council.[6] At the same Council, however, official sanction
was conclusively given to the practice of granting a plenary indulgence
to *crucesignati*, in a formula which remained static until the end of the
crusading era.[7] There was no sudden transformation of the doctine
of indulgences in the early thirteenth century,[8] but a coalescence of
ideas into an increasingly coherent body of teaching. The crusading
decree of 1215 was undoubtedly a strong influence on the rapidity
with which this coherence was achieved.[9] It was with a considerably

---

[4] Cf. P. Anciaux, *Le Sacrement de la pénitence*, Louvain, 1957. The Appendix,
"Origine et signification des 'indulgences' ", pp. 145-165, gives a good summary
of the ideal relationship between indulgences and the sacramental life of the
Church.

[5] Cf. B. Poschmann, *Der Ablass im Licht der Bussgeschichte*, pp. 63-68.

[6] *Mansi*, xxii, col. 1050, (Can. 62) "Ad haec quia per indiscretas et superfluas
indulgentias, quas quidam ecclesiarum praelati facere non verentur, et claves
Ecclesiae comtemnuntur, et paenitentialis satisfactio enervatur; decernimus
ut . . ." etc.

[7] *Mansi*, xxii, cols 1058-1067.

[8] This has been argued by certain Protestant historians of dogma such as
A. Harnack, *Dogmengeschichte*, Tübingen, 4th edition, 1905, pp. 373 *et seq.* For a
discussion of the opposing view, cf. N. Paulus, *op. cit.*, especially i, pp. 259 ff.

[9] It must not be overlooked that this same Council decreed, in conformity
with an ancient practice of the Church, that all the faithful should confess their
sins at least once a year during Lent, partly in response to heretical denials of the
need for sacerdotal absolution (cf. P. Anciaux, *La théologie du sacrement de pénitence
au XIIe siècle*, Louvain, 1949, p. 605, on the influence of heretical teaching)
and partly as a defence of the priestly intervention in the sacrament in the remission
of sins. This fact must also have had its influence on the great scholastic theologians of the sacrament, and of indulgences, William of Auvergne, Alexander of
Hales, Albert the Great, St. Bonaventure and St. Thomas Aquinas.

greater mass of evidence of abuses in the practice of indulgences that Humbert de Romans spoke of the need for reform in this matter in discussing the more general reform of the clergy.[10]

In dealing with indulgences not simply as they were granted in the penitential system, but as instruments of papal crusading policy, one is faced with the apparently irreconcilable facts that plenary indulgences became far more widespread as the thirteenth century advanced, and yet remained theoretically linked to crusade. It is impossible to tackle the problem of reconciling these two facts without some brief consideration of the notion of penitential satisfaction as understood by the contemporary theologians and canonists. It is equally impossible in attempting to do this, not to agree with Teetaert when he speaks of the development of the doctrine of satisfaction as,

> une des évolutions les plus mouvementées, qui aient jamais existé au sein de l'Eglise catholique.[11]

The notion of satisfaction was two-sided; considered objectively it was the necessary demand of God's justice on sinful man.

> Ordo justitiae hoc requirit ut peccato poena reddatur. Ex hoc autem quod ordo servatur in rebus, sapientia Dei gubernantis apparet. Pertinet igitur ad manifestationem divinae bonitatis et Dei gloriam quod pro peccato poena reddatur. Sed peccator peccando contra ordinem divinitus institutum facit, leges Dei praetergrediendo. Est igitur conveniens ut hoc recompenset in seipso puniendo quod prius peccaverat: sic enim totaliter extra inordinationem constituetur.[12]

Subjectively it was man's voluntary submission to the penalty thus incurred, and his co-operation in fulfilling the penitential works of satisfaction sacramentally imposed, or extra-sacramentally substituted. This voluntary co-operation in charity to God, self and neighbour, were for St. Thomas absolutely basic to all his teaching on the Christian life, and fitted indulgences into a far wider scheme of Christian perfection even than their connection with the sacrament of penance implied. This is stated elsewhere in the *Summa Contra Gentiles*.

---

[10] Cf. *Opus Tripartitum* (printed by E. Brown in *Appendix ad Fasciculum Rerum Expetendarum et Fugiendarum*, London, 1690), Pars 3, Cap. VIII and IX.

[11] Cf. A. S. T. Teetaert, "La Doctrine pénitentielle de Saint Raymond de Penyafort, O.P.", in *Analecta Sacra Tarraconensia*, IV, 1928, p. 159 (p. 39).

[12] St. Thomas Aquinas, *Summa Contra Gentiles* (Editio Leonina Manualis), Rome, 1934, III, clviii.

nam mens nostra debite ad Deum converti non potest sine caritate, caritas autem sine gratia haberi non potest ... ... Haec igitur mentis reordinatio, quae in contritione consistit, ex interiori procedit, idest a libero arbitrio, cum adiutorio divinae gratiae.[13]

The same spiritual, rather than juridical, approach to penitential works is to be found in others of the scholastics of whom St. Raymond of Penafort may be taken as typical:

Eleemosyna aute[m] est triplex, Prima consistit in cordis contritione, quando aliquis se offert Deo, ... Secunda consistit in co[m]passione proximi, qua co[m]patimur alienis adversitatibus, tamquam nostris: ... Tertia consistit in largitione manuali, advocatione cura corporali, & spirituali, & breviter in quocumque consilio, et subsidio, quod impe[n]dimus proximo ...[14]

Basic to all scholastic theology was the urgent sense that by sin man incurred the liability of eternal punishment for which he could not of his own capacity make satisfaction; nor could he set himself back on the way to salvation. The theologians of the early Church had acknowledged that only God could remit this eternal punishment, but had looked on ecclesiastical penances as a gesture of willingness to make satisfaction. This willingness was an earnest of contrition, and was at the same time an impetration for forgiveness. This view was gradually modified both by the very severity of ecclesiastical penances which had resulted in the practice of allowing commutations and redemptions,[15] and by the changes which had taken place in the rite of sacramental penance, eliminating the lapse of time between confession and reconciliation, and attaching the impetratory absolution prayers immediately to the sacramental rite where they took the place of the reconciliation. Since this telescoping of the rite of penance obviously stressed the efficacy of the penitent's contrition, theologians by the eleventh century were at pains to find some justification for the satisfactory works still imposed by the minister of the sacrament, even though the eternal punishment had been remitted when the sin was forgiven. The answer to this problem was of major importance in the development of the notion of indulgences.

----

[13] *Ibid.*, IV, lxxii; cf. III, cli.

[14] *Summa Sancti Raymundi de Peniafort Barcinonensis O.P. De Poenitentia et Matrimonio*, Rome, 1603, lib. 3, p. 468, cols 1 and 2.

[15] There were, of course, wide variations of practice in the application of the penitential system. For some discussion of this, see the article by T. P. Oakley, "Alleviations of penance in the continental penitentials", *Speculum*, XII, 1937, pp. 488-502.

The theory which came to be generally postulated was that, by virtue of the penitent's contrition, confession and absolution, the eternal punishment was commuted to temporal punishment which had some possible proportion to the penitent's capacity for satisfaction.[16] This was a much more reliable hypothesis of the connection between penitential works imposed by the Church, and the remission of punishment due to sin, and it gave rise by the thirteenth century to refinements such as that of St. Bonaventure. In discussing the validity of indulgences he postulated three steps in the commutation of eternal punishment, first a commutation by contrition to temporal punishment still out of proportion to man's capacity to make satisfaction, then a further commutation by sacramental absolution to temporal punishment proportioned to man's strength, and finally a commutation of this major penance to a minor one by means of an indulgence.[17]

As St. Thomas pointed out, the control of the Church over eternal punishment was absolutely essential for the validity of indulgences. If these were merely a remission of ecclesiastical penance (*poenæ iniunctæ*), with no effect on eternal punishment, then they would do the penitent more harm than good, since they would effectively prevent his obtaining the remission promised by the ecclesiastical penance, and would leave him liable to meet his debt in the next life.[18]

To the hypothesis outlined above concerning the commutation of eternal to temporal punishment, Hugh of St.Victor added another important distinction in dividing sin into two logically separable parts, the *culpa*, or guilt, and the *poena*, or punishment. Though the teaching which Hugh based on this division was not generally accepted, the distinction itself became an integral part of the scholastic

---

[16] Cf. B. Poschmann, *Busse und Letzte Ölung*, pp. 83-84.

[17] St. Bonaventure, *In Quartum Librum Sententiarum* (Vol. 4, 1889, of *Opera Omnia*, 10 vols, Quaracchi, 1882-1902), IV, Dist. XX, P II, A I Q 2. Cf. also St. Albert, *Commentarii in IV Sententiarum* (Vols 29-30 of *Opera Omnia*, ed. A. Borgnet, 38 vols, Paris, 1890-99), IV, Dist.XVIII, C, Art.VII. For a discussion of the significance of this whole notion in the works of St. Albert and its relation to the reconciliation of the sinner to the church see B. Kurzawa, *De effectibus sacramentorum relate ad Corpus Christi Mysticum apud St. Albertum Magnum*, Friburg, Switzerland, 1950, pp. 74 *et seq.* St. Thomas, on the other hand, denied that indulgences were commutations; cf. *Summa Theologiae*, ed. De Rubeis, Billuart, P. Faucher, O. P. *et al.*, cum textu ex recensione Leonina, Rome, 1948, *Supplement*, Q 25 a 2 Resp.

[18] *S. T. Supp.*, Q 25 a 1 Resp.

discussion of penance.[19] This was to contribute much to the justification of indulgences, more specifically plenary indulgences, in the
context of the contritionist teaching on the sacrament of penance,
and the nature of the sacramental grace. This is implied in statements
such as that of Alexander of Hales:

> Dico ergo quod susceptio poenitentiae iniunctae ex virtute clavium
> cum proposito poenitendi, et cum absolutione in contrito, hoc totum
> est signum et causa dimissionis peccati quoad culpam et poenam.
> Et nota quod causa in sacramentis non est efficiens, sed causa adaptens,
> quia causa efficiens est ipsa Deus.[20]

Among the extra-sacramental methods of adapting man's works of
satisfaction to his capacity on the one hand, and his debt of punishment on the other, were indulgences, which took their efficacy from
the power of the keys, but which were at one more remove from the
efficient cause of remission than the sacrament itself.[21]

Despite these advances in the theology of satisfaction there remained two contradictory elements in the development of plenary
indulgences up to the period immediately following the Fourth
Lateran Council. One of these was the lack of a theory which would
guarantee unlimited supplies of vicarious satisfaction, and the other
was the related conviction that a remission could be granted only
after the performance of a condign work of satisfaction. From this
standpoint crusade was obviously better fitted than any other penitential work to warrant the grant of a plenary indulgence, since it
subsumed all forms of penance, prayer, fasting, and alms. As Alexander
of Hales remarked,

> maxima poena est obligari voluntarie ad periculum mortis pro fide
> Christi vel pro adversariis fidei impugnandis. [22]

As a condign work of satisfaction crusade conformed more nearly to
the early ecclesiastical penances. On the other hand, up till the time of

---

[19] Cf. P. Anciaux, *La théologie du sacrement de pénitence au XIIe siècle*, pp. 191
et seq., and B. Poschmann, *Busse und Letzte Ölung*, p. 86.

[20] Cf. Bodleian MS 859 f. 354a, quoted by K. F. Lynch in "The doctrine of
Alexander of Hales on the nature of Sacramental Grace", *Franciscan Studies*,
19, 1959, p. 348.

[21] Cf. also B. Kurzawa, *op. cit.*, pp. 81-82, on St. Albert's view of indulgences
as extra-sacramental extensions of the sacramental remission.

[22] Alexander of Hales, *Glossa in Quatuor Libros Sententiarum Petri Lombardi*,
ed. PP Collegii S. Bonaventurae, 4 vols, Florence, 1951-57 (Bibliotheca Franciscana Scholastica Medii Aevi, Vols XII-XV), IV, Dist. XX, 14, IV r. It is to be
noted here in passing how loose is Alexander's definition of crusade.

Hugh of St. Cher's formulation of the doctrine of the treasury of the Church, it was held that all remissions, redemptions and commutations of ecclesiastical penance cast the burden of satisfaction on the body of the faithful. There were difficulties enough in this with regard to assuring the validity of partial indulgences to provoke Abelard's earlier objections to abuse of the power of the keys in episcopal grants of indulgence. Others also were troubled by the uncertainty, since indiscriminate and irresponsible grants meant that an undue strain was being put on the resources of the Church.[23] It is obvious that if there were doubts about the ability of the faithful to satisfy vicariously for partial indulgences, then plenary indulgences imposed an almost insupportable obligation. This accounts for the insistence on the need for discretion in granting indulgences, not only in the relevant canon of the Fourth Lateran Council,[24] but also in contemporary theological definitions.[25]

Always there remained the difficulty of preserving the claims of God's justice which could never be laid aside,[26] and therefore of making provision for condign works of satisfaction performed by some member or members of the body of the faithful. There was no shirking the issue since plenary indulgences were well established in practice, and had to be fitted into any theory. William of Auxerre's solution was unsatisfactory in its almost total subjectivity and reliance on personal moral worth of the *crucesignatus* who was thus given no objective assurance of the efficacy of the indulgence. Though observing that the Church's claims to be able to grant indulgences were not invalidated if the effect of any particular indulgence should fail, he went on to remark,

> Frequenter eni[m] illi qui accipiunt cruce[m] parati sunt mori pro christo et in hoc proposito augmentatur in eis contritio et sic per co[n]tritione[m] dimittitur eis pe[ccata] sicut dicitur de magdelena.[27]

---

[23] Cf. N. Paulus, *op. cit.*, i, pp. 234 *et seq.*, and B. Poschmann, *Der Ablass im Licht der Bussgeschichte*, pp. 79 *et seq.*, discussing the difficulties of the theologians of the early thirteenth century on this score.

[24] Canon 62.

[25] See, for example, William of Auxerre, *Summa Aurea in quattuor libros sententiarum*, ed. Magister Guillermus Quercu, Paris, 1500, IV, tit. De relaxationibus que fiunt per claves Cap. De iusta estimatione, tertia questio, Solutio (f. cclxxxiii r.), Innocent IV, *Apparatus*, V, tit. De poenitentiis et remissionibus Cap. IIII (Quod autem) § 6 and St. Thomas, *S. T. Supp.*, Q 25 a 1 ad 4.

[26] Cf. St. Thomas, *Summa Contra Gentiles*, III, clviii. See also William of Auxerre, *Summa Aurea*, IV, tit, De relaxationibus Cap. De iusta estimatione, tertia questio ad quartum (f. cclxxxii v.).

[27] *Summa Aurea, loc. cit.* (f. cclxxxiii r.).

This merely begged the question. Alexander of Hales' solution was not a major advance on this,

> Ad illud vero quod obicitur de suscipiente crucem pro omni suo peccato, dicimus quod maxima poena est obligari voluntarie ad periculum mortis pro fide Christi vel pro adversariis fidei impugnandis. Potest ergo fieri quod ex passione Christi et ex meritis Ecclesie, cuius unitas in fide consistit, ex hac poena generali satisfactum sit quoad Deum, sed non quoad forum Ecclesie.[28]

Hugh of St. Cher, as quoted by Hostiensis,[29] attributed the remission of sins to the merits of Christ's passion, and the sufferings of the saints, an inexhaustible treasury which at once guaranteed all the Church's obligations, and assured the penitent of an efficacy independent of his own efforts. At one stroke this doctrine removed all difficulties in the way of granting plenary indulgences as far as distributors were concerned; yet it also gave rise to two very divergent schools of thought about the nature and extent of plenary indulgences. What remained an obstacle to an entirely satisfactory definition of doctrine was the question of condign works of satisfaction. St. Thomas adopted a view to which none of his contemporaries subscribed, namely that the efficacy of the treasury was such that the question of condign necessary works was suspended.[30] It must clearly be understood that St. Thomas was assuming in the penitent the desire and capacity to fulfil all the conditions generally agreed as necessary for gaining the indulgence. He was, besides, assuming those qualities of soul considered inherently Christian and without which the life of grace posited by the reception of indulgences could not flourish. The work prescribed by the indulgence was in no degree the efficient cause of the remission of sins, whether it were prayer, fasting or alms. This work was rather the motivating cause which urged the distributor of the indulgence to exercise his power over the treasury of the Church. The extent of the remission depended on the decision of the distributor, and not on the nature of the work.[31] St. Thomas pointed out in this same article that the distributor must protect the intentions of those whose merits were being dispensed, by having a reason for the distribution, but that this reason was not the efficient cause of the indulgence. Even in a case where a distributor

---

[28] *Glossa IV Sent.*, IV, Dist. XX, 14, IV r.
[29] *Summa Aurea*, V, tit. De Remissionibus § 7 (Ad quid valent).
[30] *S. T. Supp.*, Q 25 a 2 Resp.; cf., however, Q 25 a 1 ad 1 & 2.
[31] *S. T. Supp.*, Q 25 a 2.

might grant too large a remission the penitent still received the prescribed remission, though the distributor incurred sin by his imprudence.[32] It was quite in keeping with St. Thomas' general teaching on charity as the form of all the virtues,[33] as the bond of Christian perfection and Christian unity, to attribute such transcendent value to the treasury of the Church. It was also in keeping with his general synthesis of the Christian life, and insistence on its integrity that he should not only stress the sufficiency of merit of Christ's passion "ad omnia peccata totaliter tollenda",[34] but should clearly express the twofold nature of acts of penance, the remission of sin, and the more profound reality of union with God and neighbour.

> Ad residuum sua iniunctione obligat poenitentem: cuius quidem obligationis impletio *satisfactio* dicitur, quae est *tertia* poenitentiae pars; per quam homo totaliter a reatu poenae liberatur, dum poenam exsolvit quam debuit; et alterius debilitas naturalis boni curatur, dum homo a malis abstinet et bonis assuescit; Deo spiritum subiiciendo per orationem; carnem vero domando per ieiunium, ut sit subiecta spiritui; et rebus exterioribus, per eleemosynarum largitionem, proximos sibi adiùngendo, a quibus fuit separatus per culpam.[35]

Yet there is a *caveat*, which in the context refers to sacramental remission, but may be applied more generally:

> sed tamen non omnes effectum remissionis perfecte consequuntur sed unusquisque in tantum consequitur in quantum Christo pro peccatis patienti coniungitur.[36]

Though St. Thomas did thus preserve a balance, there was an evident risk of formalism in removing the absolute necessity for condign works of satisfaction while insisting on the objective efficacy of plenary indulgences.

Elsewhere St. Thomas had discussed the case of a *crucesignatus* dying before he set out to fulfil his vow.[37] Basing himself on the formula contained in the papal letters granting the indulgence St.

---

[32] *S. T. Supp.*, Q 25 a 2 ad 1.

[33] Cf. for example, A. J. Falanga, *Charity the Form of the Virtues according to St. Thomas*, Washington, 1948. Cf. also, O. Lottin, *Psychologie et morale au XIIe et XIIIe siècles*, 6 vols in 7, Gembloux, 1948-1960, Vol. III, *Problèmes de morale*, Part II, pp. 200 *et seq.*

[34] *Summa Contra Gentiles*, IV, lxxii; cf. IV, lv which gives a summary of St. Thomas' view of the whole economy of salvation.

[35] *Summa Contra Gentiles*, IV, lxxii.

[36] *Ibid., loc. cit.*

[37] St. Thomas Aquinas, *Quaestiones Quodlibetales*, ed. R. Spazzi, Rome, 1949, Quod. II, Q VIII a 2 [16].

Thomas declared that the essence of the indulgence lay in the *votum itineris* and not in the *iter* itself, there being no insistence in the letter on the actual fulfilment of the intention. The intention was actually that of aiding the Holy Land rather than the journey considered in itself. If the letters stated that the indulgence was available only to those crossing the sea then those alone would be eligible who did so, but this was not the sense of the letters.[38] Alexander of Hales had also considered that the *crucesignatus* prevented by death from fulfilling his vow would receive the effects of the indulgence,[39] but in this case, as we have seen above,[40] the burden of satisfaction was transferred elsewhere in the Church on earth. The implications of St. Thomas' view for the papal practice of allowing widespread redemption and commutation of crusading vows with a retention of the indulgence, are of far wider significance than its immediate application to the relatively small numbers of *crucesignati* whom an *untimely* death prevented from fulfilling their vows.[41] Once more it is necessary to see this particular view in the context of St. Thomas' more general statement on whether indulgences avail anyone who does not fulfil the necessary conditions.[42] The simple answer is that such a person does not receive the benefit of the indulgence, an answer also given by St. Albert.[43] St. Thomas and St. Albert both add the significant comment that the willingness to perform the works required, and to fulfil the conditions, avail to increase the charity of the penitent, and that this is to be taken as the essential aim of all

---

[38] St. Thomas must have been basing himself on letters of Innocent IV, or even on the crusading decrees of the Fourth Lateran Council and the First Council of Lyons since these conciliar decrees were practically identical, and were not formally enrolled as canons. They could therefore be referred to as "littera". It would be nice to think that St. Thomas was in fact writing with the letter before him which Innocent IV had sent to the prior of the Paris Dominicans on April 2nd, 1253, ordering the preaching of a crusade to be led by Alphonse of Poitiers to Louis IX's aid in the Holy Land (Innocent IV, *Register*, 6469).

[39] *Glossa IV Sent.*, IV, Dist. XX, 14, IV r.

[40] Cf. pp. 41-3, above.

[41] As will be seen in the chapter on the redemption of vows, it was far more common for *crucesignati* to die without fulfilling their vows because they recurrently postponed their departure so long that death from old age intervened. This was the case with Henry III of England. Raymond of Toulouse did, however, die on the seashore, as it were, and thus presents a case of simple intervention by death.

[42] *S. T. Supp.*, Q 27 a 3.

[43] *IV Sent.*, IV, Dist. XX, E, Art. XIX.

indulgences. It does not suffice for the accidental reward which is the remission of sins.[44]

It is not therefore that St. Thomas dismissed completely the notion of proportionate works of satisfaction, but that his stress was on the work as subordinate to the sufficient cause which was the treasury of the Church. The only condition with regard to the work was that it should tend to the honour of God, or the good of the Church, a condition obviously allowing a wide interpretation.[45] This teaching lent a far greater objective validity to the granting of indulgences; if it seemed to cancel some of the personal responsibility of the penitent for meriting the remission of the punishment, yet it was still in direct line with the traditional practice of the Church in assuming a strongly vicarious element in all penitential satisfaction, and in assuming that degree of union in charity of the faithful which was intent on mutual aid to salvation:

> Christus autem pro Ecclesia sua sanguinem suum fudit, et multa alia fecit et sustinuit, quorum aestimatio est infiniti valoris propter dignitatem personae . . . . . . Similiter etiam et omnes alii sancti intentionem habuerunt in his quae passi sunt et fecerunt propter Deum, ut hoc esset ad utilitatem non solum sui, sed etiam totius Ecclesiae.[46]

Moreover St. Thomas more than once insisted that the recipient of an indulgence must beware of allowing the remission of his sins thus gained to constitute an obstacle to his spiritual advance:

> crucesignatis, dum vivunt, consulendum est ut non praetermittant satisfactionis opera, in quantum sunt praeservativa a peccatis futuris licet reatus poenae sit totaliter solutus. Nec ad hoc requiritur aliquis labor; quia sufficit labor passionis Christi. Morientibus autem non est necessaria huiusmodi praeservatio, sed solum liberatio a reatu poenae.[47]

Indulgences, especially plenary indulgences, were thus not to supersede the normal Christian obligation to co-operate by penitential acts in the mystery of God's plenteous redemption through the merits of Christ's passion. Indulgences, whether plenary or partial, were objectively valid to St. Thomas insofar as redemption and salvation were objectively valid to him who co-operated with redeeming grace.

---

[44] This leads St. Albert to the further, strictly logical, but seemingly overlegalistic conclusion that a person who has gained many indulgences may reach heaven sooner than one with more intensity of charity but with fewer indulgences to his credit. The latter would, however, enjoy greater glory in heaven by reason of his more intense charity.

[45] *S. T. Supp.*, Q 25 a 2 Resp.

[46] *Quaest Quod.*, II, Q VIII a 2 [16] Resp.

[47] *Ibid., loc. cit.*, (ad III).

Despite these implications which St. Thomas drew from the doctrine of the treasury of the Church, his greatest contemporaries did not follow him in abandoning the notion of condign satisfaction. St. Albert and St. Bonaventure both insisted on the importance of personal moral achievement, and a just proportion between the indulgenced work and the size of the remission granted:

> Ille autem, qui dat indulgentias, cum eas tribuit, considerat causam pro qua reputat eum dignum tanta gratia; et secundum quod plus vel minus accedunt homines ad illam causam, plus vel minus participant de indulgentia; [48]

> Dicendum ergo ad primum, quod Deus se non negat confirmando indulgentiam Ecclesiae, sed potius se veracem ostendit in hoc quod dixit: 'Quorum remiseritis peccata, remittuntur eis': et verba ista implet, quia secundum mensuram delicti est poena dupliciter proportionata, scilicet in quantitate, et hoc attendit clavis in confessione: vel valore Ecclesiae, et hoc attendit clavis in relaxatione, quando praecipit fieri quod magis valet Ecclesiae, in qua peccata omnia remittuntur.[49]

It is to be noted that Innocent IV in discussing indulgences comes closer to the position of St. Thomas in that he attributed the remission granted by a plenary indulgence to justice on account of the works performed, and liberality on the part of the distributor, since all remission is an act of liberality. On the other hand partial indulgences, for which great works are not demanded, remit sin by sheer liberality.[50]

The greater the insistence on personal moral worth, the less objective validity can be attributed to the remission of temporal punishment by indulgences.[51] Logically this view would serve to tie indulgences more closely to the sacrament than St. Thomas', and would considerably limit the distribution of plenary indulgences, even though crusade was considered a suitably condign work of satisfaction. From the point of view of thirteenth century papal

---

[48] *IV Sent.*, IV, Dist. XX, P. II, A I Q 6.

[49] St. Albert, *IV Sent.*, IV, Dist. XX, E, Art. XVII.

[50] Innocent IV, *Apparatus*, III, tit. De poenitentiis et remissionibus Cap. IIII (Quod autem).

[51] Though not the same thing, this whole question is not unrelated to a point of far greater interest to the scholastics in their discussion of the sacrament of penance, and the power of the keys therein, namely the distinction between attrition and contrition and their respective effects within and outside the sacrament. All these questions were, in fact, symptomatic of, and influenced by, growing awareness of the psychological elements involved; cf. O. Lottin, *op. cit.*, for a very lengthy discussion of precisely this increase in psychological awareness.

crusading policy, St. Thomas' view was far more widely applied in practice, though in theory the popes would probably have claimed to subscribe to the notion of the necessity of condign works of satisfaction.

However fundamental a difference this may seem to postulate, there was in fact, fairly general agreement about the conditions necessary for the efficacious grant and reception of an indulgence. The distributor had to possess the necessary authority, that is, the power of the keys,[52] and must use that authority with discretion.[53] In illustrating an invalid cause for such a grant, St. Bonaventure ruled out going to see tourneys, an example which one would hope was a theological joke, but which may have had some basis in a confusion between the warlike pursuits of *crucesignati* when directed towards crusade, or simply when pursued for their own sake as pleasure by *crucesignati*. No doubt the trouvère who spoke of his venture overseas as a "glorious tornoi" [54] expressed a common attitude, and bears witness to a likely confusion. The recipient of the indulgence was required to be in a state of grace, that is, to be contrite and to have at least the intention of going to confession.[55] He had to believe in the power of the keys over the remission of sins,[56] and to have a serious reason for seeking the remission of his sins by means of an indulgence, rather than by penitential works; normally an indulgence was a valid substitute for penitential works only for the bodily infirm. However, the penitent could also be considered eligible for an indulgence if he were motivated by the needs of a particular place, so

---

[52] Cf., for example, Alexander of Hales, *Glossa IV Sent.*, IV, Dist. XX, 14, I c; William of Auxerre, *Summa Aurea*, IV, tit. De relaxationibus que fiunt per claves Solutio (f. cclxxxii r.); St. Albert, *IV Sent.*, IV, Dist. XX, E, Art. 16, Solutio; St. Bonaventure, *IV Sent.*, IV, Dist., XX, P II, Q 6; St. Thomas, *S.T. Supp.*, Q 25 a 2 Resp.; Innocent IV, *Apparatus*, V, tit. De poenitentiis et remissionibus Cap. IIII (Quod autem).

[53] See p. 42, footnote 25, above.

[54] "Douce dame, cui j'ain en bone foi", printed in J. Bédier, *Les chansons de croisade*, Paris, 1909, No. xxviii, p. 290.

[55] St. Bonaventure, *IV Sent.*, IV, Dist. XX, P II, Art. I Q 6 Conclusio; cf. William of Auxerre, *Summa Aurea*, IV, tit. De relaxationibus Solutio (f. cclxxxii r.); Alexander of Hales, *Glossa IV Sent*, IV, Dist. XX, 14, 1 c; Innocent IV, *Apparatus*, V, tit. De poenitentiis et remissionibus Cap. IIII (Quod autem); St. Thomas, *S.T. Supp.*, Q 27 a 1 Resp.

[56] The question of the power of the keys over the remission of sin was an integral part of the discussion of the sacrament of penance, and was also intimately linked with opposition to heretical denials of the efficacy of sacerdotal absolution, and of the need for a sacramental priesthood. See also p. 37, footnote 9, above.

as to contribute in person, money, or kind.[57] The bodily infirm were accorded an indulgence because they were unable to perform penitential works; those who engaged in works, such as crusading, or building churches, which were not within the penitential system proper were accorded indulgences because the works in which they engaged were more profitable to the common good. Finally it was considered that the recipient must have the permission of his confessor for the remission of temporal punishment for which penitential works had been prescribed in the sacrament.[58]

Despite this common body of doctrine, the relative newness of the coherent teaching on indulgences led to a certain looseness of terminology which produced its own problems and misunderstandings. There was a tendency early in the century to use the terms *absolutio*, *remissio*, *relaxatio* and *indulgentia* interchangeably. Even when *absolutio* became more specific in its application in the sacrament, the problem remained. Attendant difficulties are to be seen in the learned altercation which arose in 1265 between the English clergy and the papal legate, Cardinal Ottobuono Fieschi, who, in the course of his legatine duties issued letters granting a "remissio peccatorum" without making specific use of the word *indulgentia*.[59] No doubt the English clergy were perturbed by their knowledge that defective legal form constituted an invalidating factor, as a goodly proportion of letters in every episcopal or papal register bear witness. Ottobuono's response was tart, and would have gladdened the heart of many a sixteenth century reformer,

> Scimus autem quoniam Dominus omnium et magister qui neminem capere volebat in verbo, cum dixit 'Remittuntur tibi peccata tua', non dixit omnia set peccata, et in sacris eloquiis vix aut numquam indulgentiam, remissionis autem vocabulam sepius inuenimus.[60]

He did, however, promise new letters in conformity with the English demand. In relation to this sort of problem, St. Thomas, who was

---

[57] This embraced pilgrimages, crusade, helping to build or repair monasteries, churches, chapels, shrines, hospitals and bridges, and contributing to their upkeep.

[58] Alexander of Hales, *Glossa IV Sent.*, IV, Dist. XX, 14, I c. This condition was not generally observed in its strictest form in the thirteenth century, especially as indulgences became more detached from the sacramental rite itself. The obligation of confession remained. Cf. St. Albert, *IV Sent.*, IV, Dist. XX, E, Art. XVII, Solutio.

[59] Cf. "Letters of Cardinal Ottoboni", ed. R. Graham in *English Historical Review*, XV, 1900, pp. 87-120, Letter xiii to Henry III, pp. 102-3.

[60] *Ibid.*, p. 103.

always careful to accept the legal position, scrupulously stressed the fact that God's grace can be hindered only by defective intention of the recipient, and does not depend on legal forms.[61] The precise problem of the English clergy was the notion that the will of the distributor was of primary importance in ensuring the efficacy of the indulgence, granted that all other conditions had been fulfilled.[62]

The question of legatine grants of indulgence points to another important development in the theory of indulgences subsequent to the formulation of the doctrine of the treasury of the Church. Previously the granting of indulgences had been considered to come under the ordinary power of the keys as exercised by any priest with jurisdiction over souls in virtue of his ordination. Such was the nature of the treasury of the Church that its sole guardian was seen to be him who alone had plenitude of power, namely the pope. There was thus substituted the notion of a reserved power of the keys which was one purely of jurisdiction, and not of the essence of the priesthood, to be exercised only by the pope or by those specifically delegated by him. Not even bishops had this right *ex officio*.[63] It was because indulgences belonged to this category of delegated power of the keys that legates, even if they were not in orders, were able to grant indulgences. St. Thomas makes specific mention of bishops elect as enjoying this delegated authority,[64] having in mind no doubt such contemporaries as Peter of San Giorgio, bishop elect of Ferrara, and papal legate to Germany during the reign of Innocent IV. This served still further to separate indulgence from the sacrament by very reason of the distinction drawn between the two modes of operation of the power of the keys, a separation not counteracted by the insistence of all letters of indulgence on the need for the recipients to be "vere corde contriti et ore confessi", since the practice of requiring a confessor's permission for the taking of a crusading vow had fallen into desuetude.

The reservation of the power of the keys over the treasury of the Church to the pope, or his specific delegates, was connected with the reservation to the pope of crusading vows. Only Alexander of Hales makes a causal connection between the reservation of the vow,

---

[61] Cf. pp. 45-6, above.

[62] Cf. St. Thomas, *S. T. Supp.*, Q 25 a 2 ad I, and Hostiensis, *Summa Aurea*, tit. De remissionibus, § 8 (Item).

[63] Cf. St. Thomas, *S. T. Supp.*, Q 26 a 1-4; St. Bonaventure, *IV Sent.*, IV, Dist. XX, P II, A I Q 3; Innocent IV, *Apparatus*, V, tit. De poenitentiis et remissionibus Cap. IIII (Quod autem) § 5.

[64] *S. T. Supp.*, Q 26 a 3 Resp.

and the plenary remission of sins.[65] Because of the difficulties in guaranteeing the Church's ability to meet her obligations of vicarious satisfaction in the matter of plenary indulgences, it is plain why Alexander of Hales should have sought to take proper precautions against any indiscriminate redemption of crusading vows. This implies, of course, that such a redemption did not cancel the plenary indulgence; it did, however, remit the condign work of satisfaction which the *crucesignatus* himself would have performed in fulfilling his vow, and by which he would have decreased the burden of vicarious satisfaction to be borne by the faithful. Alexander's statement also implied that the reservation of the vow was aimed solely at avoiding too heavy a burden of satisfaction, and neglected any consideration of the practical need of thus guaranteeing the crusading force against indiscriminate diminution by a widespread redemption of vows. Both Innocent IV and Hostiensis accept the reservation of crusading vows to the pope without advancing any such reason as Alexander of Hales, Hostiensis concentrating rather on the practical aspects of redemption and commutation of vows.[66] In effect, though all indulgences were reserved to the pope, the ordinary delegation of jurisdiction to bishops sufficed for partial indulgences provided that they did not exceed the due limit.[67] In practice, therefore, only crusading indulgences required a special delegation of authority by the pope, and this accorded with the normal view that crusade was peculiarly the business of the pope. The effect of his control of plenary indulgences was not only to support his control of crusade, but also to tighten the bond between plenary indulgence and crusade. It also resulted in a tendency to manipulate crusade in the interests of a wider spread of plenary indulgences, rather than to grant such indulgences outside crusade. In this the popes seemed to be subscribing to the idea of the necessity of a condign work of satisfaction, while at the same time their liberal grants of redemptions and commutations in the interest of finance or politics, argued an approach to St. Thomas' rejection of the absolute necessity for condign satisfaction. Consistency has never been a marked characteristic of practical politics, and this applies no less to the theological consistency of thirteenth century popes than to those of any other century, or to the politics of any other recorded attempt at theocratic government.

---

[65] *Glossa IV Sent.*, IV, Dist. XXXVIII, 6 f.

[66] Hostiensis, *Summa Aurea*, III, tit. De voto § 12 (Qualiter); Innocent IV, *Apparatus*, III, tit. De voto Cap. I (De peregrinationis).

[67] Cf. St. Thomas, *S. T. Supp.*, Q 26 a 3.

CHAPTER FOUR

INDULGENCES IN PRACTICE

(a) INTRODUCTORY REMARKS

From the text of the conciliar decrees discussed above, it is easy to distinguish the general rules for the grant of crusading indulgences. Plenary remissions of sin were to be given to all *crucesignati*. This appears to be a simple and straightforward principle until one realises that *crucesignati* were of three different kinds:

(i) the first type was the man who took the cross with the intention of going on crusade in the next general passage,[1] or of leading the next general passage himself. He went at his own expense, though this did not preclude a subsidy.[2] Such a *crucesignatus* was expected to lead a number of warriors proportionate to his wealth, and status.[3] This type of *crucesignatus* was, in fact, one of

---

[1] What follows applies, *mutatis mutandis*, to clerical and lay *crucesignati* alike. The cleric was prohibited from fighting, though he sometimes forgot himself in the heat of a crisis. (Cf. Jean de Joinville, *Histoire de Saint Louis*, ed. N. de Wailly, ninth edition, Paris, 1921, lii, § 258-9). His vow was strictly one of pilgrimage, and his service was to provide spiritual aid and comfort to the combatants. If he were a prelate he led a band of fighting men, and was in all respects, save taking part personally in the fighting, a *crucesignatus* of the first type. (Cf. Hostiensis, *Summa Aurea*, V, tit. De voto § 12 (Qualiter et)). Prelates did not always refrain from personal participation in the fighting. Joinville tells the story of the bishop of Soissons, whom he wrongly names Jaque de Castel, who attacked a group of Saracens single handed after the defeat at Damietta. The seneschal attributes this action to the bishop's great desire to be with God (lxxvii, § 393).

[2] Going at one's own expense can only have meant accepting ultimate responsibility for the raising and management of funds, and not meeting all expenses out of one's own pocket. All the princes and magnates received papal subsidies; many received royal subsidies as well. Even St. Louis could be suspected of having spent none of his own money, but only what he had received by way of subsidy. (Cf. Joinville, lxxxiii, § 427). Joinville's own case is to the point. He mortgaged his property so that he should take with him nothing to which he did not have a right (xxv, § 113), but he was also in the pay of Peter de Courtenay (lxxx, § 412). He declared to King Louis his intention of staying in the Holy Land at his own expense, or at someone else's. In fact the king provided for his needs (lxxxvi, § 439-441).

[3] Joinville, for example, took with him nine knights, three knights-banneret, and presumably a proportionate number of lesser *crucesignati*. Richard Giffard, a relative of Alexander III of Scotland, is recorded as intending to take five knights with him (Innocent IV, *Register*, 4814; cf. *Calendar of Entries in the Papal Registers relating to Great Britain and Ireland*, ed. W. H. Bliss, Vol. I, London, 1893,

a relatively small group who constituted the leaders of any crusade.[4] It is clear from the observations of Hostiensis that this group might technically include women who chose to take the cross and follow their husbands or to recruit a band of followers, and accompany this band on crusade.[5]

(ii) The second type of *crucesignatus* was the man who assumed the cross with the intention of setting out at the next general passage, but at the expense of someone else. This type constituted the majority of any band of crusaders, and were, one might say, non-professional mercenaries.[6] They were not always connected by strict feudal ties to their immediate leader, but hired themselves out to the man who would pay them.[7]

(iii) The third type of *crucesignatus*, distinct from the group immediately above, was the man who acted as a substitute for someone unable to fulfil his own vow, or for someone who had taken a vow with the full intention of providing substitutes according to his means.[8] This group was far more likely to embrace the simple mercenary, though substitution could be a family arrangement.[9]

---

p. 261). Gibaud de Saint-Verain's number of followers is unspecified (Innocent IV, *Register*, 3317. This man is wrongly styled Giraudus in the letter of grant). Barral des Baux, doing homage to Alphonse of Poitiers, swore to go to the Holy Land with ten followers for a year, with the interesting stipulation that if one of the followers died Barral should not be held responsible for providing another, but should serve the required time with the remaining men (*Layettes du trésor des Chartes*, eds A. Teulet and J. de Laborde, 3 vols, Paris, 1863-75, iii, No. 4037).

[4] As is shown by Joinville's case, the delimitation of the first two groups of *crucesignati* is not always simple.

[5] *Summa Aurea*, III, tit. De voto § 9 (Quis). He distinguished elsewhere between vows taken out of devotion to visit the Holy Land, and vows to go to the aid of the Holy Land (§ 14 Et utrum). Women accompanying their husbands would normally take vows which belonged to the first category. Alice, countess of Blois, was presumably a *crucesignata* of her own right. She was granted a subsidy by Urban IV if she should assume the cross with her husband who was already *crucesignatus* (*Les Registres d'Urbain IV*, 1261-64, eds L. Dorez and J. Guiraud, 4 vols, Paris, 1899-1958, 690). She eventually set out from Marseilles for Acre in 1286-7 with a great company of men-at-arms, and died in Acre in 1288. (See *Annales de Terre Sainte*, ed. R. Röhricht in *Archives de l'Orient latin*, ii, 1884, pp. 459-60, and Marino Sanudo, *Secreta Fidelium Crucis*, in Bongars, lib. iii, pars xii, cap. xx, for the year 1287, p. 229).

[6] Some *crucesignati*, like Joinville, made certain provision on their own behalf, others, described in papal letters as "poor", were either wholly subsidised, or encouraged to redeem their vows so as not to put too great a strain on the general resources. To this group of *crucesignati* belong the lesser clergy who acted as chaplains and confessors.

[7] This is most clearly shown in the general upheaval following St. Louis' decision to stay in the Holy Land, and Joinville's narration of his own recruiting.

[8] This matter will be discussed more fully in the section on redemption of vows.

[9] Henry III, for example, used Edmund as his substitute in 1268 (Clement

It is clear that all three groups of *crucesignati* described above, would in the ordinary course of events, become crusaders in fact, and so would fulfil the conditions necessary for gaining the promised indulgence. There were no complicating factors here. What did serve to complicate the matter of crusading indulgences, within the context of crusade to the Holy Land itself, was the provision in the decrees from 1215 onwards for the grant of plenary indulgences to yet another group of people who became in effect, quasi-*crucesignati*, by reason of their indulgence, and their assumption of the cross. These people were not the ordinary *crucesignati* who were prevented by some major impediment from actually setting out, and for the redemption of whose vows the 1215 decree made special provision. On the contrary, it is made clear in the context that there was envisaged a group of people to whom the full crusading indulgence was granted on account of their material contribution to the crusade. In the light of the theological teaching on indulgences already discussed, it is to be presumed that a simple monetary contribution, no matter how large, was never considered a sufficiently condign work of satisfaction to merit a plenary remission. The contribution had to be accompanied by a *votum itineris*, and therefore by the assumption of the cross, even though the journey was to be undertaken by a substitute. One is still left to account for the anomaly of having a merely ostensible intention of going on crusade accepted as fulfilling the conditions for the efficacious reception of a plenary remission of sins. The practice of taking crusading vows with the intention of redeeming them is sufficiently well-attested for there to be no doubt that this group of contributors were regarded as *crucesignati* even though they never intended to be crusaders.[10]

The admission of such crusaders-by-proxy helped to swell crusading funds, but ultimately constituted an active menace to the recruitment of crusaders-in-fact. While they were taken only from the rank of those genuinely prevented from going on crusade by some impediment existing prior to their taking the cross, there was no real danger. In practice, however, the opinion that there was no absolute necessity

---

IV, *Register*, 609), and later, Edward I sought to do the same (See *Registrum Epistolarum Fratris Johannis Peckham, Archiepiscopi Cantuariensis*, ed. C. T. Martin, Rolls Series, 3 vols, London, 1882-85, i, No. cxviii and *The Register of William Wickwane, Lord Archbishop of York 1279-85*, Surtees Society Vol. CXIV, London, 1907, No. 467, also printed in *Historical Papers and Letters from the Northern Registers*, ed. J. Raine, Rolls Series, London, 1873, No. xxxviii).

[10] This will be discussed in the section on redemption of vows.

for the performance of any condign work to gain an indulgence, prevailed, and ultimately contributed to the dwindling efficacy of crusading indulgence as a means of recruiting forces to go to the Holy Land. It should be made clear at this stage of the discussion that this group of *crucesignati*, like those who redeemed their vows, were not eligible for the material rewards promised to those intent on fulfilling their vows.[11] Likewise it should be kept in mind that the motives for granting a full indulgence to this group were not all interested. The popes were genuinely concerned to offer the same chances of salvation to all the faithful, but the tergiversations of men like Henry III, Hakon of Norway and Alfonso X of Castille point the dangers of such a democratic notion of plenary indulgences.

Within the terms of the conciliar decrees there is to be noted a further extension of the plenary remission of sins, namely to those providing ships for transport overseas, or for contributing to the building of such ships.[12] Undoubtedly the plenary indulgence would depend on the proportion of the contribution to total revenue, but of all recipients of the crusading indulgence, the donors of ships would appear to have reaped the richest return for their efforts. They do not seem to have provided free transport, if one can judge by the negotiations carried out for the hire of ships,[13] but they did have to forego the profits from trade while the ship was engaged as a transport. There was undoubtedly a heavy risk that the ship would be lost in the course of the campaign, but if it were not, it was then at the

---

[11] Further discussion of this point will be included in the section on crusader privileges and protections. See below, pp. 168-9, 175-6.

[12] The wording of the decrees on this matter is obscure, but transport was a notoriously difficult problem. It is, therefore, safe to assume that shipowners would be offered the maximum inducement. Unless the owners were also the masters of the vessels, they probably did not rank as *crucesignati*; although the position of the clause concerning the provision of ships differs in the decree of 1274 from that of the other two decrees of 1215 and 1245, none of the decrees seems to indicate more than the grant of "an indulgence according to contribution".

[13] There is a certain amount of evidence for the money paid for hiring ships by King Louis (*Layettes*, ii, 3537, and R. Sternfeld, *Ludwigs des Heiligen Kreuzzug nach Tunis 1270* (Historische Studien, IV), Berlin, 1896, Exkurs iii, pp. 363-368) and Alphonse of Poitiers (*Layettes*, iii, 3789). Joinville hired a ship in conjunction with his cousin the lord of Aspremont (xxiv, § 109). Henry III wrote to the patriarch of Jerusalem concerning help with the provision of ships for his crossing (T. Rymer, *Foedera, Conventiones Literae, ex cujuscunque generis Acta Publica*, 16 vols, London, 1704-1715, i, p. 473). Urban IV specifically requested the Venetians to provide transport "sine naula" for those going to help against Michael Palaeologus in 1262 (*Register*, 131).

owner's disposal. No doubt the loss of trade and the heavy risks were considered a sufficient cause for the grant of a plenary indulgence, to entice the co-operation of shipowners in a crusading venture. Urban II had declared quite explicitly that an indulgence would be granted to anyone who set out to liberate the Church in Jerusalem "pro sola devotione, non pro honoris vel pecuniae adeptione", [14] but by the thirteenth century to make a profit from a crusade was a common enough expectation. There was, however, a calculable difference between Henry III's attempts to claim his subsidy without going on crusade, for example, and the almost wholly commercial transaction connected with the provision of ships and the gaining of the indulgence.

The decrees also made provision for the grant of partial indulgences to those making minor contributions to the crusade, contributions which ranged from money to the undefined "auxilium vel consilium".[15] The operative factor in determining the difference between a plenary and a partial remission of sins was not the *amount* contributed but the proportion which this amount represented of the donor's wealth. The extent of such partial indulgences was dependent on the decision of the distributor, and was not a threat to crusade so long as grants were not rationalised for convenience, and the rate of exchange remained high.[16]

---

[14] Mansi, Vol. XX, col. 816.

[15] The giving of "consilium" seems to have been a special function of the clergy, their usefulness in providing which hindered the redemption of their vows in the opinion of Hostiensis, *Summa Aurea*, tit. De voto et voti redemptione § 12 (Qualiter).

[16] The Fourth Lateran Council strictly limited the amount which bishops might grant by way of indulgence (cf. Canon 62), but the popes tended to differ in the amounts which they normally granted. A statistical survey of the amounts of partial indulgences granted by the popes in the latter half of the thirteenth century shows that Innocent IV, though he tended to give more generously for contributions to the building of churches, was the most moderate, and that the general level tended to rise. It is interesting to note that whereas Innocent IV is recorded in the *Calendar of Papal Letters* for England as having granted in England nine indulgences, ranging from twenty days to one year and forty days, at the end of the century the Franciscan, Nicholas IV, is recorded as having granted one hundred and twenty six partial indulgences of which one hundred and twenty three were for one year and forty days. It must be remembered that most of the local indulgences were within the competence of the local hierarchy. Thus the registers of John Le Romeyn record episcopal grants for visiting churches, altars, newly built chapels and shrines, for contributing to the building repair and upkeep of cathedrals, abbeys, churches, hospitals, bridges and a leper hospice, for praying for the dead, and for the Austin friars, as well as for listening to crusading sermons. The registers of Walter Gray, archbishop of York add to this list the building of causeways and roads.

(b) CRUSADE INDULGENCE TO THE HOLY LAND

After these general remarks it is possible to proceed to a more particular examination of evidence of the widening of the grant of crusading indulgences first in relation to the Holy Land, and then for crusading not directed at the traditional goal. It is evident that no new category of *crucesignati* could be added to those already defined by the conciliar decrees. The next logical step, that of substituting a work unrelated to crusade had to wait until after the loss of Acre, and the end of the crusading era.[17] New groups of participants in a crusading indulgence tended, therefore, to be connected, even if peripherally, with crusade itself, or with *crucesignati*. Most closely connected were the crusader wives to whom Innocent IV granted a full plenary indulgence.[18] These were the wives of English *crucesignati*, proposing to set out with Henry III. This practice seems to have begun as a placatory gesture to wives who might wish to prevent their husbands' departure on crusade. The sort of feminine reaction against crusade reported by the trouvères and minnesingers [19] was noticed in a different way by the theologians and canonists. While the poets dramatised the plaints of lovers and their mistresses at being torn apart by the exigencies of crusade,[20] the theologians were drily discussing the question whether or not a man was justified in taking the cross, should his wife be unwilling for him to do so, and should his absence be a potential danger to her virtue. Alexander of Hales roundly declared that the man, as head of his wife, might go on crusade without her consent, and that she must follow him if she would otherwise consider herself defrauded of her marital debt.[21]

---

[17] By this is meant the era of effective crusade, covering the period of the existence of the mainland kingdom. It is not intended to enter into discussion of the nature of the crusade after the fall of Acre.

[18] Innocent IV, *Register*, 5980; cf. *C.P.L.* I, p. 279.

[19] Typical of these are "Jherusalem, Grant damage me fais" and "Chanterai por mon corage", both printed in J. Bédier, *Les chansons de croisade*, Paris, 1909, xxvi, pp. 278-9, x, pp. 112-4. The question is discussed at greater length by P. Throop, *Criticism of the Crusade*, pp. 156 *et seq.*; see also A. Lecoy de la Marche, "La prédication de la croisade au treizième siècle", *Revue des Questions Historiques*, xlviii, 1890, p. 20. One must not overlook the fact that not all the ladies reacted against *crusade*; some expressed great grief at the separation, but acknowledged the superior demands of the Holy Land. See for example the lady's reply in "Douce dame, cui j'ain en bone foi", J. Bédier, *op. cit.*, No. xxviii, p. 290, stanza ii.

[20] One must not overlook either, the fact that such plaints were coloured by equally exigent demands of the courtly love tradition in which the poets were writing.

[21] *Glossa IV Sent.*, IV, Dist. XXXII, 6.

The husband had this right because taking the cross against heretics, or for the purpose of liberating the Holy Land, was a greater good than respect for his wife's conjugal rights.[22] As if dissatisfied with the apparent slight to women contained in this decision, Alexander explained that the husbands only enjoyed this right because they were competent to fight, and that it was on this account not reciprocal.

Hostiensis discussed the question at length [23] and arrived at the conclusion that women could take a vow to go to the Holy Land without the consent of their husbands. The real question was whether they could fulfil the vow without his consent. This depended entirely on the circumstances, whether the lady was too young, likely to fall into bad repute, and such dangers. If this were likely she would redeem her vow, as one unable to set out. If, however, she was of mature age, good repute, and able to take many fighting men with her, she was obliged to fulfil her vow, even seemingly without her husband's consent.[24]

St. Thomas, on the other hand, denied to husbands the right to go on crusade without their wives' consent, since crusade was not necessary for individual salvation, but the proper care of their wives was an essential obligation of all husbands.[25] If the wife were legitimately impeded from following her husband on crusade, and was placed in jeopardy of salvation by his absence, then the man might not justly go on crusade. None of these conclusions about the status of women bore any strict relation to the love-lorn situations evoked by the poets, since the dramatic essence of the poems lay so often in the absence of any legitimate bond between lover and lady, but they did show an awareness of the problems which arose in the domestic arrangements of a *crucesignatus*. One may safely conclude from a letter of Gregory X in which reference is made to the redemption of vows by those "propter . . . sexus fragilitatem inhabiles vel impotentes . . . ad pugnandum vel transfretandum" [26] that women could be included in their own right in that group of *crucesignati* whose plenary indulgence depended on contribution, and not on personal service. From this

---

[22] Alexander of Hales, *Glossa IV Sent.*, Dist. XXXII, 6.

[23] *Summa Aurea*, III, tit. De voto § 9 (Quis).

[24] Hostiensis went on to consider with an engagingly scholastic lack of a sense of the ridiculous whether a prostitute who could take a large number of followers with her, should be allowed to redeem a vow to go to the Holy Land (*Summa Aurea*, III, tit. De voto § 10).

[25] Cf. *Quaest. Quod.*, IV, Q VII a 2 [11].

[26] Gregory X, *Register*, 497.

letter one may further conclude that the grant of an indulgence on
account of their husbands' service, implies that the women had neither
to make a contribution, nor to accompany their husbands. It is uncertain whether this indulgence was operative only if the husbands
fulfilled their vows, or whether it applied equally to the wives of
crucesignati who redeemed their vows, or who had earned an indulgence by means of a contribution.

Quite a different case was the grant of a full indulgence to the
proctors of crusaders while the latter were overseas, and had to
commit their business entirely into the hands of their officials.[27] The
reason assigned for such a grant by Innocent IV in a letter to the
treasurer of St. Hilaire concerning the procurators of Alphonse of
Poitiers is not wholly satisfying:

> cum sacra dicente scriptura, equa debeat esse pars descendentis
> ad prelium et ad sarcinas remanentis . . . [28]

It is easy to see that the purpose of the crusaders was to achieve for
their officials a grant of the same privileges and protections as they
themselves enjoyed. This would be an inestimable help in allowing
the officials maximum freedom and safety in the conduct of business.
While the central aim of the crusader was to protect his rights in his
absence, and to expedite his business, the grant of a crusading indulgence for the execution of his business enhanced the status of the
crusader, and that of the official. The latter became, in effect, a
crucesignatus. It is curious to note that not one of the privileges and
protections accorded to crusaders was peculiar to that state,[29] and that
any, or all of these privileges and protections might have been obtained for the official without his becoming a *crucesignatus*, with a full
crusading indulgence. Moreover the fact that the indulgence was
gained in the pursuit of everyday duties which were connected with
crusade only at a few removes, established a dangerous precedent.
Urban IV seems to have feared that this was a dangerous precedent,
or else he was aware of already existing abuses, for in a letter to
Alphonse of Poitiers in 1264 he specified that the count's officials
could enjoy a crusading indulgence,

---

[27] A. Potthast, *Regesta Pontificum Romanorum inde ab A. Christum natum 1198-
1304*, 2 vols, Berlin, 1874-75, 13416. On the functions of these proctors see
D. E. Queller, "Thirteenth Century Diplomatic Envoys: Nuncii and Procuratores", *Speculum*, XXXV, 1960, pp. 196-213.

[28] Innocent IV, *Register*, 6440.

[29] See the section specially reserved for a discussion of this subject in Chapter
Six, below.

si crucesignati fuerint et alias essent transituri in ejusdem terrae
succursum et de bonis congrue missuri sint in subsidium dictae terrae.[30]

Perhaps in the same category could be placed the envoys despatched
by Philip III of France to the Holy Land in 1273, to ascertain the state
of the Crusader Kingdom.[31] It is not altogether clear if these men were
the recipients of a crusading indulgence because they were the envoys
of a king, *crucesignatus*, or because their journey was to the Holy Land,
or because that journey was particularly hazardous at the time.
Whatever the pretext—and it can have been no more than a pretext—
this was yet another extension of crusade indulgence ostensibly
within the framework of crusade to the Holy Land.

Extension of full crusading indulgence to those making monetary
contributions without personal service is easier to reconcile with the
traditional norms only insofar as financial support was a perpetual
necessity. The *amount* of the contribution being open, the extent of
the indulgence depended on the proportion which this amount represented of the donor's income. The conciliar decrees leave this
proportion open, but later papal letters relieved the collectors of
some of the pressure of *ad hoc* decisions by specifying the minimum
contribution to gain a plenary indulgence as a quarter.[32] Urban IV
seems to have reverted to a less specific standard of measurement in
his letters of October, 1263, ordering the preaching of a crusade in
France.[33] For King Louis' second crusade Clement IV made a further
concession of a plenary indulgence to tax payers who voluntarily
extended their tenth or twentieth for a fourth year.[34] This spelt a grave
emergency in the Holy Land, now being troubled by the campaigns
of Baibars. Strangely enough, in his letters to the Mendicant pro-
vincials in France appointing the two orders to the preaching of a
crusade in France against Baibars, Clement did not even specify the
ordinary indulgences in detail.[35] On the other hand, the pope's instructions to his legate Simon de Brie, cardinal priest of St. Cecilia,
do outline the ordinary indulgences.[36]

It is not therefore surprising that this period saw the extension

---

[30] Urban IV, *Register*, 2181.
[31] Gregory X, *Register*, 337.
[32] Cf. Innocent IV, *Register*, 6469.
[33] Urban IV, *Register*, 467-468.
[34] Clement IV, *Register*, 627.
[35] Cf. T. Ripoll, *Bullarium Ordinis FF. Praedicatorum*, Rome 1729, i (Clement IV) xxxvi.
[36] Clement IV, *Register*, 1493, 1504.

of full crusading indulgences to the agents concerned with the implementation of crusading policy, the preachers and collectors. The nature of the effort expended by these agents differed from that of crusaders proper, but it also differed between the two groups, though both were striving to promote crusade. St. Thomas listed preaching crusade as one of the purely spiritual activities for which an indulgence could be granted.[37] What happened in both these cases of grants to preachers and collectors was that there was usually a specified minimum time of service. Innocent IV granted a crusading indulgence in 1252 to the preachers appointed for the crusade to be led by Alphonse of Poitiers.[38] In 1262 Urban IV granted a plenary indulgence to friars preaching a crusade to the Holy Land,[39] and in the following year granted the same indulgence to all preachers and other officials engaged in promoting the crusade, provided that their service was of one year's duration.[40] This minimum period of service was reduced by Clement IV to six months,[41] but Gregory X, typically, raised it to three years.[42] Death in the course of such service was considered the equivalent of having fulfilled the whole term.[43]

From the time of Clement IV letters of appointment of collectors specified a crusading indulgence for these officials, at first for the collector in chief, with a partial indulgence for his deputies, but on occasions without such a distinction.[44] The collector in chief had greater responsibility not only in deciding difficult cases, but in keeping an eye on all deputy collectors.[45] The difficulties of collecting cru-

---

[37] *S. T. Supp.*, Q 25 a 3 ad 2. It is interesting to note that St. Thomas remarks that the same indulgence is *sometimes* granted to those who preach as to those who go on crusade. The practice seems to have become more general after the pontificate of Innocent IV.

[38] *Register*, 6469.

[39] Ripoll ,i (Urban IV) xv.

[40] Urban IV, *Register*, 469, 2973.

[41] Clement IV, *Register*, 1627, 1683.

[42] Ripoll, i (Gregory X) xxxii; *C.P.L.*, I, p. 449.

[43] Ripoll, *loc. cit.*

[44] Cf. W. E. Lunt, *Papal Revenues in the Middle Ages*, 2 vols, New York, 1934, i, No. 44, pp. 187-90. This is a collector's commission issued by Gregory X in 1275, and accords a full indulgence to deputy collectors. It is useful to compare this with No. 343, p. 186, which is a similar commission issued by Alexander IV with much less detail; cf. also *Les Registres* (de Grégoire X et) *de Jean XXI*, ed. (J. Guiraud &) E. Cadier, Paris, 1892-1960, 13, 110; *Les Registres de Nicholas III*, ed. J. Gay, Paris, 1898-1938, No. 537; *Les Registres de Martin IV*, ed. L'Ecole française de Rome et F. Olivier-Martin, Paris, 1901-1935, No. 436.

[45] See, for example, the warnings issued by Clement IV, *Register*, 1608, and Nicholas III, *Register*, 545.

sading taxes increased during the course of the century, and the business was not unattended by danger, as witness the report of his trials submitted by Aliro, canon of San Marco of Venice, collector in Salzburg and neighbouring areas.[46] Justifiable as these extensions of crusading indulgence were in terms of effort expended, and of the goal of that effort, they still represented a diminution of strength in the bond between actual crusade endeavour, and crusading indulgence. Plausible enough to argue parallel difficulties and dangers, but unreasonable to go on expecting these same instruments of policy to be as effective in the enticement of actual crusaders. The more alternative means of acquiring a plenary indulgence there were, the less faith there was possible in crusade's unique spiritual value. Crusade as the sole condign work of satisfaction was rapidly becoming a legal fiction at a time when the Crusader States were more desperately vulnerable than ever before in their existence.

(c) Partial Indulgences

The elevation of the partial indulgence granted to deputy collectors into a plenary one is the only example of its kind in this period for a work related to crusade. The same tendency to widen the scope of partial indulgence in the context of crusade is, however, observable. The conciliar decrees had provided for the grant of partial indulgences for various minor contributions to the work of crusade. At the same time as the major contribution was fixed at a quarter, the minor one was reckoned at a tenth.[47] There is one extremely interesting grant of a partial indulgence for an indirect contribution to crusade contained in a letter of Innocent IV to Eudes de Châteauroux concerning a confraternity of the lesser *crucesignati* of Châteaudun. For those making donations to the confraternity (of whom one would dearly love to know more) there was a remission of forty days.[48] From the pontificate of Innocent IV it became customary to grant a partial indulgence to all the faithful attending crusading sermons, and other liturgical, or semi-liturgical functions specially decreed by way of intercession for the success of a crusade. For Henry III's crusade these were litanies and processions.[49] Eudes de Châteauroux, legate appointed to preach Louis IX's crusade, was given faculties to grant

[46] *Les Registres d'Honorius IV*, ed. M. Prou, Paris, 1886-1888, No. 5.
[47] Innocent IV, *Register*, 6469.
[48] *Ibid.*, 2644.
[49] *Ibid.*, 6035-6; *C. P.L.*, I, pp. 279-80.

an indulgence of up to one hundred days to all those attending his crusading sermons,

> ut ad audiendum verbum ipsum copiosior confluat multitudo, ac volentibus signaculum predictum suscipere nullum impedimentum obsistat . . .[50]

There is plenty of evidence to suggest that the promise of an indulgence was not sufficient to draw a large enough audience, and that resort was had to moral suasion. Humbert de Romans in his treatise on preaching summed up the causes why people might come to be negligent of listening to sermons.[51] The evils which he envisaged as a result of this negligence were such that it would be quite consonant with contemporary attitudes to resort to ecclesiastical censure to bring these sinners into the way of salvation. Similarly it would be an easy step to turn this compulsion to the benefit of the crusade preacher. Innocent IV's unusually urgent letter to the Dominican prior of St. Jacques in Paris concerning the preaching of the crusade of Alphonse of Poitiers speaks of compelling the faithful under pain of censure to come to the sermons,[52] and there are similar instructions among the correspondence of prelates such as Eude Rigaud, archbishop of Rouen,[53] and Walter Giffard.[54] There was a safe enough scriptural precedent for such compulsion in the parable of the wedding feast, though it is difficult to see how such compulsion could be reconciled with the voluntary nature of penitential works.

For Alphonse of Poitiers' crusade Innocent IV granted a maximum indulgence of forty days for attending crusading sermons.[55] For Henry III's crusade the surviving correspondence does not specify the amount of the indulgence but records its extension to attendance at litanies and processions, at the request of the king himself. By the time of Urban IV the grant for sermon attendance had been increased to one hundred days.[56] The practice of granting an indulgence for attending processions as well as sermons continued in England as is

---

[50] Innocent IV, *Register*, 4663.

[51] Humbert de Romans, *A Treatise on Preaching*, ed. W. M. Conlon, London, 1955, Chapters V and VI.

[52] Innocent IV, *Register*, 6469.

[53] *Journal des visites pastorales d'Eude Rigaud, archevêque de Rouen*, 1248-69, ed. T. Bonnin, Rouen, 1852, pp. 737- 41. This is a letter from Innocent IV to the French hierarchy.

[54] *Northern Registers*, xxxiii. This is a letter from the archbishop to the clergy of his diocese.

[55] Innocent IV, *Register*, 5556, 6469.

[56] Urban IV, *Register*, 373, *Cameral Register*, 311; *C.P.L.*, I, p. 394.

shown by Urban's letter to Walter de Cantilupe, bishop of Worcester, and chief promoter of crusade.[57] The obvious reason for the inclusion of an indulgence for processions as well as sermons is that such a form of devotion was much more likely to attract the faithful. In one of the entries in his register Eude Rigaud speaks significantly of the faithful gathered processionally in the newly built market of la Vieille-Tour, Rouen, in the presence of the legate, Raoul de Grosparmi, to listen to a crusade sermon.[58] Clement IV raised the maximum indulgence for a crusade sermon to one year forty days,[59] an amount retained by Gregory X, though by 1274 the list of religious services had grown considerably with the inclusion of general congregations of the faithful, translations of relics of saints, consecration of churches, and other solemnities.[60] The influential factor in this expansion of the list was not crusade to the Holy Land, but the necessities of the legatine offices closer to home. In England, for example, legates intended to deal with the baronial revolt were given every assistance to be able to reach as wide a public as possible with pro-royalist propaganda, and this included the grant of indulgences for attendance at any religious service at which the legate or his deputies might preside.[61] Such a policy could not help influencing the use of indulgence with regard to crusade proper, and it is indicative of the possible degree of confusion at which it was possible to arrive by the manipulation of the instruments of crusade policy in favour of a campaign that was far from being reconcilable with the traditional concept of crusade.

No doubt Gregory X, in continuing this practice in his grants of faculties to legates, thought to turn this wider category of 'liturgical' indulgences to the advantage of crusade, for of all the popes of the period he was least likely to be interested in political expediency. The chief effect, however, was to deprive crusade yet further of any unique spiritual value. Nor can it be too much emphasised in this

---

[57] *C.P.L.*, I, p. 394.
[58] *Journal*, p. 597. Joinville, in the incident mentioned above, p. 26, testifies to the popular belief in the efficacy of processions, even if one were not aware of this from a host of other sources of various kinds, and from continuing 'liturgical' practice.
[59] Clement IV, *Register*, 1519.
[60] Gregory X, *Register*, 544.
[61] For these legatine powers in England of Guy de Foulquois see Urban IV, *Register*, 596, 609-613, and *C.P.L.*, I, pp. 396 *et seq.* For those of Ottobuono Fieschi see Clement IV, *Register*, 58-61; *C.P.L.*, I, pp. 419 *et seq.*

connection, that, with the general belief that indulgences were dependent for their full effect on the degree of personal moral achievement, accumulation of partial indulgences could seem just as valid and assured a means of gaining remission of sins, with considerably less effort. Just a little beyond the period under examination, the registers of John Pontissara, bishop of Winchester, provide a splendid example of the way in which participation in the liturgy on behalf of the Holy Land could easily seem to provide a substitute for crusade, with its rich offers for all classes of indulgence-seekers.[62] Basically indulgences aimed at individual salvation; the work performed was not the essential object, no matter what its nature.[63] In effect the more indulgence was used as an enticement to the performance of a certain work, were it crusade, or building churches, or any other temporal work, the more confused thinking about indulgence became. Substitute works tended to take their equivalence from the urgency of the distributors' need, and not from any more absolute standard such as was implied by theories based on the necessity for a condign work of satisfaction. The distributor with a genuinely urgent cause on hand was dangerously open to the temptation of offering indulgences at bargain prices for the sake of a maximum immediate gain.[64] This could not end otherwise than in long term debasement of value. The major temptation for the recipient of indulgences was to develop a habit of looking for maximum remission for minimum of effort. As an instrument of crusading policy indulgence served its purpose only so long as it retained a certain exclusiveness but this notion was in reality inimical to the truly democratic and egalitarian element in Christian spiritual thought. In the light of contemporary opinions and teaching about the spiritual value of indulgences, it is no wonder that the popes were conscious of a wider responsibility than simply that demanded by their crusading policy. Not only did they insist on the need to urge on the faithful the transcendence of the spiritual

---

[62] *Registrum Johannis de Pontissara*, ed. C. Deedes, 2 vols, Canterbury and York Society, London, Vol. XIX, 1915, Vol. XXX, 1924, pp. 191-3, letter of 4 May, 1295, from John Peckham.

[63] Not even those who argued the absolute necessity for a condign work of satisfaction believed that the work was any more than a means to salvation.

[64] It must be remembered that the sole distributor of crusade indulgences was the pope. Putting aside the question of forged letters of credence, all extensions of crusade indulgence emanated from the papacy. Hostiensis specifically denied to bishops the right to give authority for preaching the cross. Cf. *Summa Aurea*, tit. De Voto § 19 (In quo casu).

rewards for their good deeds,[65] but they were logically placed in the position of making these rewards available to all. This seemed to promise well both for the faithful and for the cause of crusade. Paradoxically, however, the more the exponents of crusade tried to promote their cause by bringing it nearer to the everyday life and religious devotions of the faithful the more they devalued the actual effort of going on crusade. To open the possibility of a plenary indulgence to all the faithful was in accord with the democratic notion of the universal possibility of salvation, but it accorded ill with the unique value placed on crusading effort while this remained the sole work of satisfaction considered meritorious of a plenary remission of sins.

Crusade and indulgence suffered separation through the process of democratisation, and as a result of ecclesiastical pragmatism. Were these observations based solely on the evidence already presented from a consideration of crusading indulgence within the context of crusade endeavour to the Holy Land, the argument would sound tenuous. What remains to be examined is the use to which crusade indulgence was put outside the context of crusade to the Holy Land, but with conscious retention of all the organisational forms of that traditional crusade.

(d) Diversion of Crusading Indulgences

(i) *Against the Moors*

Campaigns against the Moors in Spain were already an established way of life when the first crusaders set off for Jerusalem. Though final victory over the Moors was to wait until 1492, their progress into Europe itself had, in effect, been arrested as far back as the era of Le Cid. Thereafter expulsion of the Moors became in a sense a national problem, rather than one which vitally concerned the West as a whole. Crusade to the Holy Land, going beyond national boundaries, could fire the imagination of Christendom more than the still desperate, but not generally threatening, situation in Spain. It was for this reason that holy war in Spain which had lent many of its ideas and forms to crusade came eventually to be estimated as a Christian endeavour in terms of its approximation to crusade to the Holy Land. This was partly the result of the introduction into Spain of peculiarly crusading ideas such as the formation of Military Orders, and partly

---

[65] See, for example, *Les Registres d'Alexander IV*, ed. C. Bourel de la Roncière, J. de Loye, & A. Coulon, 3 vols, Paris, 1895-1953, 1673, 1981; Urban IV, *Register*, 373.

the result of an idealisation of crusade to the Holy Land as a form of Christian endeavour. In fact fighting against the Moors needed no external justification for the granting of plenary indulgence. It was an effort on behalf of Christendom which, of its nature, demanded a reward equivalent to that granted for crusade to the Holy Land,[66] and was not a diversionary crusade in the same sense as other European ventures which will receive notice.

For this reason there is scarcely any need to detail the innumerable grants of plenary indulgence issued on behalf of the almost incessant campaigns which marked the half century following the victory of Las Nevas in 1212. These indulgences, granted "as for the Holy Land", followed the same pattern as those discussed above in the section on indulgences for crusade actually to the Holy Land. Crusade in Spain became diversionary only when Ferdinand III of Castille's victory in the south, and James I of Aragon's recapture of the kingdom of Valencia allowed Spanish attention to be seriously directed away from Moorish campaigns.[67] In any case Pedro III of Aragon's crusade against Tunis was refused the grant of an indulgence, because the pope, Martin IV, suspected that it was a political ruse.[68] In the second half of the thirteenth century Spain was rather the victim of diversionary crusading indulgences than the recipient.[69]

(ii) *Against the Tartars*

After Spain, the simplest of all the diversions of crusade because it took its rationale from an immediate external crisis, and not from any political motives, was the conferring of crusader status on campaigns against the Tartars. It is true that time brought about an ambivalence in the attitude of the West to the Tartars, but this did not seriously affect the general acceptance of repulsion of the Tartar invasions as a fair equivalent of crusade to the Holy Land. These were

---

[66] Many of the troubadours were not slow to make this point. Cf. K. Lewent, "Das altprovenzalische Kreuzlied", *Romanische Forschungen*, XXI, 1905 (1907), pp. 321-448, especially pp. 369-73.

[67] This does not mean to suggest that all problems were solved by the mere defeat of the Moors. The sorts of difficulties that remained have been examined in detail for the kingdom of Valencia by R. J. Burns, *The Crusader Kingdom of Valencia*: Reconstruction on a Thirteenth Century Frontier, 2 vols, Cambridge, Mass., 1967. See also footnote 204, below.

[68] Cf. Potthast, 21877. See also *The Chronicle of Muntaner*, 2 vols, The Hakluyt Society, Second Series, Vol. I, No. 47, 1920, Vol. II, No. 50, 1921, Chapter LVI.

[69] See below, pp. 72; 87-8; 97.

pagans threatening the frontiers of Christendom, not only in the East itself, but on the eastern frontiers of Europe, they were quite patently enemies of the faithful, and constituted a serious threat to Christians. Resistance to their incursions was one of the projects laid down by Innocent IV for discussion at the First Council of Lyons; two years earlier Innocent had issued a full crusading indulgence to all the Germans who should take up arms against the Tartars invading Hungary.[70] In an acute crisis four years later, crusade against the Tartars in Hungary touched crusade to the Holy Land more nearly when Innocent IV agreed to the use of *crucesignati* destined for the Holy Land against these invaders.[71] It does not seem that Innocent considered such diverted service as actually fulfilling a vow of crusade to the Holy Land. Certainly twenty five years later Gregory X refused to accept the abortive expedition of Louis IX to Tunis as having fulfilled a vow of crusade to the Holy Land, although in this case there had been no actual fighting.[72] It became the accepted thing for a plenary indulgence to be granted for vows taken specifically to combat the Tartars. This was by no means a unique provision, since crusade to the eastern frontiers of Europe was a long established practice. By 1248 the Teutonic Knights were fast outstripping everyone else in gaining power and possessions in this area of Europe, having transferred their chief interests thither from the Holy Land, no doubt because they could not compete there with the two older military orders, and also because their relations with Frederick made Europe a more mutually satisfactory base for activities.[73]

From 1248 Innocent placed the direction of the various crusades in Eastern and North Eastern Europe largely in the hands of the Teutonic Knights [74] who were empowered to grant full crusading indulgences to all assuming the cross against the Tartars. Even in the height of preparations for King Louis' crusade, indulgences were being freely and justifiably granted for combatting the Tartars. There could in any case scarcely have been a heavy recruitment for the

---

[70] Innocent IV, *Register*, 30.

[71] *Ibid.*, 2957.

[72] These were not commutations of vows in the strictly legal sense.

[73] J. Riley-Smith suggests a major reason for the dissatisfaction of the Teutonic Knights in the East was their subordinate position to the Hospitallers. See *The Knights of St. John in Jerusalem and Cyprus c. 1050-1310*, London, 1967, especially pp. 397-8, 447-8.

[74] Innocent IV, *Register*, 4000, 4088-4090, 4092; Potthast, 11103, 11136-11137, 11143-11145, etc.

French crusade in this threatened area. The major problem in the crusade against the Tartars came from the connection which gradually arose between the expulsion of the Tartars and the ambitions of the Teutonic Knights in North and Eastern Europe. Though it was convenient for the pope to have such a well organised body as the Teutonic Knights on the spot, and ready to assume responsibility for the conduct of the campaigns against the Tartars, yet it was scarcely in keeping with the good of the Holy Land to allow these knights to use all their crusading powers and privileges to the detriment of that crusade from which they took their *raison d'être*.[75]

(iii) *Against the Hohenstaufen*

Alexander of Hales took heresy for granted as a cause for crusade;[76] this was a frame of mind consolidated by the Albigensian crusades, not initiated by them. The rectors of Berkshire implied their acceptance of crusade against heretics when they refused to answer a papal call for a subsidy to be used in a campaign against Frederick II, on the grounds that he was not a declared heretic.[77] Theologians and canonists were all in agreement that heretics and schismatics could be compelled by main force to return to the fold, and the Fourth Lateran Council had explicitly decreed the same indulgence for those combatting heretics, as for those going on crusade to the Holy Land.[78] The temptation to identify the two forms of crusade was increased by the twofold advantage accruing from the grant of a crusading indulgence. In the first place this was as good a recruiting gambit as had yet been devised for a holy war: to the *crucesignati* it offered spiritual reward; it opened the way to not inconsiderable material rewards, and it was a guarantee of the justice of the war. In the second place, from the standpoint of those waging the war, the indulgence which turned the campaign into a crusade gave licence for the employment of other instruments of crusading policy, of more practical value in organising and prosecuting the campaign than indulgence itself. The result of using indulgences as an enticement to assume the cross was immediately

---

[75] This subject will be taken up again in the section below on crusade indulgences in Northern and Eastern Europe, pp. 88-91.

[76] *Glossa IV Sent.*, IV, Dist. XXXII, 6.

[77] Cf. Matthew Paris, iv, p. 39; *Annales Burtonienses*, ed. H. R. Luard (*Annales Monastici* I), Rolls Series, London, 1864, p. 265. The discrepancy in dates in the two annals does not materially affect this remark.

[78] Canon 3.

effective, if ultimately destructive.[79] It is easy enough in retrospect to develop a sense of urgency about the state of the Crusader Kingdom after the final fall of Jerusalem in 1244, and to overlook the fact that the West was not in a position to make an objective and accurate assessment of the true state of the Crusader Kingdom. The Christian East was itself deceived, and pursued its normal Christian way of life in the intricacies of family quarrels, state and city rivalries, ecclesiastical squabbles and unawareness that the day of judgement was at hand.

In the West the enmity of Frederick II was much more urgent to Innocent IV, and such enmity on the part of a Christian was far worse than the ignorant enmity of Saracen or other pagan. In a famous passage of his *Apparatus* Innocent IV showed a remarkable degree of objectivity in discussing the rights of pagans to the conduct of their own affairs.[80] His correspondence with Saracen and Tartar rulers,[81] though sharing in certain too simplified attitudes of his contemporaries about the nature of conversion,[82] show him to have been reasonable and tolerant in his approach to these external enemies of the Church, even though he might be ready to smite them when the occasion arose. In a letter to Peter

---

[79] It must be noted that the cross which was assumed for crusades other than one to the Holy Land, was distinguished by its colour, or the position in which it was worn. As early as the Second Crusade this was an established practice. The author of *Annales Stadenses* (*M.G.H. SS*, XVI), wrote: "Tertius exercitus se accinxit ad Slavos — Conradus de Within cum pluribus. Et hic tali se signabant contra Slavos karactere ☥ " (p. 327). Otto of Freising, speaking of the same thing says that the crosses assumed by crusaders against the Slavs differed from those of Otto's own crusaders by the fact that they were not simply sewed on, but were brandished aloft, surmounting a wheel (*Gesta Friderici I Imperatoris*, ed. G. Waitz, (Scriptores Rerum Germanicarum in usum scholarum), Hanover 1884, Lib. I, Cap. 42). It has been thought worthwhile to reproduce the liturgical ceremony of the taking of the cross, and to include it with some appropriate observations in Appendix B. The matter is not without importance in connection with the redemption of crusading vows.

[80] III, tit. De voto Cap. VIII (Quod super).

[81] Cf. Innocent IV, *Register*, 1364-5, 1994, 3031-4; R. Röhricht (ed.), *Regesta Regni Hierosolymitani, 1097-1291*, Innsbruck, 1893, Nos 1134, 1138-9, 1142; Raynaldus-Baronius, *Annales Ecclesiastici*, 8 vols, Rome, 1646-1663, xiii, §§ 18-23 for the year 1245. Innocent's letters to the Moslems, save those to the king of Morocco, have not been preserved, but one can infer something of their contents and tone from the Sultan's replies.

[82] This is most evident in Innocent's anxiety that the Tartars, having once heard the Word of God expounded, and not having received it, had incurred automatic responsibility for rejecting the true faith.

of Verona,[83] and Vivian of Bergamo, whom he was constituting Inquisitors in Northern Italy, Innocent sanctioned the use against heretics of *crucesignati* destined for crusade in the Holy Land,

> cum non minus expediat, immo magis, fidem in locis prope positis quam procul distantibus defensare.[84]

This phrase might well be seen to epitomise Innocent IV's attitude to the use of the instruments of crusading policy for the organisation of campaigns much nearer home. This frame of mind was not without some troubling of the Christian conscience as can be seen by the numerous criticisms of every such diversion of crusade from the beginning of the movement. Perhaps the most dramatic thirteenth century statement of the case is to be found in the *Chronica Rolandini Patavini*,[85] and is effectively recorded as a dialogue between the heretical tyrant, Ezzelino di Romano, and the legate, Philip of Ravenna who, in leading a crusade against the tyrant, had fallen captive to him in 1259. The author of the chronicle elsewhere makes it clear that Ezzelino was a monster of evil,[86] and, this being so, either the writer had a remarkable sense of dramatic irony, or he was reporting an actual conversation, and was quite oblivious of the impact of Ezzelino's words which render the legate's defence so unsatisfactory. In either case one is left with an appreciation of the problems of conscience involved. Unlike Ezzelino's speech which is immediate in its impact, because based on a particular example, the legate's reply loses its force by relying on a formulation of the principles involved which, though theologically correct, lacked circumstantiality. One is reminded of the funeral orations of Brutus and Mark Antony, as presented in dramatic form by Shakespeare.

> Dompne mi legate, dudum meus animus sub ingenti dubitacionis articulo pendet, qualiter scilicet et quomodo sancta mater ecclesia substinet, quod sub umbra alarum eius inferat christiano christianus iniuriam, aut nitantur ad tributa ministri apostolice sanctitatis, nitantur et ad rapinas. Scitis enim, quod illa die, qua Paduam introistis, hii, qui vobiscum crucem Domini baiulabant, dicentes se christianos et milites sancti Petri, christianos bonis propiis spoliatos quosdam interfecerunt, extorserunt exactiones ab aliis, et alios, utpote pupillos et orphanos ac viduas, compulerunt ad mendicandum. Et est mirum,

---

[83] St. Peter Martyr who was murdered by the heretics shortly after setting out on this mission.

[84] *Register*, 5345.

[85] *M.G.H. SS*, XIX, Lib. XI, pp. 133-4.

[86] *Ibid., loc. cit.*, p. 136.

quod manifeste confitebantur se ab ecclesia hoc habere mandatum et erant a sede apostolica absoluti, nec debent unquam predam illam restituere vel ablatum; quamvis et ipsi videant, quod aliquando manus Domini extenditur ad vindictam.

Vestre altitudini supplicamus, ut ad verba Domini sapientie vestre animus more nobilium inclinetur. Scimus namque vos plenarie nosse, quod est aliud precipere et aliud consentire. Similiter vobis satis extat notorium, sanctam Romanam ecclesiam, tocius christianitatis baiulam et magistram, sumpsisse regni celorum claves ab ipso Christo secundum evangelicam sanctionem, ut quodcunque ligaverit super terram, sit et ligatum in celis, et quodcunque solverit super terram, sit et solutum in celis. Quare libere potest ecclesia de licencia Iesu Christi, si iustam causam invenerit, illas castigare personas, quas noverit ecclesiastice libertati rebelles. Nec ex hoc possunt ecclesie ministri digne redargui, si gentes pluries monitas, cum in sua contumacia perseverant, in rebus huius mundi castigant, cum possent, si vellent, eciam in personis citra mortem vel sanguinem castigare. Nec ob hoc ista dicimus, quod non fuisset honestius tempore capcionis civitatis tam catholice condam, abstinuisse a preda, aut quod non credamus hodie, salubrius esse quibuslibet, si restituant quecunque post civitatis introitum rapuerunt, precipue si propter hodium vel avariciam rapuissent. Nam et si compunctus aliquis nostrum super hoc consilium peteret, confortaremus eum utique, ut, sibi quam cicius possibilitas foret, ablata redderet vel illis, quorum fuerant si eos habere posset, vel pauperibus et egenis.

Such was the divided conscience of the West which saw crusade indulgence as a just reward for service against the Lord's enemies, or as a cloak for decidedly unchristian behaviour or sometimes, as here, as a mixture of both. Muntaner in the seventy-eighth chapter of his *Chronicle* similarly stresses the division of conscience resulting from Martin IV's diversion of crusading indulgences against Pedro III of Aragon since Rome cannot but act with justice, "And so all faithful Christians must believe, and so do I believe."

There is a significant change of emphasis from the idea of crusade as a sufficiently penitential work to earn a plenary remission of sins to that expressed by Innocent IV in a letter to the duke of Austria concerning a war on the Prussians,

> ... quod dignum est ut hii qui se divinis exponunt obsequiis remune-rationem recipiant congruentem.[87]

Instead of demanding that the work be condign, the pope was intent upon seeing that the reward be congruent. The personal nature

---

[87] *Register*, 711.

of the struggle between the pope and the Emperor tended to augment the degree of papal gratitude, and to preclude any objective assessment of the relative congruence of any reward for service against the Emperor, and service on behalf of the Holy Land. As early as 1243 in giving an indulgence to those assisting the papal legate, Cardinal Raynerio, and the Viterbese against Frederick, Innocent had remarked:

> . . . Nos igitur attendentes quod dignum sit ut benignitas ipsius Ecclesiae in condignis gratie premiis respondeat meritis filiorum . . .[88]

This was before Innocent's flight to Lyons, and the open declaration of hostilities between the two.

Frederick himself was aware of the propaganda value of combatting heresy, and was quite prepared to make use of it against the pope. He declared Gregory IX a heretic, and wrote to the cardinals complaining of his unjust excommunication in the following terms:

> Petrus fit petra scandali, qui tenebatur zelare pacem, circa quam nostra versatur intencio, et Paulus reversus in Saulum iterum colligit lapides ad cedendum. [89]

In a manifesto published at the same time the Emperor accused Gregory of anti-crusade activities which had ruined his earlier campaign in the Holy Land.[90] The themes of heresy and crusade were to run through all the papal-Hohenstaufen struggle from that time onwards, and even beyond the extinction of the Hohenstaufen into the vexed history of Sicily. Anti-Hohenstaufen crusade in Sicily eventually became pro-Angevin crusade against any opponent of that dynasty. What set out to be simply an assertion of the rights of the papacy against the claims of its enemies, turned into a manipulation of papal policies, and even the papacy itself, against its own interests, and against those of the Holy Land, in favour of Angevin ambitions in Europe and the East.

It was for heresy that Innocent IV denounced Frederick II at the Council of Lyons in 1245, and for the nearly related crimes of sacrilege, consorting with Saracens, and being a manifest enemy of the Church and the faithful.[91] Thaddeus of Suessa refuted these accusations somewhat unconvincingly,[92] and later, Frederick, writing to Louis

---

[88] *Register*, 179.

[89] Winckelmann, *Acta inedita*, i, No. 355, pp. 314-5.

[90] *Ibid.*, ii, No. 31, pp. 29-36.

[91] Matthew Paris, iv, p. 435; cf. also, pp. 445-455.

[92] *Ibid.*, pp. 435-6. The reference in this defence to usury shows clearly the kind of irrelevant abuse which served for an accusation of heresy. In Frederick's

IX, specified more exactly the nature of these accusations, and his refutation of them.[93] He had been condemned for contempt of the power of the keys, for sins against nature, and for unorthodox beliefs. Frederick declared his adherence to all articles of faith, but the accusation was a recurrent one, directed again and again at Frederick, and Manfred especially among his sons.[94] Innocent did not immediately follow Frederick's deposition with a crusade, partly because he was still hoping for the Emperor's submission, and partly because the preaching of Louis' crusade had just got under way throughout Europe. The first signs of a coming campaign against the Emperor were manifested in a letter to the archbishop of Cologne ordering the withdrawal of indulgences granted "in recompensionem dampnorum et laborum gravium" from any who should in the meantime have proved unenthusiastic in the Church's cause or even rebellious.[95] Shortly afterwards Innocent ordered the preaching of a crusade against Frederick, on behalf of Henry Raspe, with an indulgence as for crusade to the Holy Land. As in Louis IX's crusade there was an indulgence of from twenty to forty days for hearing a crusading sermon.[96] Later in the same year Innocent ordered a similar crusade to be preached by his Vicar in Urbe in Rome and the surrounding districts, with a full crusading indulgence because Frederick was responsible for the great tribulations which had befallen "non solum Ecclesiam, sed etiam fere totum Christianum populum." [97]

Once committed to full scale crusade against the Hohenstaufen, Innocent IV concentrated all the instruments of crusade on that effort. Though he continued to support Louis IX's crusade, he plainly would have preferred the French king to remain at home as a threat to Frederick should he menace the pope.[98] Though Eudes de Châ-

---

propaganda there was a tendency to confuse sin with heresy, on the papal side the tendency was to read the Emperor's actions in terms of the heresies of which he stood accused.

[93] Winckelmann, *Acta inedita*, ii, No. 43, pp. 44-47.

[94] Cf., for example, Innocent IV, *Register*, 4062, 7758; Rymer, i, p. 548; Urban IV, *Register*, 633; G. del Giudice (ed.), *Codice diplomatico del regno di Carlo I e II d'Angio dal 1265 al 1309*, 2 vols, Naples, 1863-69, i, xvi; Ripoll, i (Clement IV) xxxi.

[95] *Register*, 1928. Presumably this refers to waverers who had returned to the support of Frederick, after deserting his cause.

[96] *Ibid.*, 2931.

[97] *Ibid.*, 2945; cf. also, 2999.

[98] This seems to be the tone of Innocent's letter to Louis, *Register*, 3040; cf. *Chronica Fr. Salimbene de Adam*, ed. O. Holder-Egger, *M.G.H. SS*, XXXII, Hanover, 1905-13, pp. 211-2. That he felt in need of protection is shown plainly

teauroux was committed to preaching King Louis' crusade throughout France, Germany, Scandinavia, Eastern Europe and the British Isles, Innocent IV ordered him to supersede this in Germany by the preaching of a similar indulgence against Frederick because there the call to King Louis' crusade was only "modicum fructuosa". Possibly out of respect for Louis, or perhaps through fear of his reaction, this change of object in the crusade, and the indulgence, was to be kept secret.[99] The Friars Preachers, to whom had been committed the promulgation of the papal sentence against Frederick in Germany, were promised a full remission of their sins for the suffering they might thereby incur.[100] The indulgence against Frederick was extended to Lombardy by the preaching of Cardinal Ottaviani Ubaldini.[101]

After the death of Henry Raspe, William of Holland became an object of crusading assistance, also equivalent to the Holy Land. Innocent IV informed the bishop of Curlandia that William's cause was in no way a private one, but was that of the whole Church.[102] The hierarchy of Germany was, therefore, to preach the crusade against Frederick "saltem bis in mense".[103] There is no record of any such injunction for St. Louis' crusade. This preaching was to be accompanied by the promise of a full crusading indulgence.[104] The period of service required for such an indulgence was three years, if the grant made to Thomas de Bellomanso and other supporters of William can be taken as a norm.[105]

This crusade against Frederick and his followers was quite closely connected by Innocent with the Holy Land itself. In fact, Frederick, by acquiring dominion over the Crusader States, and by emphasising his crusadeı status, had inevitably connected his cause generally in the minds of his contemporaries, with that of the Holy Land. This allowed a more cogent rationalisation of the connection between

---

in his reluctance to allow Henry III to set out on crusade until this other champion, King Louis, should return. Cf. Rymer, i, pp. 451-2, letter of April 6th, 1250. Matthew Paris heavily stresses the loss which this imposed on the Holy Land, v, pp. 102-3. Innocent was, however, ungrudging in his praise of King Louis' zeal in going on crusade; cf. *Register*, 3040, 3661, 4662.

[99] *Register*, 2935.
[100] Ripoll, i (Innocent IV) clxxiii.
[101] *Register*, 3002.
[102] Potthast, 12844.
[103] *Ibid.*, 12902.
[104] *Ibid.*, 12920.
[105] Innocent IV, *Register*, 3886; Potthast, 12935.

anti-Hohenstaufen crusade, and crusade to the Holy Land. Whether or not Frederick gave his friend the Sultan of Egypt what information he had about King Louis' projected crusade, as he was generally supposed to have done, the general distrust of Frederick's policy of alliance with the Saracens is evident in the very existence of the rumour. When Innocent spoke of Frederick's disturbance of almost the whole Christian Church he did not exclude the Crusader States to whom he wrote begging loyalty to the Church, and rejection of Frederick.[106] Other letters prohibiting the display of Frederick's standards at Acre, and threatening the Emperor's adherents with loss of all privileges, made crusade against Frederick implicitly crusade on behalf of the Christians in the Crusader East.[107]

Similarly the crusading indulgence declared in Sicily in 1248 for those "qui contra Fredericum in subsidium Ecclesiae curaverint crucis insigniri caractere" [108] received its ultimate rationale in a letter written in 1253 in which Innocent expounded the importance of Sicily for crusade to the Holy Land,[109] a reason which the pope had used much earlier in his pontificate to explain the importance of crusade in support of the Latin Empire of Constantinople.[110] This Sicilian crusade was to prove even more a threat to the integrity of the organisational forms of crusade than that in Germany. With the death of Frederick in 1250, Innocent IV thought to be at an end of his struggles with the Hohenstaufen, though he had already had resort to the granting of a crusade indulgence against Conrad in Germany,[111] and had given his voice for the candidacy of Melissende for the regency of Jerusalem.[112] Early in 1251 Innocent issued orders to William of Holland's chaplain, John de Dist, to commute the indulgence for aid against Conrad.[113] A similar order was directed to Sicily.[14] Such indulgences continued to be preached in both Germany and Sicily until the end of Innocent's pontificate,[115] though by

---

[106] Innocent IV, *Register*, 4050.
[107] *Ibid.*, 4104, 4107.
[108] *Ibid.*, 4681; Potthast, 13007.
[109] *Register*, 6818.
[110] *Ibid.*, 22.
[111] Ripoll, i (Innocent IV) ccxiii, (27 November, 1250); Potthast, 14116.
[112] *Register*, 4427. This decision did not wholly accord with the need of the Crusader States, but tended rather to add to the general lack of settled government.
[113] Innocent IV, *Register*, 5031-2.
[114] *Ibid.*, 5339.
[115] *Ibid.*, 5339, 6303-5, 6322, 7312.

1253 the emphasis had changed slightly in Sicily to the declaration of an indulgence for aid to Charles of Anjou.[116] The papal enticement of Louis IX's younger brother to the throne of Sicily not only cut across the French king's expressed belief in the right of the Hohenstaufen to their hereditary land, and his constant refusal to have his own family involved in this quarrel,[117] but it also militated against the success of the crusade which even then was being preached in favour of Alphonse of Poitiers to relieve King Louis' situation in the Holy Land.[118]

Allowing for Matthew Paris' prejudices there is still a good deal of evidence to suggest that public reaction to King Louis' defeat in 1250 was directed against the pope's diversion of crusading energies against the Hohenstaufen. Paris represents the king's two brothers as arriving back in France determined to allow nothing to prevent their organisation of a crusade which Louis had dispatched them to lead to his aid. To this end they threatened to expel the pope from Lyons should he refuse his aid, and proposed that peace be negotiated with Frederick who was clearly the chief obstacle.[119] From Joinville comes a more reliable report that neither of the counts was willing to stay in the Holy Land with the king, and that both were as unwilling for him to stay.[120] On the face of it their rough handling of the pope, and their headlong zeal for crusade seem unlikely, more especially in view of their considerable decline in zeal as reported by Matthew Paris some two years later.[121] Whether the cause of Alphonse of Poitiers' waning enthusiasm may have been simply the result of ill health,[122] it seems probable that Charles of Anjou was more interested

---

[116] *Ibid.*, 6812.
[117] Cf. Matthew Paris, iv, pp. 523-4; v, pp. 22-23, 70, 171.
[118] Innocent IV, *Register*, 6469.
[119] Matthew Paris, v, pp. 175, 188.
[120] Cf. Joinville, lxxxiii, § 422-4. The seneschal rather obviously refuses to commit himself on the point of whether Louis IX actually ordered his brothers to return to France, or whether they requested to be so ordered (lxxxvi, § 438). Joinville's previous account of the two councils of war held in Acre, and his story about the counts' neglect of the king on the journey to Acre (lxxix, § 404-5), show that he probably believed that they wished to go. The count of Poitiers had plenty of reason for wishing to be back in France, since Raymond of Toulouse had died in 1249 and Alphonse had not yet taken possession of his territories.
[121] v, p. 281.
[122] Matthew Paris, v, p. 311, suggests, characteristically, that the count of Poitou's illness was a heavenly visitation for deserting his brother's cause, whereas Alphonse seems to have been genuinely of a delicate constitution. The count's chaplain, Philip, writing to Louis of Alphonse's having assumed the cross again late in 1252, speaks of him as having been "gravi satis infirmitate detentus"

in the prospects of a crown than in following the behests of his elder
brother.

Popular reaction, as so often, was vehement and irrational. Salimbene
records public scorn for the Mendicants no doubt because they
were connected with the preaching of the crusade which had failed.[123]
In France there sprang up one of those spontaneous but incoherent
spiritual movements which had frequently taken the shape of a
crusade since the time of Peter the Hermit, namely the crusade of the
Pastoureaux. Eschewing the organisational forms of official crusade,
these groups of the poor and simple faithful needed no plenary indulgence to spur them on their way to rescue their king, and the
Holy Places. In her anxiety to aid the king by whatever means were
available, Blanche of Castille seems to have overlooked the potentially
explosive nature of this movement, and lent it her countenance, to be
quickly disappointed.[124] For the purposes of this study, the significance of this spontaneous popular crusade lies in its utter neglect of
the forms which gave shape and meaning to any venture overseas.
While there were popular attempts at correcting the balance by posing
sheer spontaneity as an antidote to utter concentration on organisational forms, crusade had a chance of surviving.[125]

With the news of Innocent's revival of the anti-Hohenstaufen
crusade in 1251, despite the hopes raised by Frederick II's death,
Queen Blanche took stern measures to prevent the preaching of this
crusade within French territories, threatening to confiscate the lands
of any of her subjects who should take the cross against Conrad.

(*Layettes*, iii, 4030). See also C. C. J. Webb, "Roger Bacon on Alphonse of Poitiers",
in *Essays in History presented to R. Lane Poole*, ed. H. W. C. Davis, Oxford, 1927,
pp. 290-300.

[123] Salimbene, pp. 444-5.

[124] Cf. J. Viard, (ed.), *Les Grandes Chroniques de France*, 10 vols, Paris, 1920-53,
(Société de l'histoire de France), Vol. VII, Chap. LXII; Le Nain de Tillemont,
Vie de Saint Louis, ed. J. de Gaulle, 6 vols, Paris, 1847-51 (Société de l'histoire
de France), Vol. III, Chaps CCCXIV-CCCXV; E. Berger, *Histoire de Blanche
de Castille, reine de France*, Paris, 1895, p. 401, remarks that the queen's tolerance
was uncharacteristic if she did lend her countenance to such unruly behaviour.

[125] Thomas de Cantimpré is no doubt right in speaking of the imprudent devotion to Christ which manifested itself in such movements as the Children's
Crusade, and the *Pastoureaux*, and which was so easily led astray by antichrist
(*Bonum universale de apibus*, French edition, translated and ed. V. Willart, *Le Bien
universel ou les abeilles mystiques*, Brussels, 1650, Book II, Chap. 3). This does not
invalidate the view that popular reactions such as these, considered from the
point of view of motivation, and not of the mode of expression, were potentially
corrective of excessive organisation.

Though no evidence is available it seems highly improbable that anyone should have been content to sacrifice all for the spiritual reward of a plenary indulgence, or the doubtful material support suggested by the queen.

"Qui Papae militant, de Papalibus sustineantur et eant irredituri." [126]

In view of all the above it is ironic that Innocent IV should have granted an indulgence to the bishop of Orléans who accompanied Charles to the discussions of terms for accepting the Sicilian throne "quatinus predictum negocium ad optatam perfectionem perducens."[127] It is even more ironic in view of the difficulties which the papacy was storing up for itself in offering Sicily to Charles. In the event this particular attempt to place Charles on the throne proved abortive, possibly because of the influence of King Louis.

Innocent's pursuit of victory over the Hohenstaufen led to one other, theologically very interesting, diversion of crusade indulgence from the mainstream of crusading practice. This was the promise of Christian burial to those killed in tourneys should they have made a sufficient contribution to the crusade of William of Holland.[128] This could be done only by means of a plenary remission of sins, which alone could guarantee the removal of the excommunication that had prevented Christian burial in the first place. In his *Apparatus* Innocent claimed that an indulgence granted by the pope was effective for the dead.[129] However, there is something theologically very doubtful about this provision of a plenary indulgence in advance for sins not yet committed, since it looks no better than a licence to commit that sin, and, despite an almost universal defiance of the ban on tournaments such a provision seems somewhat too tolerant. It is scarcely possible to read the grant as referring to a vicarious indulgence applicable to those already dead by relatives, or even executors. No matter what explanation fits the case, the grant was potentially a grave danger to the credibility of crusading indulgences and even more so to the force of ecclesiastical censures; in fact there is no other record of such a grant in the period under review. It was but a straw in the wind.

---

[126] Matthew Paris, v, pp. 260-1.

[127] Innocent IV, *Register*, 6813.

[128] *Ibid.*, 7457.

[129] V, tit. De penitentiis Cap. IIII (Quod autem) § 7. For a discussion of contemporary notions on the question of applying indulgences to the dead, see Paulus, i, pp. 39-57, ii, pp. 160-183, especially 160-174.

Hailed as a man of peace, Alexander IV turned out to be a man of passivity,[130] and if he did little to earn blame for diverting the instruments of crusade from their proper object, he merited as little praise for his neglect to employ them on behalf of the Holy Land.[131] Though he was a man of neither vigour nor decision, Alexander was forced very early into granting a crusading indulgence against the true heir of all Frederick's evil propensities, Manfred. This ambitious young man was manifestly guilty of his father's crimes of heresy, consorting with heretics, schismatics and Saracens. He formed alliances with Michael of Epiros, and, by reason of this, with Michael's ally, William, prince of Achaia.[132] He also made alliance with Baibars Bunduktari.[133] There seemed nothing to choose between Manfred and his father as worthy objects of crusade. In 1255 Alexander extended a crusading indulgence to the campaign he ordered to be conducted against Manfred's ally, the notorious tyrant, Ezzelino, di Romano. The charge was heresy, a long standing one against Ezzelino,[134] but in reality the chief crime was alliance with the Hohenstaufen.[135] Innocent IV had issued various warnings to Ezzelino to present himself at the Holy See to purge himself of his crimes and suspected heresy.[136] Every possible concession had been made [137] before the final anathema was pronounced against Ezzelino as a manifest heretic.[138] It was Alexander who finally launched the campaign against Ezzelino under the leadership of Philip, archbishop elect of Ravenna.[139] This prelate fell into Ezzelino's hands in 1259,[140]

---

[130] Matthew Paris, v, pp. 472-3.

[131] For a concise summary of the disastrous effects of Alexander IV's lack of positive action, see E. Jordan, *Les origines de la domination angevine en Italie*, Paris, 1909, Chap. VI.

[132] Manfred thus showed himself to have inherited his father's genius for putting his enemies in a false position by appearing to support the same cause, in this case by his alliance with the prince of Achaia. Later Manfred was to promise to go on crusade to the Holy Land if Urban IV should grant him peace.

[133] Cf. R. Grousset, *Histoire des Croisades*, iii, p. 625. Cf. also, E. Blochet, "Les relations diplomatiques des Hohenstaufen avec les sultans d'Egypte", in *Revue historique*, LXXX, 1902, p. 64.

[134] In a letter of 4 March, 1244, Innocent IV had ordered an investigation of reports of Ezzelino's suspected heresy (*Register*, 518).

[135] This question of the connection between charges of heresy, and crusade against Ezzelino as an ally of the Hohenstaufen is discussed by E. Jordan, *Les origines de la domination angevine en Italie*, Chap. V, especially pp. 74 *et seq.*

[136] Innocent IV, *Register*, 4095, 5344.

[137] *Ibid.*, 5793.

[138] *Ibid.*, 7761.

[139] Alexander IV, *Register*, 1013.   [140] Cf. pp. 71-2, above.

and the crusade did not revive till the following year when Ezzelino was finally defeated. In September the Guelf crusaders suffered a sore defeat at the hands of Manfred and his supporters at Montaperti, a defeat from which the morale of Alexander never recovered. Popular reaction to the flow of the tide against the indulgenced crusaders was not, as it had been in France a few years earlier, an upsurge of confidence in the military power of simple faith to conquer all. These dire calamities cried to the conscience for reparation, but crusade had lost its credibility as a work of penance. There sprang up instead in Northern Italy the *flagellati* with their strong emphasis on intensely and directly corporeal forms of penance.

Northern Italy was by no means the only place in which a crusading indulgence was preached against Manfred. Henry III, in pious emulation of his brother-in-law, had taken the cross in 1250, and had obtained the grant of plenary and partial indulgences from Innocent IV. Although the fulfilment of this vow was delayed with the consent, and even at the seeming request, of the pope the subsequent history of non-fulfilment leaves one in grave doubt as to the actual instigator of the delay.[141] At any rate the transfer of the Sicilian throne to Henry's second son, Edmund, in 1255, brought the anti-Hohenstaufen crusade into the forefront of English foreign policy. Rostand, appointed collector for the Sicilian crusade in England, preached a crusading indulgence against Manfred in terms which recall denunciations of Frederick.[142] Matthew Paris, nothing loath to welcome a story of the discomfiture of his enemies, the friars, even unto blood, here, however, with a more impartial eye, bemoaned the alacrity with which Christian promised to shed Christian blood, for the sake of an indulgence.

Quod cum audirent fideles, mirabantur, quod tantum eis promitteret pro sanguine Christianorum effundendo quantum pro cruore infidelium eliquando.[143]

This diversion of crusade, and crusading indulgence, in England, was simply a beginning in that country of a long history of manipulation of the instruments of crusading policy in the interests of

---

[141] Matthew Paris, v, pp. 102-3, 134-6, actually leaves no doubt that Henry, rather than the pope, was responsible for the delay.
[142] Matthew Paris, v, pp. 521-2.
[143] *Ibid.*, p. 522.

papal claims in Sicily. Baronial opposition, when it was finally made explicit, necessarily involved protests against the amount of English money being poured into papal coffers for the conduct of the Sicilian affair. The barons were not opposed in principle to Henry's involvement in Sicily,[144] but their objections may well have seemed to papal eyes an added cause for declaring a crusading indulgence against Simon de Montfort and his supporters. From 1258 his baronial troubles occupied Henry beyond possibility of making good his Sicilian promises but, although Alexander revoked the grant of the throne to Edmund, Manfred's victory at Montaperti prevented his concentration on the task of finding another candidate.

Urgent as he was about bringing aid to the Holy Land, Urban IV spent his short pontificate counteracting the effects of his predecessor's lack of vigour. Urban's determination to settle affairs in the West in order to be free to organise a crusade could almost be said to have resulted in his conducting most of his affairs in terms of crusade. The crusade against Manfred was given a fresh impetus with the issue of new crusading indulgences. Urban once more offered Sicily to Charles of Anjou. The latter's skilful management of the negotiations, and the pope's failure to have any of his important conditions carried into effect [145] should have acted as a warning that Charles was not likely to serve papal purposes any better than the Hohenstaufen. Instead of taking such a warning, Urban further compromised the value of crusading indulgences by using them in support of Charles, and against Manfred.[146] In a letter ordering the preaching of a crusading indulgence by his legate, the cardinal of San Martino, against Manfred and his Saracens as enemies of the faith, Urban specified the indulgence as for,

> Omnibus qui contra illos efficax in personis vel bonis juvamen impenderint. [147]

Presumably the pope did not intend the indulgence to depend on the efficacy of the campaign, but on the recipient's making a large enough contribution of military power, or financial help, to prove an effective aid. This was not an attempt to confine the indulgence to those who were rich and powerful, but to preclude mere promises or niggardly

---

[144] Cf. F. M. Powicke, *King Henry III and the Lord Edward*, 2 vols, Oxford, 1947, i, 378.
[145] Cf. E. Jordan, *Les origines de la domination angevine en Italie*, Chap. VII.
[146] Urban IV, *Register*, 321, 633, 860, 870, for example.
[147] *Ibid.*, 633.

contributions from reaping an indulgence. The further implication is that Urban IV was aware of the abuses which were rendering the grant of plenary indulgences ineffectual, and was taking steps to counteract those abuses.

Although Urban set the minimum service of one year for all engaged in preaching crusade to the Holy Land, or collecting for it,[148] he granted a full crusading indulgence to all who should serve for three months against Manfred, Peter de Vico, and their followers, or to those who should provide substitutes for a similar length of time.[149] One cannot quarrel with the equating of three months personal service in the field and one year spent contributing to the organisation of the crusade; paying the expenses of a substitute for exactly the same period of time is another matter. The crusading decrees examined in chapter two had laid down a period three times as long for supporting substitutes as for rendering personal service. Perhaps this grant was attributable to Urban's sense of urgency about the situation, because victory favoured neither side for long; perhaps it was the result of the pope's desire to avenge the murder of his nephew by one of Manfred's followers early in 1264.[150] At any rate Urban issued three letters in July ordering renewed preaching of the crusade indulgence against Manfred.[151]

This same sense of urgency seems to have been responsible for Urban's extensions of normal legatine powers to favour the Sicilian campaign. Simon de Brie, legate to France, was given a general faculty to grant an indulgence of one year to all those attending dedications of churches, translations of relics, festal solemnities, solemn religious congregations, and sermons, to promote the Sicilian crusade.[152] This seems to have been a remission over and above that normally accruing from attendance at these ceremonies, since elsewhere the cardinal was given faculties for granting an indulgence of three years for the dedication of the churches of Chartres, Rouen and Laon,[153] though it is possible that these were regarded as churches apart from the general, and worthy of a greater indulgence. The legate dispatched to deal with the baronial troubles in England,

---

[148] Cf. p. 61, above.
[149] Urban IV, *Register*, 778.
[150] *Ibid.*, 757, 764. The murderers were actually followers of Peter de Vico.
[151] *Ibid.*, 860, 870, 2991.
[152] *Ibid.*, 818.
[153] *Ibid.*, 819.

Guy Foulquois, was given similar powers, related specifically to crusade.[154] Though essentially a domestic quarrel, this affair carried its implications beyond the boundaries of England, not only because it was potentially a disturbance of the general peace, but because it cut across papal policies in Sicily, and elsewhere. The baronial party was seen to be "cruciabilis", however remote the re-establishment of the political *status quo* in England might seem to a more objective observer, from the salving of what remained in Christian hands of the Holy Places, already seriously threatened by Sultan Baibars.

Guy Foulquois was given unrestricted powers to proceed against the rebels with the preaching of a full crusading indulgence for all offering personal service, or the other usual contributions.[155] Most serious of all from the point of view of the Holy Land was the legate's power to allow the retention of this indulgence by those commuting their crusading vows from the Holy Land to Sicily.[156] Those listening to the legate's sermons were to receive an indulgence of one hundred days whereas his deputies' sermons were valued at a remission of forty days.[157] One can only suppose that this hierarchical arrangement observable elsewhere with regard to collectors and their deputies, for instance, was not based on a calculation of the relative quality of the sermons as works of penance for the audience.

When Guy Foulquois succeeded Urban IV to the papacy he continued this practice of enlarging legatine powers in the direction of crusade. Ottobuono Fieschi, whom Clement IV sent to England in his own stead, received the same faculties for granting indulgences as the pope himself had enjoyed.[158] In France Simon de Brie remained legate, but received powers to grant an augmented indulgence for those listening to sermons—his own were valued at a year, and those of his deputies at one hundred days.[159] When Simon was ordered to preach St. Louis' second crusade, however, a gesture was made in the direction of recognising the greater importance of this crusade over the Sicilian one by having the legate's sermons rated at one year and forty days.[160] In Sicily, where the bishop of Alba was empowered

---

[154] Urban IV, *Register*, 596, 609-13; cf. *C.P.L.*, I, pp. 396-400.

[155] *Ibid.*, 596.

[156] The gravity of this will be discussed in the section on commutation of vows.

[157] Urban IV, *Registers*, 609-10.

[158] Cf., p. 64, footnote 61, above.

[159] Clement IV, *Register*, 1446.

[160] *Ibid.*, 1519; cf., however, the pope's report to Charles on 11 July, 1265, of the substance of the former's letter to King Louis, in del Giudice, i, vi.

to preach a crusading indulgence as for the Holy Land,[161] the value of the legate's sermons was rated at only forty days.[162] The French pope seems to have intended a richer reward for his countrymen for listening to crusading sermons than for the English or the Sicilians performing a similar work of penance. St. Thomas had pointed out that different indulgences were often granted for the same work, urging this as a proof that the work itself was not the sufficient cause of the grant, but only the motive.[163] Presumably Clement IV expected more help for Charles of Anjou among his own compatriots, but King Louis' response was far from encouraging.[164] In one of his early letters to Simon de Brie Clement had outlined his reasons for abhorring Manfred, whose crimes not merely resembled those of his father, but seemed even to exceed them in savagery. Charles was the "athleta Ecclesiae" to whose cause Simon was to rally supporters "non solum piis exhortationibus, set etiam superabundantibus gratiis", that is with promises of crusading indulgences as for the Holy Land. One wonders how far a man of Clement IV's experience could have believed in the cogency of the reason given to Simon for the granting of an indulgence,

> ut universi et singuli ad id eo libentius et animosius intendant, quo exinde dona spiritualia, quae temporalibus praeferenda sunt . . .[165]

To the Dominicans called to preach this crusade, as to Simon de Brie, Manfred was represented as "de venenosa genere, velut de radice colubri, virulentia progenies".[166] On Charles' behalf a plenary indulgence was also granted to those taking the cross in the patriarchate of Gran against certain enemies of the count who were impeding the progress of soldiers coming to his aid.[167]

With the death of Manfred came final defeat for the Ghibelline cause, the horrors of the sack of Benevento, which provoked a papal rebuke for the victorious crusaders,[168] and a dawning recognition of the fact that Angevin Sicily was no more in papal control than

---

[161] Clement IV, *Register*, 297.
[162] *Ibid.*, 263.
[163] *S. T. Supp.*, Q 25 a 2 Resp.
[164] Cf. del Giudice, i, xxvii. It is perhaps the supreme irony of crusading history of this period to have the pope pleading with St. Louis not to cherish a "pectus saxeum" against this (diversion of) crusade.
[165] *Ibid.*, i, xvi, p. 51.
[166] Ripoll, i (Clement IV) xxxi.
[167] Clement IV, *Register*, 168.
[168] del Giudice, i, xlv.

Hohenstaufen Sicily had been. Despite the precarious state of the Crusader Kingdoms, all crusading energies since the return of King Louis to France in 1254, had been directed elsewhere, largely into the anti-Hohenstaufen campaign. Had the matter ended there, with the papacy free at last to concentrate on the Holy Land, with King Louis eager to sacrifice everything for that cause, and with the large quarrels which had beset the West for so long finally settled, the diversion of crusading energies might have seemed a regrettable, but justifiable, preparation for a major effort in the East. So at least Gregory X must have thought when he summoned the Second Council of Lyons to organise just such a crusade to rescue the fast dwindling Crusader States. Before seeing how these hopes foundered in the years between the Second Council of Lyons and the fall of Acre, it will be as well to look briefly at the diversion of crusading indulgences into other fields of activity than that of anti-Hohenstaufen crusade, and campaigns immediately linked with that.

(iv) *Against the Greeks*

Although the first major diversion of crusade in the thirteenth century had been to Constantinople, it is largely to be doubted that Innocent III's ultimate approval made good in retrospect the indulgences of those taking part.[169] The Latin Empire was supported in its first years more by subsidy, than by the use of indulgences, and Greece did not present an example of a major diversion of this spiritual instrument until Angevin ambition drew this area, too, into the orbit of the Sicilian crusade. Innocent IV had argued the necessity of Constantinople as a base for those going on crusade overland [170] and had granted crusading indulgences to those going to aid the Latin Empire.[171] The recapture of Constantinople by Michael Palaeologus

---

[169] Villehardouin represents the clergy as assuring the *crucesignati* who were about to attack Constantinople, that they would be eligible for the indulgences granted to the expedition, not because it was a crusade proper, but because the war was a just one (G. de Villehardouin, *La Conquête de Constantinople*, ed. N. de Wailly, Paris, 1872, §224-5). Robert of Clari represents the bishops as promising absolution in the name of God, and by the authority of the Apostolic See. (Robert de Clari, *La Conquête de Constantinople*, ed. P. Lauer, Paris, 1924, lxxiii). In view of the interchangeability of the terms absolution, indulgence and remission, it is difficult to say with certainty whether Robert of Clari is saying the same thing as Villehardouin, or not.

[170] Innocent IV, *Register*, 22. This had also been one of the basic arguments for the diversion of the Fourth Crusade.

[171] *Ibid.*, 6829, 6845.

in 1261, and the offer of the Sicilian throne to Charles of Anjou combined to mark the beginning of a period of more actively encouraged crusade against the Greeks. Pope Urban IV had the Mendicant Friars preach an anti-Greek crusading indulgence on the eastern frontiers;[172] in another letter [173] he insisted on the importance of possessing Greece for the sake of the Holy Land. He also persevered, however, in negotiations for reunion.[174] Clement IV, partial as he was in all that concerned the Angevin cause in Sicily, refused to grant a crusading indulgence at the outset of Charles' active interference in the Byzantine world to enable the latter to seize Corfu.[175]

Gregory X was determined to effect a final reunion with the Greeks, and great efforts were made by him and his immediate successors towards this end. Charles of Anjou was a stumbling block, and it is notable how many of the documents concerning Greece in the papal registers of this time are admonitions to Charles not to molest the Greek envoys of Michael Palaeologus.[176] The Greek Emperor professed himself ready to further the cause even as early as the abortive setting out of James of Aragon.[177] The tergiversations of the Greeks over reunion finally gave Martin IV, however, the excuse he needed to support Charles' crusade against the Byzantine Empire with a full crusading indulgence and all the consequent material advantages.[178] The pope's refusal to give similar support to the venture of Pedro III of Aragon to Northern Africa

---

[172] Urban IV, *Register*, 131; cf. Ripoll, i (Urban IV) xii.

[173] Urban IV, *Register*, 132.

[174] For an extensive discussion of Urban's dealings with Michael Palaeologus during the period of this projected crusade, see W. Norden, *Das Papsttum und Byzanz*, Berlin, 1903, pp. 399-433.

[175] Clement IV, *Register*, 1131; cf. Potthast, 19824.

[176] See, for example, M. H. Laurent, *Beatus Innocentius PP V*, Rome, 1943, [130] p. 446; Nicholas III, *Register*, 378-80, 896, 993.

[177] Cf. *The Chronicle of James I, king of Aragon*, ed. and trans. by J. Forster, 2 vols, London, 1883, Chap. cccclxxxi. A letter of Innocent V (in M. H. Laurent, *op. cit.*, [135] p. 447) to Michael Palaeologus telling him of the assumption of the cross by Rudolf of Germany, Philip III of France, Alfonso III of Portugal and the son of Charles I of Sicily, indicates that the Greek Emperor was still showing his interest in crusade at this time (23 May, 1276).

[178] In strict fact Charles had taken the cross to go to the aid of the Holy Land, and it was ostensibly for this that he was granted crusade privileges; cf. Martin IV, *Register*, 116. It was no secret that he intended to move first against the Byzantine Emperor who had been excommunicated the previous year; in that year also a treaty had been made with the Venetians and Philip de Courtenay, the Latin claimant of the Empire; cf. G. L. F. Tafel and G. M. Thomas, *Urkunden zur Alteren Handels- und Staatsgeschichte der Republik Venedig*, 3 vols, Vienna, 1885-7, iii, Nos ccclxxiii-ccclxxv, pp. 287-308.

shows all too clearly that war against Saracens was no longer considered to confer an automatic right to privileges of crusade. If Pedro of Aragon was using his Tunisian venture as a camouflage for his real purpose of invading Sicily as the pope obviously thought he was,[179] then this is as excellent an example of a cynical attempt at misusing indulgence and all the trappings of crusade, as is Charles' more successful attempt to have his ambitious attempt at seizing an eastern empire labelled crusade. The destruction of Charles' ambitions by the occurrence of the Sicilian Vespers, and by the Aragonese seizure of the island led to an assimilation of both Greece and Aragon into the cause for which the Sicilian crusade was being waged, a cause once tenuously connected with the Holy Land by reason of its strategic position, and the union of crowns of Sicily and Jerusalem in the persons of Conrad and Conradin.

By virtue of the heavy concentration of the instruments of crusading policy in the interests of papal claims in Sicily, there had been a distinct shift in emphasis in the pretexts advanced to justify the free use of crusading indulgences. From speaking of the necessity of achieving a peaceful settlement in Sicily in order to ensure an atmosphere in the West conducive to a successful crusade in Syria, official documents had changed to speaking of Sicily as the focal point of all crusading energies, to which other causes were assimilated, and from which crusading indulgence had begun to draw its efficacy.

(v) *In Northern and Eastern Europe*

By the end of Innocent IV's pontificate crusade against the Tartar invasions, under the direction of the Teutonic Knights, had become inextricably mingled with the longer standing crusade against pagans on the eastern frontiers. It is easy to see from such sources as *The Chronicle of Novgorod* [180] and Matthew Paris [181] how confused reports were about the Tartars; nor are John de Plano Carpine and William

---

[179] The pope replied to Pedro's request for crusading help by sending the bishop of Grosseto to discover the king's plans; cf. Potthast, 21877. It is significant that Muntaner speaks of Martin as giving Peter "neither money *nor a crusade*" (italics mine), Chap. LVI. By crusade Muntaner meant simply indulgence.

[180] Translated R. M. Michell and N. Forbes (Camden Third Series, Vol. XXV), London, 1914. In such an area as Novgorod, "a raid was a raid was a raid" and there was little difference between a raid by the "new" Tartars, or by the "old" Lithuanians as far as the immediate impact was concerned. The chronicler is not so much intent on disinguishing between raiders, as on tracing the history of the city which was the object of the raids.

[181] iii, pp. 488-9; iv, pp. 76-8, 109-20, 270-7, 386-90.

Rubruck, for all their first hand information, models of clarity.[182]
If, in the early years of Innocent IV's pontificate, crusade against
Tartars was distinct from crusade against *pagani*, this was not the case
later. One suspects that the issue was deliberately confused by rulers
such as Hakon of Norway who had a vested interest in having the
sanction of a crusading indulgence for his aggression against his
neighbours. This man had taken the cross to go to the Holy Land with
King Louis who was eager to have a contingent of Norse ships at his
service.[183] Hakon was a man on the make, and had his own reasons
for taking the cross to go to the Holy Land, and for then turning his
crusading intentions against his neighbours. Hakon was but one of a
group of doubtfully Christian rulers in Scandinavia who used the
invasion of Tartars and other pagan tribes as an excuse for land
grabbing on the frontiers of their territories.[184]

In 1245 Innocent IV granted full crusading indulgences to those
taking the cross to assist the Teutonic Knights against pagan tribes in
Livonia and Prussia.[185] This crusade had been assigned to the preaching of the Dominicans in 1243, with full crusading indulgence and a
partial indulgence for all those coming to listen to the exposition of
the *verbum crucis*.[186] In the following year, granting a crusading indulgence to those assisting the duke of Austria against pagan enemies
of the faith in Prussia, Innocent wrote in explanation:

> quod dignum est ut hii qui se divinis exponunt obsequiis remune-
> rationem recipiant congruentem.[187]

The general pattern repeats itself endlessly all over the area, with
crusading indulgence, the key to all other instruments of crusading
policy, put at the disposal of each petty princeling who conceived a
pious design of border warfare. Such minor variations as emerge are
probably unique only in their survival in record.[188] The difficulty
about this kind of extension of the instruments of crusading policy
was that, once begun, there was no rationally-based ending since,

---

[182] Their accounts of their experiences among the Tartars are to be found
in A. van den Wyngaert, *Sinica Franciscana*, Vol. I, Florence, 1929.

[183] Matthew Paris, iv, pp. 651-2; Raynaldus, xiii, § 35 for the year 1246.

[184] Cf. P. Riant, *Expéditions et pèlerinages*, pp. 343-349, and Raynaldus, xiii,
§ 36 for the year 1246, for example.

[185] Potthast, 11657, 11803.

[186] Innocent IV, *Register*, 162-3; cf. Ripoll, i (Innocent IV) xiv-xxxi.

[187] Innocent IV, *Register*, 711.

[188] See, for example, Innocent IV, *Register*, 1029, a grant of an indulgence
of forty days for helping to build fortifications in Kulm.

if any of the campaigns was "cruciabilis", all were. If none was, then extensions of crusade indulgence was a wilful abuse of spiritual powers.[189] The matter was further confused by the presence in the area of the Teutonic Knights who used their status in proceeding with full crusading rights against pagans and Tartars. Eventually the two forms of crusade inevitably fell together as a defence of Christendom against those thirsting for Christian blood.[190] Even if men such as Humbert de Romans were not inclined to see the enemies on the eastern and northern frontiers as a serious threat,[191] it suited the land grabbers to represent them as such. Tartar invasions presented an excellent excuse for enlarging boundaries under a cloak of pure zeal. Quarrels over land settlement between the hierarchy and the Teutonic Knights, between these two and local rulers were a grave scandal, but were remarkably similar to the situation in the Crusader East.[192]

For all that Innocent IV described crusade in this area in terms of Moses wielding his sword against idolators, and so either consciously or not, widened the scope of crusading indulgence enormously,[193] the fact remains that secular and ecclesiastical rulers alike made use of crusade indulgence for their own territorial advancement. Hakon of Norway serves as a typical example.[194] It is true to say that crusading policy in this area was not, in any strict sense, papal. Too intent on affairs nearer home, and prevented by distance and bad communications from being well informed about the frontier situation, the popes too readily allowed the exploitation of the instruments of crusading policy in the interests of local ambitions. Before the end of the pontificate of Alexander IV the Teutonic Knights were so far in the forefront of crusading endeavour, that the clerics of the order were actively engaged in preaching crusade in Livonia and Prussia,[195] an advance in the assumption of control of

---

[189] The question of papal conscience about the grant of indulgences will be illustrated from their letters at the conclusion of this section.

[190] Innocent IV, *Register*, 6791.

[191] *Opus Tripartitum*, Pars I, Cap. V.

[192] A cursory reading of the *Regesta Regni Hierosolymitani* is enough to show the endless quarrels in the Crusader States over material possessions, not stopping short of murder, or internecine war. For examples of 'crusade' quarrels in Eastern and North Eastern Europe; cf. Innocent IV, *Register*, 1561, 1565-6, 3222, 5223-4, 8050.

[193] Raynaldus, xiii, § 93 for the year 1245.

[194] *Ibid.*, § 32-35 for the year 1246; cf. also, Innocent IV, *Register*, 2218-9, 3439, 3488, 6090, 6147.

[195] Alexander IV, *Register*, 3068-9.

the organisational forms of crusade without recorded parallel in the history of the Templars and the Hospitallers.

Forcible, or politic, conversions, with subsequent lapse into paganism of the border tribes contributed largely to the plausibility of many of these crusades, since heresy was an undoubted reason for crusading action. Occasionally the tribes were members of an Eastern rite sect, and were therefore schismatic, thus providing another reason for the grant of a crusading indulgence.[196] Strangely, one of the chief reasons for the ambivalent attitude of the West to the Tartars was the fact that many of these people were Nestorian Christians, and seemed, therefore, more open to conversion, though the schism of the Greeks was regarded a major cause for crusade. On the eastern and northern frontiers, as well as the confusion between Tartars who might have been Nestorian Christians, pagans who might have been lapsed Christians, and heretics, Christians who might have been schismatics, and pagans who were genuinely pagan, there were the further complications of the establishment of the In-quisition, and of simultaneous missionary activites to Tartars, Slavs and countless other pagan tribes throughout the known world.[197]

(vi) *Missionary activities*

Missionary activity only very rarely touched crusade policy im-mediately by the arrogation to itself of the instruments of crusading policy. Lopez, the Friar Minor appointed by Innocent IV to be the first bishop of Morocco, was granted a plenary indulgence for his lay entourage, presumably because they were envisaged as a species of armed bodyguard.[198] Despite the elaborate preparations made for Lopez' mission, including some interesting letters from the pope to Mirammamolinus, the sultan of Morocco, setting out the rights of

---

[196] Alexander IV, *Register*, 1578.

[197] These missionary activities in general lie beyond the scope of this dis-cussion, except when the missionaries are known to have been granted crusading privileges. The missionaries themselves differed in their attitudes to crusade. John de Plano Carpine was an advocate of crusade, and of beating the Tartars at their own game, with their own weapons. He did not share Humbert de Romans' optimism about their convertibility. William of Tripoli, by contrast, was opposed to crusade, and optimistic about converting the Saracens; so was Ramon Lull. Robert Grosseteste offered to go to preach to the Saracens, but did not take the cross. Roger Bacon, on the other hand, advocated the use of scientific war-fare, suggesting the use of large mirrors to burn up the Saracen hosts. King Louis' army need then consist only of two or three men, including the humble friar.

[198] Innocent IV, *Register*, 2514; cf. Potthast. 12470.

the Christians,[199] the venture did not get under way, and Lopez was next to be found preaching an ordinary crusading indulgence against the Saracens of North Africa, including the sultan of Morocco, presumably on behalf of Alfonso X of Leon and Castille.[200] Innocent IV made extensive efforts to convert Tartars, Saracens and schismatic sects in the East both by personal appeal,[201] and by missionary activities. Dominican missionaries to the Holy Land were granted by Alexander IV crusading indulgences on account of the good example of their way of life.[202] In addition to the school of Arabic studies already founded in Toledo, Innocent IV established another within the University of Paris.[203] There can be no doubt that crusade and true missionary zeal were mutually exclusive, a fact well attested by the situation in Spain, for example, with regard to Jewish and Moorish converts.[204]

(vii) *The Inquisition*

The establishment of the Inquisition had closer affinities with crusade against heretics. We have already seen how crusade against the Hohenstaufen was plausibly linked with campaigns against heresy, and against individual heretics such as Ezzelino di Romano. In the last years of his pontificate Innocent IV turned his attention to the extirpation of heresy in Northern Italy. As well as imposing the constitutions laid down by Frederick II against heresy,[205] Innocent established the Inquisition, and gave to the Inquisitors the faculty to grant crusading indulgences to those taking the cross against heretics,[206] and partial indulgences for those listening to the preaching of the *verbum crucis* against these heretics.[207] It was specifically en-

---

[199] Innocent IV, *Register*, 5172-5173.
[200] Alexander IV, *Register*, 483.
[201] Cf. p. 70, above.
[202] Alexander IV, *Register*, 1032.
[203] Honorius IV, *Register*, 274. Reference is made in this letter to the action of Honorius' predecessor in founding this school of language studies.
[204] Cf. R. J. Burns, "Journey from Islam: Incipient Cultural Transition in the Conquered Kingdom of Valencia, 1240-1280", *Speculum*, XXXV, 1960, pp. 337-356, and "Christian-Islamic Confrontation in the West: The Thirteenth-Century Dream of Conversion", *The American Historical Review*, 76, 1971, pp. 1386-1434. Unfortunately I have been unable to make use of Burns' most recent work on the subject, *Islam Under the Crusaders:* Colonial survival in the thirteenth century Kingdom of Valencia, Princeton, 1973. This has appeared too late for me to incorporate its findings where they may be relevant.
[205] Innocent IV, *Register*, 7800-7802; cf. Ripoll, i (Innocent IV) xxxiv.
[206] Innocent IV, *Register*, 7792, 7794.
[207] *Ibid.*, 7793.

joined that those combatting heresy should wear the cross; at the same time all 'converted' heretics also bore a penitential cross.[208]

It is notable that crusading indulgences on behalf of the Inquisition fused with crusade against relapsed pagans in Eastern Europe with the institution of the Inquisition in that area. In August, 1255, Alexander IV appointed Brother Bartholomew, of the Friars Minor, to preach a crusade with an indulgence as for the Holy Land, against the Lithuanians and various other pagan tribes on the frontiers, invading and killing or capturing Christians in Poland, Bohemia, Moravia and Austria.[209] The same friar, or another Brother Bartholomew of Bohemia, was appointed Inquisitor in 1257 along with Lambert the Teuton, another Friar Minor, in the area of Poland and Bohemia. These friars were granted a plenary indulgence, as were their assistants. All those giving military aid, or other help in combatting the heretics, for a period of three years, were also granted a plenary indulgence. Should they be killed before the expiry of their term of service they received the crusading indulgence.[210] In such an area as this crusade was an excuse for temporal and spiritual aggression—the seizing of desirable lands, and the forcible conversion of the vanquished tribes. Even St. Bernard had advocated that the Slavs against whom he preached a diversion of the second crusade must be either converted, or killed.[211]

Writing for the Second Council of Lyons, Bishop Bruno of Olmütz advocated these frontiers as the most suitable place for a concentration of crusading energies.[212] Like the Teutonic Knights who had in principle abandoned the Holy Land as their *raison d'être*, this prelate could see no great obstacle to the general abandonment of the Holy Land as the object of crusade. Obvious as his political motives were, Bruno must seriously have considered that his suggestions would make some mark. Diversion of crusade, and the instruments of crusading policy, was so commonplace that the bishop certainly did not see his proposal as a monstrous travesty of crusade. Missionary zeal could find a surer field of activity on the frontiers of Europe than it could among the Saracens, and there was a far greater emphasis on

---

[208] Innocent IV, *Register*, 7794.
[209] Alexander IV, *Register*, 704-6.
[210] *Ibid.*, 1975.
[211] Cf. *The Letters of St. Bernard*, No. 394.
[212] The memoir is printed in *Abhandlungen der historischen Classe der Bayerischen Akademie der Wissenschaften*, Munich, 1846.

the missionising side of imperialistic expansion in that area than there ever had been in the Holy Land. Bruno's patron, Ottokar of Bohemia, was not a man to cherish romantic ideals about the Holy Places and, though there was probably more naïvety than sinister intent in his alliance with Baibars in 1275,[213] one can read from his actions the sort of attitude which inspired Bishop Bruno's suggestion that the centre of crusade be no longer Jerusalem. In fact, Bruno might well have argued that, since the centre had already moved to Europe, and since the popes had so extensively put crusade to the political purposes of Western princes, it was more fitting to use the instruments of crusading policy against those who were pagan, and at least semi-barbarian, than against fellow Christians.

(e) Papal Rejections of Suggested Diversions

Bruno was not the only one to make interested suggestions about the use of crusade and its instruments. Gregory X answered the Bishop of Olmütz by silence. Fortunately there are preserved in the *Registers* of Clement IV and Nicholas III papal responses to two specific attempts to misuse crusade indulgences. It is not unexpected that these requests both came from the French royal family, one from the Capetian branch itself, and one from the Angevin. Shortly after his defeat of Manfred, Charles of Anjou, who had inherited all the Hohenstaufen ambitions in the East, cast his eyes in the direction of Greece. The first object of his wishes was Corfu, which he claimed to be his by right of Manfred's wife, Helen of Epiros, whom Charles held prisoner. The island had been governed for Manfred by an old supporter of the Hohenstaufen cause, Philip Chonardi.[214] Charles seems to have prevailed upon the latter's sons to raise a revolt against their father; to gain them not only military support, but a cloak of righteousness he appears to have appealed to Clement IV to grant a crusading indulgence to those going to the assistance of the rebels.[215] The pope refused the request because, though Philip was "excom-

---

[213] Cf. *Regesta Regni Hierosolymitani*, 1407, and R. Röhricht, "Etudes sur les derniers temps du royaume de Jérusalem", in *Archives de l'Orient latin*, Vol. I, Paris, 1881, pp. 617-652, Vol. II, Paris, 1884, pp. 365-409, especially p. 369, footnote 14.

[214] There are references to Philip's career as a supporter of the Hohenstaufen in Winckelmann's *Acta inedita*, i, Nos 916, 918, 920; cf. also, Huillard-Bréholles, iii, p. 536. Philip was ousted from Corfu, and succeeded by his son, Gazzo, whom Charles appointed.

[215] Clement IV, *Register*, 1131; cf. Potthast, 19824.

munacatissimus", it was not fitting that indulgences should be given for a war between two lots of Greeks any more than it should be to give one for a war between Tartars and Saracens. What is most enlightening, especially in view of papal experiences in Sicily itself, is that Clement added a rider to the effect that the campaign could be considered '*cruciabilis*' if those who desired the possession of the island should become vassals for it to the Holy See, or the Latin Emperor of Constantinople. This can leave little doubt about Clement's idea of the complete acceptability of the territorial possessions of the papacy, or of papal allies, as valid objects of crusade, and crusading indulgences.

The other letter is a lengthy reply from Nicholas III to Philip III of France, and a group of French barons who had sent a deputation to the pope requesting an extraordinary grant of crusading indulgences.[216] Philip III had assumed the cross in response to the appeal of the Second Council of Lyons, but had become embroiled in the quarrels over the succession in Navarre and Castille. The unsuccessful outcome of this dispute for the French was to lead indirectly to the Aragonese crusade of 1285, with the support of a pope whose conscience about crusade was distinctly French, but in the meantime, Philip was intent on building up his resources. The plan that he proposed to Pope Nicholas III in 1278 is a clear indication of the dangers made clear throughout this section of the increasing diversion of crusade indulgence from crusade to the Holy Land. The six years during which a crusading tenth had been decreed by the Council of Lyons, had by no means expired,[217] but the French king and his barons brought forward a suggestion for realising yet more money. They had followed the logic of the composition of the fourth group of *crucesignati* discussed above [218] to its ultimate conclusion. If the object of giving the cross to this whole group was to swell crusading funds, and not crusading ranks, then there seemed no reason for denying a plenary indulgence to those who made a straight contribution. The French request, therefore, was that a plenary indulgence be made available to those "non crucesignati aut voto crucis astricti" who made a sufficient contribution. Those making a lesser contribution were to receive one hundred days indulgence.[219] The

---

[216] Nicholas III, *Register*, 392.
[217] The collection began at the earliest in the latter part of 1274, and so must have had at least two years to run when this letter was written, 3 December, 1278.
[218] Cf. p. 54, above.
[219] The details are set out in the pope's reply.

French request went further to the heart of the matter by suggesting pardoners be quashed in the meantime, and all indulgences not related to the Holy Land be suspended, or at least restricted.

In his lengthy reply the pope set out his own tremendous sense of responsibility for the prudent and timely dispensing of the treasury of the Church, as well as his ardent desire to aid the Holy Land. With a palpable hit he reminded the French king of the labours which the papacy had had to effect peace between France and Castille to the detriment of the affairs of the Holy Land. He urged also the collection still being made in accordance with the decrees of the recent Council, and the generous distribution of the treasury of the Church in ways both old and new. If the French showed themselves aware of the logical conclusion to be drawn from the trend of policy in the granting of crusading indulgences, the pope showed himself aware of the logical consequences of allowing the policy to be followed to its conclusions. Not only would there be a falling off in zeal for the actual effort of crusade, if no distinction were made between personal effort and mere donation, but if once a precedent were established in France, there would be no denying other princes a similar concession Moreover, Nicholas III reminded the French king of the provision of the Council for crusader chests into which the faithful could put their mite in order to gain the indulgence. More serious still was the consideration that interference with donations to the poor, even in favour of the Holy Land, was not meritorious, but inhuman. Lest he should have seemed too adamant, the pope tempered his refusal with a promise to give his utmost help should a general passage become imminent, though the tone of the letter suggests that the pope was not very optimistic about the state of crusading fervour.

Nicholas III cannot have been unaware that the precedents which he declared himself unwilling to establish, had been established long since. To Nicholas' hesitation must be added his unexpressed conviction that Philip's zeal was not for the Holy Land, and that his motives were interested; there must also be added the fact that at that moment the papacy was not an interested party, either, in the diversion of crusade. Though Nicholas III might protest adherence to the principles traditionally governing crusading policy, and spare no opportunity to insist on the sad plight of the Holy Land,[220] yet the dam-

---

[220] *Register*, 222-3, 225, 676-8, 758, 761-2, 765; cf. also, Martin IV, *Register*, 302, 351, 570.

age done by the policies of his predecessors, was to be increased by his immediate successors, Martin IV[221] and Honorius IV, in favouring with all their power the joint cause of the Capetians and the Angevins against the house of Aragon.[222] Earlier crusade in Sicily had been an assertion of papal claims; now it was nothing more than an obstinate defence of the results of that earlier crusade, though from the papal point of view this had been a failure. Holy Land, Greek union, papal independence, were all subordinate to the affair of Sicily and Aragon. Most significantly, Muntaner stresses papal diversion of indulgence against Aragon as the justification advanced for opening to France the treasury of St. Peter.[223] Indulgence represented the essence of crusade for Muntaner, and he did not fail to note triumphantly that the Aragonese won victory in spite of the indulgence and interdict used against them.[224]

(f) Reductio ad Absurdum

From the disastrous Aragonese crusade of Philip III comes perhaps the most revealing story of the degeneration of crusading indulgence in the minds of the general body of the faithful. This story has two different versions, but they both point to the same conclusion. The French soldiers had been granted a full crusading indulgence for assisting Philip against Pedro III.[225] After the capture of Elne, the French forces were daunted by the crossing of the Pyrenees which lay before them, and by the attacks of the Aragonese troops. Many of them determined to desert Philip, and return home. One chronicler, Desclot, relates how, in order not to miss the indulgence they took up three stones, each of which they hurled in the direction of the mountain pass. One of these stones they declared to be for the soul of their mother, one for that of their father, and one for the remission of their own sins. They then gathered earth from the foot of the mountains, and bore off, each of them a quantity. In this way they had fulfilled their *votum itineris*, by journeying to Pedro's territory, by waging war thereon, and by taking possession of it; they had

---

[221] Simon de Brie, cardinal of St. Cecilia, and papal legate in France from the time of Clement IV.

[222] Martin IV, *Register*, 276-8, 570; Honorius IV, *Register*, 392-3, 395, 768-9, 807.

[223] Chap. LXXVIII. See also, p. 88, footnote 179, above.

[224] Chap. CXXVI.

[225] Bernat Desclot, *Chronicle of the Reign of King Pedro III of Aragon*, trans. F. L. Critchlow, Princeton, N. J., 2 vols, 1928-1934, Vol. II, Chapter LXXIII.

earned their plenary remission of sins.[226] In the last days of the mainland Crusader Kingdom, crusade had become a matter of political
expediency in the West. One must not be blinded by the fact that
kings and princes still assumed the cross, and with it all the appear-
ances of devotion to the cause of the Holy Land. Becoming a *crucesignatus* was for many largely a matter of trying it on, to see how
far one could enjoy the finances, or the other privileges, without
actually fulfilling the vow. The wily Philip III endeavouring to
secure more funds by extension of crusading indulgence, the less
subtle borrowing of crusading funds by Edward I,[227] or the downright
robbery by John von Nassau, bishop-elect of Utrecht, of a convent
where funds had been stored,[228] all belong to the same disintegration
of organisational forms which followed the too diverse use of the
instruments of crusading policy. It is little wonder that Tartar em-
bassies seeking immediate action against the Saracens met with no
response, and that the remnants of the Crusader States went unaided
to their destruction.

---

[226] The other version, quoted in a footnote to the above mentioned chapter
of Desclot, appears in the *Gesta Comitum Barchinonensem*, XXVIII, 41, and is
much less plausible since it represents French besiegers hurling stones at the
walls of Gerona in order to gain the indulgence, there being a shortage of arrows.
[227] See below, p. 156.
[228] See below, p. 153.

CHAPTER FIVE

COMMUTATION AND REDEMPTION OF CRUSADER VOWS

(a) THEOLOGICAL BACKGROUND

The commutation of eternal punishment merited by sin, to temporal punishment within man's capacity for satisfaction, proceeded
by two steps.[1] Pelagius had found his answer to man's incapacity to
satisfy by denying the original sin from which sprang that incapacity;[2]
as an accidental consequence of this followed a denial of the necessity,
not simply of the mode of Christ's redemptive act, but of the act itself.
Orthodox theologians, embracing the Augustinian "O felix culpa",
evolved a far more complex doctrine of sin and punishment, with an
elaborate system of penances, drawing their efficacy specifically from
Christ's redemptive act.[3] An integral part of this system was the
provision for commutation and redemption of ecclesiastical penances
which were beyond the capacity of the individual penitent. A commutation allowed for a change in the form of penance, but left the
onus of fulfilment to fall on the person of the penitent; a redemption
removed the obligation for a personal fulfilment by allowing for
substitution, or for a money payment. By the end of the twelfth century
public penances had ceased to be imposed, and were represented only
in the most extreme cases by the imposition of a solemn penance. This
was the final commutation of public penance before it disappeared
altogether, and took the form of an obligation to go on pilgrimage,
with solemn bestowal of pilgrim garb and staff in a rite which was
reserved for performance by bishops, and took place on Ash Wednes-
day or Holy Thursday.[4]

Even this form of penance was rare, and, by the thirteenth century,
was largely superseded by sacramental penance, which was not

---

[1] Cf. pp. 38-40, above.

[2] It is, perhaps, technically more correct to speak of Pelagianism as a doctrine
which sees man as capable of making the first move towards salvation on his
own, prior to any divine intervention. In other words it concerns itself with
theorising about the nature of the grace necessary for salvation. This question
is important with reference to indulgences insofar as they would never have
been instituted had Pelagius' extrinsicist concept of grace prevailed.

[3] Cf. B. Poschmann, *Busse und Letzte Ölung*, Chaps 1-3.

[4] *Ibid.*, p. 82.

intended to be other than representative of the penitent's attitude, and of the efficacy of the sacramental absolution.[5] Because of some serious doubt about the satisfaction due after the fulfilment of the sacramental penance by the penitent, the stress tended to fall heavily on extra-sacramental works of satisfaction. These were, strictly, commutations of the ecclesiastical penance no longer imposed but still used as a kind of measuring stick for the amount of satisfaction yet to be paid.[6] All ecclesiastical penances were imposed by the minister of the sacrament, and were voluntarily performed by the penitent, that is, the penitent voluntarily accepted his obligation to discharge the penance. Just as the form of solemn penance incorporated the notion of pilgrimage as a work of satisfaction, so the scope of sacramental penance extended to the imposition of pilgrimage as penance. It is important to realise, however, that the minister of the sacrament could not normally impose the taking of a vow, hence the vow of pilgrimage was the consequence, rather than the essence, of the penance imposed. In a similar manner a penitent, even should he be obliged to enter a monastery in order to fulfil his penance, could not be forced to take vows of religion. No one could be obliged by a confessor to take a crusading vow, though he might be obliged to take the cross, and, indeed the taking of the cross as a sacramentally imposed penance followed naturally from the close connection between pilgrimage and crusade. In all these cases the vow took its voluntariness from the free acceptance of the penance by the penitent.

The whole question of the degree of volition necessary for the validity of vows, oaths, and contracts, was one which received a great deal of attention from canonists and theologians, and though they were more closely concerned with marriage vows, their discussions were not without importance in the matter of crusader vows, and the commutation, and redemption of such vows. Though

---

[5] Even without any agreement among theologians on the precise function of sacramental absolution, there was still a general acceptance of the symbolic value of absolution which looked both ways, from God to the penitent, and from the penitent to God, in mutual recognition of guilt, in penitential contrition, and in divine forgiveness.

[6] This is seen most clearly in the formula of partial indulgences where the "amount" of remission was measured in terms of the temporal period for which public penance would have been prescribed. Such "measurements" decreased in meaning as the period of public penances faded into antiquity, but it is typical of the history of dogmas that the phraseology should have long outlived their meaningfulness; reference to indulgences in terms of temporal periods has been abandoned only in 1968.

even a mental reservation was considered a sufficiently invalidating factor, yet moral suasion does not seem to have been so considered.[7] The commutation of crusader vows was governed by the relatively simple principle that all vows were open to dispensation,[8] though some were reserved to the pope.[9] A vow which was dispensible was, subject to the same conditions, open to commutation. It must be remembered that mediaeval society was far more prone to give its activities a religious orientation by elevating to the status of a vow, deeds which a more sophisticated society would consider little more than a pious intention.[10] It is beyond the scope of this thesis to discuss the spiritual dangers of this proliferation of vowable acts, but what touches the discussion nearly is the practical effect which the extension of vows had on recruitment for crusade. Vows were of roughly two types—those which had in view the remission of sins, and those which symbolised a higher, and more total form of dedication. One might say that the broad distinction lay between vows proper, and pious intentions.[11] St. Thomas' discussion of the reason why a *crucesignatus* who died without fulfilling his vow, could still receive the full indulgence,[12] is based on such a distinction. In this regard it is instructive to read in a letter of Pope Nicholas IV that Edmund of Lancaster and his fellow *crucesignati* were to be absolved

---

[7] The canonists do not discuss moral suasion as such, but according to both Matthew Paris (iv, p. 502), and Joinville (clxiv § 733), it would seem that people could be manoeuvred into a "free" acceptance of an obligation which was held to be binding. Of course, King Louis' courtiers were bound in honour rather than in strict legal justice, as the snippet of conversation reported by Joinville shows them to have been aware. Caesarius of Heisterbach also speaks of a certain Gottschalk, a usurer, as having been forced to take the cross by the pressure of those around him. Cf. *Dialogus Miraculorum*, ed. J. Strange, 2 vols, Cologne, 1851, Distinctio Secunda, De Contritione Cap. VII.

[8] Innocent IV, *Apparatus*, III, tit. De voto Cap. I (De Peregrinationis); Hostiensis, *Summa Aurea*, III, tit. De voto § 16 (Utrum).

[9] Innocent IV, *Apparatus, loc. cit.*; Hostiensis, *Summa Aurea, loc. cit.*

[10] Martin Luther is, perhaps, the most famous example of someone who fell victim to the popular confusion between a vow proper, and a merely pious intention. His original vow would have been questionably valid, even in his own day, in the strict legal sense. His case is of interest here as examplifying what was undoubtedly a very common occurrence in mediaeval life. Any visitor to Italian churches will recognise the modern equivalent of the "vow" of pious intention in the proliferation of *votive* offerings, and *votive* lamps.

[11] The canonists, of course, are more refined than this in their distinctions. On the development of the theology of vows, see J. A. Brundage, *Mediaeval Canon Law and the Crusader*, Madison, 1969, Chapters II and III.

[12] *Quaest. Quod.*, II, Q VIII a 2 [16].

of *perjury* for not having set out on crusade at the appointed time.[13] Considering Edmund's record as a crusader, and as a *crucesignatus*,[14] it seems more likely that he should have simply failed to set out at the time he had contracted on oath to do so, rather than that he had falsely sworn to set out at a certain time. In any case, even if the use of the word *perjurium* is inaccurate, it still indicates the category into which crusader vows were considered to fall. They were more akin to oaths, than to vows proper; this judgment is corroborated by the fact that there is no clear evidence to prove that there was a public emission of crusader vows.[15] This less binding nature of a crusader vow was somewhat obscured by the fact that, along with vows of religion and chastity, it was reserved to the pope, or his accredited official. Such a reservation, however, proceeded not from the intrinsic solemnity of the object of the vow, but from the desire to prevent wanton extravagance of redemptions from ruining crusade recruitment, and to keep the direction of crusade within papal control. Essentially the crusader vow was cognate with that of pilgrimage, though not synonymous. Joinville shows that the two functions were distinguished, even in the matter of religious ceremony, since he speaks of having received his pilgrim's staff and wallet from the abbot of Cheminon on the very day he left home to go on crusade.[16] One can only assume that the ceremony of taking the cross had been held much earlier. Like pilgrimage, crusade was a commutative act of extra-sacramental penance; canonically and theologically it was as open to commutation as pilgrimage itself, and there is plenty of thirteenth century evidence to suggest that it was not difficult to commute a vow of pilgrimage.[17] The simple difference lay in the

---

[13] *Les Registres de Nicholas IV*, ed. E. Langlois, Paris, 1886-1893, 1710[2].

[14] On his qualities as a *crucesignatus* see the laudatory letters in Peckham, i, cxviii, and Wickwane, 467, recommending that Edmund should act as substitute for the king, Edward I.

[15] See Appendix B. The rite was that of taking the cross. See Brundage, *op. cit.*, pp. 118 ff.

[16] Joinville, xxvii, § 122.

[17] Cardinal Ottobuono Fieschi who took a vow of pilgrimage to Santiago de Compostella, seemingly because he wished to cut free of all the difficulties resulting from his legatine commission in England, was readily promised a commutation by the pope, who wished him to stay on in England if possible; cf. *C.P.L.* I, p. 421. Episcopal registers also record commutations of vows of pilgrimage; cf. *The Register of Walter Giffard*, Lord Archbishop of York, 1266-1279, Surtees Society, Vol. CIX, London, 1904, pp. 281-2, for an absolution on account of poverty to Helewysa Palmer and her daughter, Isabella, from a vow to go to Compostella. Their redeeming fee was set at two shillings sterling to be paid as

reservation of the crusader vow. The major question on the commutation of this vow was practical rather than spiritual, namely the effect that this would have on a specific crusading venture, hence its reservation to the pope.

Commutation of a crusading vow presupposed an alternative, roughly equivalent, crusading venture; the commutation did not alter the nature of the participation, but merely the geographical location, and the object of the crusade.[18] Commutations of vows made to go crusading to the Holy Land were uncommon before the thirteenth century. The diversion of the English crusaders to Lisbon in the second crusade was not planned, and cannot be regarded as a commutation;[19] the Wendish crusaders took their vows specifically for that diversionary venture.[20] Vows to the Holy Land were frequently deferred, by a commutation of time and not of place; this was, perhaps, the more common way of avoiding the obligation previous to the thirteenth century. It was usual practice for vows of all kinds to be commuted to crusade to the Holy Land [21] and, until the Sicilian affair began to absorb so many crusading resources, vows of crusade other than to the Holy Land were readily commutable to the traditional goal. The general practice, and organisation, of commutations argued clearly a strong orientation towards the Holy Land as the classic object of crusade.

---

a subsidy for the Holy Land. *The Register of John Le Romeyn, Lord Archbishop of York, 1286-1296*, Surtees Society, Vols CXXIII and CXXVIII, London, 1913-1916, No. 656, contains an interesting record of an absolution from a vow to go on pilgrimage to Compostella by Henry de Brumpton of Scarborough, on account of his infirmity. The vow was already thirty six years in the fulfilling. In this case the redeeming fee was one hundred shillings sterling, without specific object. In 1288 Nicholas IV granted to a certain John de Wotton an absolution of his vow to visit Rome, inherited from his mother. In this case the redemption fee was set at the equivalent of the cost of the journey, and was to be given to St. Peter's; cf. *C.P.L.*, I, p. 492. These examples serve to give an idea of the somewhat flexible policy with regard to redemption of vows of pilgrimage, a flexibility which was not without influence on crusading policy in the matter of commutation and redemption of vows.

[18] A typical example of this is the proposed commutation of Henry III's vow from the Holy Land to Northern Africa and its eventual commutation to Sicily. On the other hand, the proposed commutation of Guy de Lusignan's vow at the request of Henry III was not a matter of geography but of a deferment of time; cf. Innocent IV, *Register*, 4056-7.

[19] Cf. Osbernus, *De expugnatione Lyxbonensi*, pp. cxlv-cxlvi and p. 14, footnote 17, above.

[20] See above, pp. 15-16, 70, note 79

[21] Cf. Innocent IV, *Register*, 4663, 6469; Urban IV, *Register*, 389, 468, 2914; Gregory X, *Register*, 569.

The tendency to encourage the taking of crusading vows for objects other than the defence of the Holy Places, was an obvious consequence of the hierarchy of importance of crusading goals. The Holy Land was the goal *par excellence*, and therefore vows to go to its aid were not simply commutable to a lesser crusade. This was a principle operative also in the matter of religious vows—normally a religious could transfer only to an order of greater austerity, could, in effect, aim only at a more perfect goal. When it became desirable to use the instruments of crusade for the conduct of a campaign other than to the Holy Land, the indulgence might be granted "as for the Holy Land", but if the vow were taken "as for the Holy Land" this would have demanded a commutation, and to commute a vow of aid to the Holy Land was not really acceptable. Thus the vow was taken to go on crusade to a place other than the Holy Land, though the indulgence invariably drew its efficacy from its relation to that traditional goal. The result of this, contrary to intention, was to enhance the importance of crusades not to the Holy Land; in the long run, by a logical process, this tended to destroy the hierarchy of crusading values, and ultimately to permit of the commutation of crusading vows to the Holy Land, for crusade elsewhere.

The redemption of an ecclesiastical penance was originally conceded on account of the penitent's manifest incapacity to perform what had been imposed. Such an incapacity could have been the consequence of the extent of the penance proportioned to the enormity of the crime committed, thus rendering it unlikely that the penitent should be able fully to satisfy during his lifetime; on the other hand it could have been the result simply of physical infirmity. In either of these cases the custom arose of allowing the penitent to redeem his penance by the use of assistant, or substitute, penitents. A man might provide his own substitutes, but it was far easier to make use of the Church's vast reserves of religious, vowed to a life of penance, and thus obvious instruments of vicarious penance. To procure the use of such substitutes the penitent was required to make a suitable payment of alms. Ecclesiastical terminology was careful to avoid the suggestion that the penitent was actually buying his exemption from personal performance of his penance, and stress was laid on the money payment as alms-giving, as, therefore, a substitute form of penance. In time, however, there was a considerable relaxation in the practice of assessing a penitent's incapacity for fulfilling his own penance, and the use of redemptions became so common as to constitute a serious threat to the coherence of the whole penitential system. This danger of formal, or even material, simony, was one of the major contributory factors to the development of a more interiorised doctrine of satisfaction.

With the passing of the old penitential system went the necessity to provide for redemptions of penances either by substitute, or by payment of alms. Despite this lack of a need, the habit of redemptions remained active in the differently orientated penitential system, though their use was changed because of the shift in emphasis to works of satisfaction voluntarily undertaken outside the sacrament.[22] By the mid-thirteenth century the bulk of redemptions were concerned with penitential vows, chiefly crusade, pilgrimage, and abstinence. Innocent IV argued that all vows were dispensible and therefore all commutable.[23] It is to be assumed that the redemption of vows was considered to be covered by their dispensation since the language constantly employed by the popes in letters concerning the redemption of vows was that the person was to be *absolved* of his vow, that is to say he was to be dispensed from the obligation of fulfilment.[24] Until the thirteenth century vows of crusade were redeemable solely under the strictest necessity, and even the later canonists allowed only the gravest reasons to prevent personal fulfilment.[25] So pressing was the obligation that a vow of crusade, quite unlike any other vow, was held to oblige a man's heirs should he not fulfil it in his lifetime, a distinction being drawn between a vow to go to the Holy Land, and a vow to go to the aid of the Holy Land.[26] The seriousness with which this obligation was accepted is to be seen in the provisions of the wills of *crucesignati* for a substitute to fulfil their vows.[27]

This is explicable in terms of the greater altruism presupposed by a crusading vow. Far from being merely an act of devotion or personal expiation like vows of pilgrimage, or abstinence, crusading vows aimed at promoting the territorial and spiritual unity of Christendom. Though in practice it was possible for a simple pilgrim to contribute more to the common fund of grace in the Church by

---

[22] See above, pp. 39-41.

[23] *Apparatus*, III, tit. De voto Cap. I (De Peregrinationis).

[24] Cf. Innocent IV, *Register*, 162, 3708, 4286 and many others.

[25] Cf. Hostiensis, *Summa Aurea*, III, tit. De voto § 12 (Qualiter); Innocent IV, *Apparatus*, III, tit. De voto Cap. I (De Peregrinationis).

[26] Cf. Innocent IV, *Apparatus*, III, tit. De voto Cap. VI (Licet Universis).

[27] See, for example, the wills of Hugh of Lusignan and Raymond of Toulouse in *Layettes*, iii, Nos 3705, 3803.

reason of the greater devotion with which he fulfilled his pilgrimage, the crusader was far richer in spiritual potential on account of his greater altruism. It was precisely this greater spiritual potential in the crusading vow which led to its being made available to a wider section of the faithful than was capable of going on crusade. While unarmed pilgrims accompanied crusading ventures, there was no radical distinction made in practice between the spiritual potential of crusading vows and those of pilgrimage, but once crusade became deliberately exclusive of unarmed pilgrims, there was a compensatory move towards widening the scope of crusading vows. This could be feasible only if the regulations concerning the redemptions of those vows were relaxed, and persons manifestly incapable from the beginning were permitted to make vows on condition of redeeming them, without ever intending actually to go on crusade. This is related to the provisions in crusading decrees for those who provided substitute warriors to receive the crusading indulgence.[28] Burning zeal, rendered incapable of fulfilling a crusading vow by physical infirmity or weakness, was able to take full advantage of a widened possibility for redemption of crusading vows, but so also was sloth, for here was an opportunity for rich benefits with little personal effort. While this extension of crusading vows and crusading indulgences theoretically served the spiritual purposes of the faithful, it also theoretically served the purposes of crusade, especially by way of financial support. The practical effects were drastically other. These can best be judged after a detailed discussion of the application of commutations and redemptions in everyday crusading policy. It is here that there becomes manifest a close parallel between the breakdown of the earlier penitential system into simoniacal redemptions, and the breakdown of the efficacy of crusading vows through the same abuse.

(b) COMMUTATION OF VOWS

Early in his pontificate Innocent IV allowed the use of *crucesignati* for the Holy Land against Tartar invaders of Hungary,[29] and later for the suppression of heresy.[30] In neither of these cases was there a suggestion that such service constituted a commutation. Should the *crucesignatus* be killed in the course of such diversionary service, he

---

[28] See Appendix A, pp. 189-90, 195, below.
[29] *Register*, 2957.
[30] *Register*, 5354; Ripoll, i (Innocent IV) ccxcviii.

was to receive the full crusading indulgence, not because of the service, but by reason of his intention of going to the Holy Land.[31] He would, in fact, have received the full indulgence even if his death were from natural causes, or from something totally unrelated to crusade, provided that the deferment of his vow had been legitimate.

While St. Louis was preparing to set out on his crusade, Innocent IV charged the legate, Eudes de Châteauroux, to take stern measures against wanton and illegitimate casting aside of crusading vows.[32] The legate was also given faculties to commute all vows to that of crusade to the Holy Land, with the usual reservations, of course.[33] Commutations of crusader vows were, in a sense, more difficult to justify in the face of King Louis' crusade than were redemptions, since commutations aimed at the redistribution of personnel, while redemptions could be justified on the grounds of financial aid. Innocent IV issued at least two letters which indicate not only that pressures were brought to bear on *crucesignati* to commute their vows, but also that the pope was prepared to co-operate in preventing such abuses from robbing King Louis of recruits. The bishop of Worcester, Walter de Cantilupe, was directed to prevent *crucesignati* from being compelled to fight any but Saracens,[34] and the confraternity of the (lesser) crusaders of Châteaudun were given papal protection against the same thing.[35] When Henry III wished to have the vow of Guy de Lusignan, who was intending to set out with King Louis, commuted to the English venture, the pope refused his permission, unless the prior consent of Louis and his regent, Queen Blanche, was obtained.[36]

While the pope was thus scrupulously careful to prohibit the commutation of vows within the French king's realm, he was not quite so protective of the interests of the Holy Land crusade in areas outside France. Eudes de Châteauroux's legatine powers originally extended to the preaching of King Louis' crusade not only in France, but also in England, Germany, Dacia, Brabant, and Scotland.[37] When the pope ordered the preaching of the crusade against Frederick II in Germany in 1247, he felt himself to be in an equivocal

---

[31] See pp. 44-6, above.
[32] Innocent IV, *Register*, 4663.
[33] *Ibid., loc. cit.*
[34] *Ibid.*, 2960; *C.P.L.*, I, p. 234.
[35] Innocent IV, *Register*, 2644.
[36] *Ibid.*, 4054, 4056-7.
[37] *Ibid.*, 2229.

position, since at first he gave instructions that the commutation of the preaching should be kept secret.[38] Menko in his Chronicle for the year 1247[39] gives some clue as to the reason for Innocent's embarrassment. In that year Brother Willibrand had come to the Holy See with a great deal of money gathered from redemptions of vows, and bearing many promises of Frisian help "in rebus et personis" for the Holy Land. Louis IX is reported as urging the pope to send preachers to stir up the Frisians on behalf of his crusade. Willibrand was chosen for the task. For this reason the pope was also in two minds about the commutation of crusading vows already taken for the Holy Land. At first the legate, Peter of San Giorgio, had been ordered to prohibit the commutation of such vows or the hindering of their fulfilment, in the border dioceses [40] where the French king might obviously have had a claim. The general legatine powers contained the faculty to commute all vows in favour of William of Holland, save those to the Holy Land;[41] the legate was, at the same time, given specific powers to commute the vows of a certain number of *crucesignati* wishing to go to William's aid—five Frenchmen and fifteen Germans.[42] These are not named, but might well have been the Thomas of Bellomanso and others specified in a different letter.[43]

Eventually, at the request of William of Holland, to whom Frisia belonged by hereditary right, the archbishop of Prussia was granted faculties to commute Frisian vows to go to the Holy Land to crusade on behalf of William, with the retention of the full crusading indulgence.[44] In the following year, 1248, Peter of San Giorgio was given the same general faculties, at William's request, to commute all Frisian vows, even, specifically, those of crusade to the Holy Land.[45] It is doubtful how far the *crucesignati* themselves were parties to this request, since a number of them seem to have taken the opportunity merely to leave their vows in abeyance.

On 22 June, 1248,[46] the pope issued instructions to the Friars

---

[38] Innocent IV, *Register*, 2935.

[39] *Menkonis Chronicon, M.G.H. SS*, XXIII, p. 540.

[40] Innocent IV, *Register*, 3384.

[41] *Ibid.*, 4065; cf. Potthast, 12755.

[42] Innocent IV, *Register*, 4060, "qui causam agit fidei et Ecclesiae".

[43] *Ibid.*, 3885-7; cf. Potthast, 12935.

[44] Innocent IV, *Register*, 4070; cf. Potthast, 12749-51.

[45] Innocent IV, *Register*, 3779; cf. Potthast, 12894.

[46] The feast of John the Baptist, June 24th, chosen because of its proximity to midsummer's day, was the traditional date for a general passage, hence the papal reminder issued near that date. It was, of course, always an approximated

Preachers and Friars Minor in Germany to warn all *crucesignati* for the Holy Land in Frisia, Holland and Zeeland to be ready to set out the following March,[47] presumably with the count of Poitiers, whose setting out had been delayed. King Louis himself was preparing to set out in the coming August. Though Joinville speaks of the count of Poitiers' arrival, he does not mention the Frisians as it seems likely he would have done, had these arrived in sufficient numbers to constitute a distinct band. The next one hears of the Frisians is in a papal letter written at the end of November, 1250,[48] after King Louis' defeat, when the friars were again instructed to see that the Frisians [49] were ready to set out in the next general passage,

quodque solent Frisones in Transmarinis Partibus prosperari.

This is undoubtedly a reference to the prowess displayed by the Frisian contingent during the siege of Damietta in the Fifth Crusade.[50] Both Frisians and Norwegians were desirable recruits on account of their fleets, and King Louis had been unfortunate in losing the services of both, though he had expectations from each. In either case the loss was officially sanctioned by the pope in his permission for the commutation of vows, even those of crusade to the Holy Land. Yet the pope made every effort to encourage the fulfilment of uncommuted vows, and to offset the general lack of enthusiasm which had been one of the consequences of the dispensation to commute all vows in favour of William of Holland. Menko represents Willibrand as having called together the hierarchy and the lay nobility especially those already *crucesignati*, and as having shown them the

---

date so far as the actual setting out was concerned. Quite apart from political, or climatic factors, it would require a detailed survey of logistical preparations to show all that was involved in determining the date of departure.

[47] Innocent IV, *Register*, 3967; cf. P. Sambin, *Problemi Politici Attraverso Lettere Inediti di Innocenzo IV* (Istituto Veneto di Scienze, Lettere ed Arti, Memorie Classe di Scienze Morali e Lettere, Vol. XXXI, Fasc. III), Venice, 1955, No. 46.

[48] Innocent IV, *Register*, 4927; cf. Ripoll, i (Innocent IV) ccxv.

[49] The letter is also concerned with Norwegian *crucesignati*.

[50] See Oliverus (Scholasticus), *Historia Damiatina*, in *Die Schriften des Kölner Domscholasters*, ed. H. Hoogeweg, Tübingen, 1894, especially Cap. 10-13. In a letter to the Frisian clergy, Oliver, in speaking of their countrymen at the siege of Damietta claimed that they had performed deeds "in qua premium eternum premeruerunt et famam temporalem, quam perdere non possunt, si in cepto itinere perseveraverint usque in finem" (Letter 4, pp. 295-6). Jacques de Vitry also testified to the religious fervour and bravery of the Frisians under Oliver. See Letter 4 in *Lettres de Jacques de Vitry* (Edition critique), ed. R. B. C. Huygens, Leiden, 1960, pp. 126 ff.

pope's letters concerning the crusade.[51] These Frisians objected that May of the following year (presumably of 1248), was too soon for them to be ready because of lack of money and uncertain transport. They demanded a delay until May, 1249. Menko telescopes the whole incident by saying that the Frisians were distracted by their participation in the siege of Aix-la-Chapelle, and that their vows were commuted by the pope's authority.[52] Despite the tone of the pope's letters of encouragement to do as their fathers had done, it is evident that the slackening of zeal had led the Frisians to cast off the cross they had assumed, and that they had little or no intention of commuting, or fulfilling, their vows.

The Norwegian contingent vowed to crusade in the Holy Land are a different case. King Hakon, an excellent example of a ruler quite prepared to manipulate the instruments of crusading policy solely for his own ends, judiciously took the cross to go on crusade with King Louis.[53] The latter responded with generous offers of harbour and provisions for the fleet,[54] but this was no inducement to Hakon who, in view of his precarious position at home, was unlikely to have entertained any serious notion of ever fulfilling his vow. On the grounds of frontier threats, Hakon quickly commuted his vow to a more localised, and territorially profitable, venture against pagan invaders.[55] By this time he was already possessed of the papal recognition, and protection, which it had been his object to procure in taking his vow. In 1254 Alexander IV offered Hakon a commutation of his vow to Sicily if he would agree to aid Henry III.[56] In the light of this easy manipulation of crusading instruments, it is amusing to read in the *Saga of Hacon* of the pressing invitation extended to Hakon by the king of Castille to accompany the latter to Jerusalem.[57] Apart

---

[51] These letters are possibly to be identified with that printed by P. Sambin, *Problemi Politici*, 46.

[52] A full crusading indulgence was granted for the campaign against the people of Aix-la-Chapelle; cf. Innocent IV, *Register*, 4181.

[53] Innocent IV, *Register*, 2218, and P. Riant, *Les expéditions et les pèlerinages des Scandinaves en Terre Sainte*, pp. 346-7; cf. also *Matthew Paris*, iv, p. 651. Hakon had actually taken the cross for the first time in 1237.

[54] Matthew Paris, iv, pp. 651-2.

[55] Innocent IV, *Register*, 6090; cf. Raynaldus, xiii, § 35 for the year 1246.

[56] Rymer, i, p. 548.

[57] Cf. *Icelandic Sagas*, Vol. IV, *The Saga of Hacon*, trans. Sir G. W. Dasent, Rolls Series, London, 1894, p. 317, for the year 1258. Urging Hakon's aid for a venture to Jerusalem the king explained that Hakon might thus fulfil his vow "for it was so by the pope's leave that the cross might be redeemed if a pilgrimage were made to Jerusalem", a form of proposal which seems to indicate some

from the Norwegian king's own commutation of vow, he must certainly have procured the commutation of the vows of such *crucesignati* among his subjects as he needed for protecting his rights, and conducting his campaigns. In Norway, as in Frisia, the general atmosphere engendered by widespread commutation led to slackness in fulfilling vows, and *crucesignati* needed to be reminded of their obligations. Once more there is no evidence of the arrival of any sort of sizeable group in the Holy Land;[58] certainly King Louis did not benefit by the aid of Norwegian forces.

In England also, the commutation of vows militated against the success of King Louis' venture. A small band of English crusaders led by William Longespée did set out almost simultaneously with the main French contingent. There seems to have been no more marked enthusiasm for military participation in this crusade than there was for financial support, but there had been, after all, a specifically English crusade, in 1240, led by Richard of Cornwall. Some of the English *crucesignati*, though they had intended to lend King Louis their aid, did not set out with him. Matthew Paris made a great story of Henry III's attempts forcibly to defer their setting out, once he had taken the cross himself.[59] Whether by his own request, or by that of the pope, Henry III deferred the fulfilment of his vow, from the very beginning,[60] and then, as a result of events in Gascony, promised to commute his vow from the Holy Land itself to participation in the venture to Northern Africa of Alfonso X of Leon and Castille.[61] This crusade had been inherited by Alfonso from his father, Ferdinand III, who, having drastically reduced the Moorish footing on the peninsula, saw that complete expulsion of the Saracens depended upon some kind of deterrent action against the African mainland whence came reinforcements. This was certainly a campaign against Saracens, even if not so purely altruistic as that of Louis IX; however, had it come to anything, it would have been an alternative goal for

---

confusion in the mind of the speaker. It also seems to indicate that Hakon was known not to have redeemed his vow.

[58] Joinville mentions one Norwegian only, with his followers, as having arrived to lend his aid to King Louis, xcvi, § 493-4.

[59] Matthew Paris, v, pp. 103, 135-6, 274; vi, p. 200.

[60] Matthew Paris' report of the pope's request to Henry to send aid to King Louis (v, p. 274) would seem to indicate that it was Henry who was responsible for the early delays, but one must remember that the death of Frederick II gave the pope a momentary sense of being out of danger; cf. Rymer, i, pp. 451-2.

[61] Cf. F. M. Powicke, *King Henry III and the Lord Edward*, i, p. 241.

crusading energies other than the relief force to be led by Alphonse of Poitiers to King Louis' aid in the Holy Land. That the commutation of Henry III's vow to North Africa did not have this effect does not excuse a dangerous attitude on the part of influential *crucesignati*, and of the pope, to the use of this particular instrument of crusading policy. Henry III's commutation failed of its effect, because more tempting fields of enterprise claimed the English king's enthusiasm.[62] After a certain amount of vacillation Henry requested a commutation of his vow to crusade in Sicily,[63] thus allowing his ill-considered family ambitions to outrun his practical judgment. In England this royal commutation resulted in the inhibition of any sense of crusading responsibility for the Holy Land until the English connection with the Sicilian affair reached its ignominious conclusion with the withdrawal of the offer of the throne to Edmund.[64] Henry III's vow then automatically reverted to the Holy Land, but he was in no position to fulfil it, being in the midst of his trouble with the barons. The papal legate, Guy Foulquois, received faculties in a letter of 27 November, 1263, to commute vows, even those to the Holy Land, to a crusade in support of the royal cause.[65] There is no record of Henry III's having commuted his vow to crusade in his own support, and, indeed, no record of any commutations to this effect. By the time the worst of the baronial troubles was over, and a new crusade to the Holy Land was being prepared by Louis IX, Henry III's vow was already upwards of twenty years in the fulfilling. Manifestly in no physical condition to embark on the venture himself, he was persuaded to appoint Edmund as his substitute,[66] though he went on maintaining his intention of setting out personally.[67] If Hakon of Norway was an example of a king able consciously to manipulate

---

[62] Alfonso likewise failed to fulfil this vow, being distracted by his prolonged efforts to secure imperial election, though he was still talking of a crusade against the Saracens as late as 1283 (See Rymer, ii, pp. 149, 196, 246, for English correspondence on this subject).

[63] See Rymer, i, pp. 517-8.

[64] Alexander IV revoked the offer in December, 1258, unless his conditions should be fulfilled. The revocation was made formal by Urban IV in 1263 when he offered the throne to Charles of Anjou.

[65] Urban IV, *Register*, 596; cf. Potthast 18725.

[66] Clement IV, *Register*, 609.

[67] See *Northern Registers*, xvi; Rymer, i, pp. 871-2, gives Henry's final proclamation of his having taken the cross once more, 16 April, 1271; N. Denholm-Young, *Richard of Cornwall*, Oxford, 1947, p. 149, gives a feasible explanation of this seemingly renewed vigour on the part of Henry III.

crusade by reason of the ease with which he could obtain a commutation of his vows, Henry III was an equally good example of a king whose emulative piety clamoured for a crusader cross, but whose irresolute and volatile policy-making necessitated frequent recourse to commutation of his vow. Redemption of that vow would not have suited Henry's cast of mind, but his frequent commutations and deferments did no good to the cause of crusade. Though Edward I's case was different, because he had once fulfilled his vow, his long deferment of the fulfilling of his second vow of crusade likewise had a disastrous effect on the possibility of a vigorous crusade in the final years of the Crusader States.[68] Had he not been *crucesignatus*, hopes might have been fixed elsewhere; the interminable delays in the fulfilment of his vows would not have been tolerated had the instruments of crusading policy not recoiled on themselves so as to hinder any effective crusading action.

England, however, was by no means the worst example of commutation of crusading vows at the expense of the Holy Land. The transfer of the Sicilian throne to Charles of Anjou introduced a period of almost total orientation of crusading policy towards victory over the Hohenstaufen claimants. Urban IV returned to the notion of the justification of crusade in Sicily by dwelling on its strategic importance for crusade to the Holy Land.[69] Though both Urban IV and Clement IV took pains to provide for the commutation of all vows in favour of crusade to the Holy Land, in order to secure recruits,[70] yet this was offset by the more urgent interest of both popes in recruitment for the Sicilian crusade. Simon de Brie, papal legate to France, enjoyed faculties to commute all vows in favour of the Sicilian campaign [71] and even to defer the whole French passage to the Holy Land.[72] Individual *crucesignati* received dispensations to commute their vows to Sicily, including such influential people as the count of Poitiers [73] and Barral des Baux,[74] formerly a strenuous opponent of the count, but his sworn liegeman from 1253.[75] Alphonse of Poitiers

---

[68] This is testified by the bulky correspondence of the popes on the subject, most of which appears in *C.P.L.*, I.

[69] *Register*, 813.

[70] Urban IV, *Register*, 389, 2914; Clement IV, *Register*, 1560.

[71] Urban IV, *Register*, 814; Clement IV, *Register*, 216.

[72] Urban IV, *Register*, 815.

[73] *Ibid.*, 813.

[74] Clement IV, *Register*, 1677.

[75] *Layettes*, iii, 4037.

is another example of a permanent *crucesignatus* whose heart was not really in the business, but whom the current use of the instruments of crusading policy permitted to be always on the verge of setting out.

The heavy concentration of energies on Sicily cannot have met with the approval of Louis IX who began preparations for his second venture during the early pontificate of Clement IV, a crusade which he launched during a papal interregnum. Until the defeat of Manfred, Clement IV was in a difficult situation because of St. Louis' refusal to accept as his concern any crusade not bearing directly on the welfare of the Holy Places. After the Sicilian crusade had been brought to a satisfactory conclusion, the crusading vows proper to it, and as yet unfulfilled, were commuted in favour of the Holy Land.[76] Gregory X seems to have had a mind to reverse the tendency towards a too open policy of commutation of crusading vows away from the Holy Land. In one of his letters to Simon de Brie he ordered the legate to compel certain *crucesignati* who had commuted their vows from the Holy Land to Tunisia to fulfil their vow, even if they had been to Tunis.[77] Presumably these *crucesignati* had accompanied Louis IX's abortive venture to Tunis in which no blow was struck for the liberation of the Holy Places, and Gregory X refused to consider this as sufficient fulfilment of a vow of crusade to the Holy Land. These vows were to be fulfilled, or redeemed, if there were legitimate cause. There are no references in the papal registers to the commutation of crusading vows to the Holy Land between the pontificate of Gregory X and the fall of Acre, but this seems to be rather because crusade recruitment had suffered a disastrous breakdown than because commutations had ceased to be allowed.

(c) CRUSADE AS COMMUTATION OF PENANCE

Perhaps the most urgently destructive form of commutation connected with crusade was not that discussed above, but one which, nevertheless, bore heavily on the whole question of the integrity of crusading vows. This was a commutation of certain ecclesiastical penances should the penitent assume the cross, and, therefore, take a vow of crusade to the Holy Land. This involved two distinct classes of crime. By far the most common was that, the absolution of which was reserved to the pope, or his specifically appointed

---

[76] Clement IV, *Register*, 496.
[77] Gregory X, *Register*, 539.

agent. Not infrequently in the history of crusade, absolution had
been granted for such reserved crimes without the penitent's journeying to Rome, provided that he contributed to the Holy Land a sum
equivalent to what he would have spent had he been obliged to go
to Rome for his absolution.[78] It is likely that this practice gave rise
to the one which became more common in the thirteenth century,
namely, that of imposing the taking of the cross as an alternative to
going to Rome for absolution. A most comprehensive list of crimes
for which absolution could be obtained by the taking of the cross is
contained in a letter of Innocent IV to the prior of St. Jacques of
Paris, ordering the preaching of the crusade of Alphonse of Poitiers.[79]
These crimes included violence offered to clerics, incendiarism,
sacrilege, the practice of sorcery, default in paying the tenth or the
twentieth, visiting the Holy Places without licence,[80] aiding heretics,
trading with Saracens,[81] assisting the Saracen cause in any other way,[82]
concubinage of clerics, clerical attendance at prohibited lectures,[83]
suspension and irregularities. In another letter of 12 February, 1253
to Eudes de Châteauroux, Innocent gave faculties to the legate to
absolve from excommunication incurred before they had set out
crusaders guilty of adherence to Frederick II or John Vatatzes, and
also those guilty of breaking into churches, robbery, and failing to
answer summonses. Where necessary the crusaders were to make
satisfaction and restitution.[84] It is clear from the episcopal register
of Walter Giffard that such assumptions of the cross were aimed rather
at increasing funds for crusade than at recruiting personnel, since

[78] *C.P.L.*, I, pp. 327-8.
[79] Innocent IV, *Register*, 6469; cf. also 4663, and Urban IV, *Register*, 468.
[80] This regulation, introduced in 1188 by Clement III after the capture of
Jerusalem by Saladin, had come to be regarded as a measure to prevent undue
Moslem profit from Christian pilgrimage.
[81] See the crusading decrees below, Appendix A. Sanctions on trade with
the Saracens, had they been effective, would have deprived the Moslems of much
needed materials for the manufacture of armaments, and for ship building.
[82] The chief offenders in this regard were the Italian merchants who tended
to ignore sanctions.
[83] Presumably this referred to unlicenced study of the prohibited Arabic
philosophers, and scientists, banned by Innocent IV at Toulouse as late as 1245.
See C. Devic & J. Vaissète, *Histoire Générale de Languedoc*, 16 vols, Toulouse,
1872-92, Vol. VIII, No. 388—CCLXXII, col. 1187, Innocent declared, "illis libris
naturalibus, qui in concilio provinciali ex certa causa prohibiti fuere, non utantur
omnino Tolose quousque examinati fuerint et ab omni errorum suspicione
purgati . . ."
[84] *Register*, 6337.

every such *crucesignatus* seems to have been given the option of redeeming his vow by the payment of a specified sum.[85] The same register contains records of a case of adultery in which a certain Simon Constable was required to take the cross. Two alternatives were offered in addition to personal fulfilment of the vow, namely, the provision of substitutes, or the payment of a redemption of £ 100 sterling.[86] From the register of Walter Giffard's successor, William Wickwane, it would seem that Simon evaded all three.[87] A fine imposed on Robert Burnell for pluralism, and payable to the Holy Land collection, does not seem to have been accompanied by a specific injunction to take the cross [88] but this may have been because the bishop had already at that stage taken the cross.[89] From the register of Urban IV comes another interesting example. Certain clerics and laymen in the diocese of Cologne had incurred excommunication at the hands of the legate, Conrad, for dubious association with nuns; these excommunicates were to be absolved provided that they went in person to the Holy Land, or made a monetary contribution.[90] The register of Eude Rigaud records the case of a knight, John de Fagicourt, who was fined sixty shillings and enjoined to go to the Holy Land for violent behaviour in a certain priory in the archdiocese of Rouen.[91]

Perhaps the most celebrated case of a commutation of a punishment for criminal behaviour to service in the Holy Land is that of Enguerrand de Coucy. It is doubly notable in that the court concerned was a lay one, though the punishment was imposed by King Louis himself, and it is therefore not surprising that the Holy Land should have been the beneficiary. Enguerrand was ordered to go to the East for three years with a suitable number of followers. In fact he was dispensed from this service with the approval of the king by the bishop of Evreux. Instead he paid £ 12,000 *parisis* which was sent by the king to the Holy Land.[92] Another case which throws light on contemporary

---

[85] Cf. *The Register of Walter Giffard*, pp. 277 *et seq.*, where every offender seems to have been given the alternative of paying a fine.

[86] *Ibid.*, p. 282.

[87] *The Register of William Wickwane*, No. 312.

[88] Cf. *C.P.L.*, I, p. 506.

[89] *Ibid.*, p. 510.

[90] Urban IV, *Register*, 2110.

[91] *Journal des Visites*, p. 490. The fine here does not seem to be an alternative to the journey.

[92] On this case see William of Nangis, *Gesta Sanctae Memoriae Ludovici Regis Franciae* (*Recueil des historiens des Galles et de la France*, Vol. XX), Paris, 1840,

attitudes to commutation of penalties to service as a crusader is to be found in the settlements following the defeat of Llewellyn by Edward I in 1282. David, Llewellyn's brother, was offered a subsidy if he would assume the cross and remain on crusade until he should be officially recalled.[93] David's reply was an indignant denunciation of the false devotion and psychology which lay behind the whole practice of commuting ecclesiastical and lay penalties to the assumption of the cross.[94]

Without a doubt the most ludicrous extreme in the practice of commuting criminal penalties to the assumption of the cross is to be found in the provision to such *crucesignati* not merely with letters of safe conduct, and a recommendation as worthy objects of almsgiving, but even with subsidies to help them fulfil their vow.[95] There was one further development which obviously arose from a close assimilation of the normal crusading practice of commutation and redemption, and that of commuting penalties to crusade. Instead of imposing the assumption of the cross on the criminal, the authorities demanded that he provide for a substitute to go to the Holy Land for a certain period of time.[96]

A different form of commutation of ecclesiastical penance is to be found in the cases recorded in the registers of Innocent IV concerning recanted heretics in the area of Toulouse. Considered too dangerous to be allowed free intercourse with the faithful, these former heretics were condemned to perpetual imprisonment. At the request of the de Montforts, themselves *crucesignati*,[97] these heretics were offered a commutation of their ecclesiastical penance to the assumption of the cross for the Holy Land. According to Hostiensis this was not, under any circumstances, a redeemable vow.[98] This form of penal crusading was, in fact, similar to the use

---

p. 398; William of St. Pathus, *Vie de Saint Louis*, ed. H. F. Delaborde, Paris, 1899, pp. 136-40; Le Nain de Tillemont, *Vie de Saint Louis*, iv, Chaps ccclxxvii-ccclxxix; and H. Wallon, *Saint Louis et son temps*, 2 vols, Paris, 1875, ii, p. 179.

[93] Peckham, ii, ccclvi.

[94] *Ibid.*, ii, ccclix. This is not the place to discuss the political implications of the proposal, or of David's reply. Such considerations are not relevant to the point under discussion here.

[95] Cf. E. van Cauwenbergh, *Les pèlerinages expiatoires et judiciaires dans le droit communal de la Belgique au moyen âge*, Louvain, 1922, pp. 159-60.

[96] *Ibid.*, pp. 173 *et seq.*

[97] Innocent IV, *Register*, 3508, 3677, 3866; cf. Potthast, 12914 and *Histoire générale de Languedoc*, VI, Book XXV, Chaps XCIX and CIX.

[98] *Summa Aurea*, III, tit. De voto § 12 (Qualiter et).

made by secular authorities of the Holy Land as a dumping ground for undesirables. Among those who saw with their own eyes the effects of using the Holy Land as a conveniently needy cause for the dispatch of turbulent and criminal elements in Western society, were Jacques de Vitry,[99] and later in the century, Burchard of Mount Sion.[100] It is possible to exaggerate the impact of this type of criminal on crusading armies, by overlooking the tendency of armies in general, and mercenary forces in particular, to act as magnets for the criminal and the lawless of all varieties. There is sufficient evidence of *crucesignati* abusing their privileges by making them an excuse for committing crime,[101] and there is also evidence to suggest that soldiers generally were not held to have a high sense of social responsibility.[102] Every army, even the crusading army led by Louis IX, depended on mercenaries to a certain extent, and any attempt on the part of historians to make much of the forcible enlistment of heretics must result in a false perspective. The real importance of the use of recanted heretics as crusaders lay in the extension of the use of commutations in connection with crusade without seeming consideration of the effect in devaluing crusader vows. The more common any form of commutation became, the less possible it was to regulate crusading policy according to the traditional norms. The more diffuse the regulations were, and the less well defined the framework of crusade, the greater effort it was to accept the credibility of any such venture as a Christian, and salvific, activity.

(d) REDEMPTION OF VOWS

There are numerous enough examples of the redemption of crusader vows throughout the first century of crusading history, though the majority of these were granted for physical incapacity occurring subsequent to the taking of the vows. For a passing infirmity a deferment of the vow was granted, a full redemption being allowed only on account of a chronic disability. The normal requirement was that the *crucesignatus* should provide a suitable substitute

---

[99] Jacques de Vitry, *Historia Iherosolimitana* (in Bongars), Cap. LXXXII. Previous chapters are devoted to a scathing denunciation of the resident Franks.

[100] Burcharus de Monte Sion, *Descriptio Terrae Sanctae*, in *Peregrinatores Medii Aevi Quatuor*, ed. J. C. M. Laurent, Leipzig, 1864, Cap. XIII.

[101] Innocent IV, *Register*, 2230.

[102] Cf. Thomas de Cantimpré, *Bonum universale de Apibus*, Lib. 2, Cap. XLIX.

before being absolved from his vow.[103] In theory this was still true of the redemptions granted in the thirteenth century. Eva, the wife of Robert Tiptoft, himself a *crucesignatus*, was granted a redemption by Nicholas IV because she was reported to be seriously ill, and because she was prepared to send suitable substitutes at her own expense.[104] In general practice, however, there was an almost inevitable movement away from the personal provision of a substitute, or number of substitutes, towards merely making provision for substitutes, in other words towards making a contribution to the crusading funds. In time the same thing happened with redemption of crusader vows as had happened earlier with the redemption of ecclesiastical penances, the money payment superseded the principle of substitution, to ensure whose easy operation it had been introduced. By the time of the Fourth Lateran Council monetary contributions had become the equivalent of personal service in ensuring eligibility for the full crusading indulgence.[105] The matter was further confused by the fact that there was no clear distinction made between the redemption of the vow of a *crucesignatus* who had genuinely intended to go to the Holy Land, and of one who had merely made a conditional vow from the beginning.[106]

For clarity in examining the practice of redemption of crusading vows in the period under discussion, one may divide the *crucesignati* involved into two main groups:

(i) those who had genuinely intended to fulfil their vows, but had been prevented from doing so by unforeseen circumstances;

(ii) Those who had little or no intention from the beginning of fulfilling their vows; they belonged to one of two groups who were either,

    a) physically and financially able to do so, but unwilling to spend time and effort going on crusade in person;

or,

    b) clearly incapable, either physically or financially, of going on crusade.

Redemptions of vows may also be resumed into four main categories:

---

[103] Early examples of redemptions are discussed by A. Gottlob, *Kreuzablass und Almosenablass*, pp. 174 *et seq.*
[104] Cf. *C.P.L.*, I, p. 528.
[105] See above Chapter Two.
[106] These conditional vows will be discussed below, p. 129.

(i) those which were justifiable, and granted by due authority acting in accord with powers delegated by the pope;

(ii) those which, even if justifiable, were granted without due authority from the pope by fraudulent officials;

(iii) those which were unjustifiable by reason of false representations on the part of the *crucesignati*, but were granted by authorised persons;

(iv) those which were both unjustifiable and unauthorised, proceeding by,

a) force exerted on an unwilling *crucesignatus*,

or by,

b) common consent in fraud by *crucesignati* and officials.

As with commutations, the redemption of crusading vows lay solely in the competence of the pope; in practice this competence was delegated to papal officials, and their deputies. A variety of phrases of no great legal precision are to be found in papal registers to express the reasons for which a crusading vow was redeemable. These phrases were deliberately unspecific in order to allow the utmost freedom of judgment to the official concerned; the frequent complaint was that this freedom was abused.[107] The popes issued instructions requiring that vows should be redeemed because of the existence of a "justum impedimentum",[108] of a "legitimum impedimentum",[109] or simply for a "justa causa"[110] or "ex causa rationabili".[111] Vows could be redeemed because of "inhabilitas"[112] or because of an unspecified "impotentia corporum"[113] or "impotentia personarum".[114] Sometimes the reason for permitting a redemption was expressed in terms of the inability of the *crucesignatus* to undertake the crossing itself, ("inhabilis ad transeundum/transfretandum")[115] or the actual

---

[107] It is safer to accept the evidence of the *Collectio de Scandalis Ecclesiae*, ed. A. Stroick in *Archivum Franciscanum Historicum*, XXIV, 1931, pp. 33-62, than that of the partisan Matthew Paris.

[108] Innocent IV, *Register*, 2017, 2238, 4166.

[109] *Ibid.*, 3523, 4038, 4286, 6469; Alexander IV, *Register*, 428; Gregory X, *Register*, 497; J. H. Sbaralea, *Bullarium Franciscanum Romanorum Pontificum*, 3 vols, Rome, 1759-65, iii (John XXI) xiv.

[110] Innocent IV, *Register*, 2758, 3723; Alexander IV, *Register*, 1104.

[111] Alexander IV, *Register*, 1253.

[112] Innocent IV, *Register*, 6285.

[113] *Ibid.*, 2758.

[114] *Ibid.*, 3723.

[115] *Ibid.*, 6910; Urban IV, *Register*, 384, 2912; Clement IV, *Register*, 1561; Gregory X, *Register*, 497.

fighting, ("inhabilis ad pugnandum").[116] The perils and exertions of the voyage are attested by a whole host of mediaeval itineraries to the Holy Places, as well as by the discussions of men like Humbert de Romans who were seeking to explain the falling off in crusade fervour.[117] Joinville leaves one in no doubt about the terrors of the deep for the crusader, and the inadvisability of going to sea in a state of mortal sin.[118] It probably needed a stronger constitution to undergo the rigours of the crossing than those of the subsequent campaign, and so it was not merely a legal fiction to allow redemptions for inability to undertake the voyage.

Infirmity and weakness were obvious reasons for allowing redemption of vows,[119] as was old age.[120] Though it was common enough for women to take the cross, Gregory X was the only pope to allow them redemptions specifically on the grounds of "fragilitas sexus".[121] On the other hand, if their means warranted, women *crucesignatae* were clearly expected to provide substitutes.[122] Allowance was also made for the fact that a *crucesignatus* might be too poor to fulfil his vow,[123] although poor *crucesignati* were subsidised, either by the pope, or by the magnates.[124] Moreover it was not unheard

---

[116] Innocent IV, *Register*, 3523, 3727, 3842, 4038, 4286; Alexander IV, *Register* 428; Urban IV, *Register*, 384, 2912; Clement IV, *Register*, 291; Gregory X, Register, 497.

[117] *Opus Tripartitum*, Pars I, Cap. XX.

[118] xxviii § 127; cf. also Joinville's description of the return journey to France, cxxii-cxxiv. Things had not much improved by the mid-fifteenth century to judge by the reports of a group of pilgrims who made the journey by sea to the Holy Land in 1458. These diaries have been used to provide a survey of the pilgrimage by Miss R. J. Mitchell, *The Spring Voyage*, London, 1964. The voyage, and its hazards, are described in chapters three and four. See also Osbernus, *De Expugnatione Lyxbonensi*, p. cxlv, describing the storm which drove the English crusaders in 1147 on to the coast of Spain. Osbernus showed his classical knowledge by placing the blame firmly on the "Syrenes".

[119] "Infirmitas aut debilitas"; cf. Innocent IV, *Register*, 162, 3842; Alexander IV, *Register*, 971, 1085, 1104; Urban IV, *Register*, 384, 468, 2912; Gregory X, *Register*, 497; Honorius IV, *Register*, 117. Joinville claimed that King Louis was too weak and infirm to undertake his second crusade, cxliv, § 737. Henry III was allowed to substitute Edmund because of his own physical incapacity; cf. Clement IV, *Register*, 609.

[120] Alexander IV, *Register*, 1104; Honorius IV, *Register*, 117.

[121] *Register*, 497.

[122] Cf. *C.P.L.* I, p. 528.

[123] Innocent IV, *Register*, 162, 3758, 6910; Alexander IV, *Register*, 971, 1085; cf. A. Theiner, *Vetera Monumenta hibernorum et Scotorum 1216-1547*, Rome, 1864, No. cxlii.

[124] See the section on crusading subsidies in Chapter Six, below.

of for the pope to make special provision for poor *crucesignati*.[125]
Only the poor who, in fact, were otherwise "inhabiles ad pugnandum"
could have needed redemptions. That these were far too numerous is,
in fact, testified by critics of papal crusading policy.[126]

The real proof of a breakdown in the administration of the redemption of crusader vows lies not so much in the phrases employed
in papal letters to describe when they might legitimately be allowed,
as in corroborative evidence to be found elsewhere in the papal
registers, or in independent sources. During the preparations for
King Louis' crusade there was need for papal intervention to curb
abuses of the system of redemptions. Innocent IV was obliged to
order stern measures to be taken against *crucesignati* who were
seeking unjustifiable redemptions in order to avoid fulfilling their
obligations.[127] The pope's letter, addressed to the French hierarchy,
indicates that the abuses were ruining the effect of crusade preaching,
and hence were impeding honest recruitment. The hierarchy were to
look to it that all wanton redemptions should cease, because of the
scandal, and that there should be a strict enforcement of vows on
those capable of going on crusade. The trouble seems to have sprung
from the fact that certain magnates who were *crucesignati* had been
granted subsidies from sources of crusading funds which included
redemptions of crusader vows.[128] The executors of these magnates
took the short way towards ensuring a quick and full payment of
the subsidy by a too eager grant of redemptions. The consequence
of this depreciation in the value of crusading effort led yet more
crucesignati to repent their vows, and discouraged potential crusaders
from taking the cross. Those who should have been wearing the
cross as a sign of their status, had cast it aside.

The pope declared all unjustifiable redemptions "irritum et inane",
ordered all scandalous traffic in such redemptions to cease, and the
resumption of the cross by all who had cast it aside. At the same
time the pope was careful to preserve the rights of the *crucesignati* to
whom subsidies had been granted by repeating the grant, excluding

---

[125] Innocent IV, *Register*, 3727, 4054, 4814; cf. Theiner, No. cxxxii.
[126] These critics will be discussed in some detail below, pp. 126 ff.
[127] Innocent IV, *Register*, 3708.
[128] How important a part of crusading funds these redemptions constituted
can be estimated only from the fact that grants of a subsidy almost invariably
listed redemptions among the possible sources to be exploited. It is to be noted
that they cease almost totally to figure in such lists from the time of the Second
Council of Lyons when the general stress was placed on the tenth.

only illegitimate sources. Evidence of the deleterious effect of a too lax policy on response to crusade preaching is to be found also in the *Collectio de Scandalis Ecclesiae*, a work attributed to Gilbert of Tournai, a Friar Minor who was himself at some time engaged in such preaching.[129]

Three months later, in June, 1248, Innocent IV issued a number of letters related to the same matter. The papal legate Eudes de Châteauroux who had been warned in July, 1247, to inhibit the wanton absolution of vows to the Holy Land in the border dioceses of Cambrai, Liège, Toul, Utrecht, Metz and Verdun,[130] was now instructed to impose the same prohibition in Marseilles, and other maritime districts,[131] while the bishops of Evreux and Senlis, the official collectors, received the same orders for the whole of the kingdom of France.[132] *Crucesignati*, whether clerics or laymen, were to be compelled to fulfil their vows, or to redeem them if such a course of action were justifiable.[133] At the same time the pope directed a letter to his official, Master Adam, archdeacon of Cambrai, ordering him to attend to the same business in the dioceses of Liège, Metz, Toul, and Verdun, where those who had precipitately, and unjustifiably, laid aside the cross without redeeming their vows, were to be compelled to resume the public wearing of the cross.[134] The Frisian *crucesignati* who had been moved by the unsettled state of affairs, and the even more ambiguous papal crusading policy in Germany, to cast off their symbolic cross, received a warning at the

---

[129] § 6 . . . "Successit altera confusio de redemptione votorum per quosdam aestimantes, qui valetudinarios debiles et eos qui crucem sub conditione praefixa susceperant, stulti manu iustitiae saecularis et censura ecclesiastica percellebant, fulminabant sententias et novas et indebitas aestimationes augentes amplius extorquebant. Revolutum est hoc scandalum in capita praedicantium, qui se denuo crucis indulgentiam praedicarent, certum <non> est, quod proficerent, sed certum est, quo varias contumelias sustinerent." (ed. A. Stroick in *Archivum Franciscanum Historicum*, XXIV, 1931). For a discussion of the authorship of this piece see A. Stroick, "Verfasser und Quellen der Collectio de Scandalis Ecclesiae, Reformschrift des Fr. Gilbert von Tournay" in *Archivum Franciscanum Historicum*, XXIII, 1930, pp. 3-41, 273-299, 433-466.

[130] Innocent IV, *Register*, 3054.

[131] *Ibid.*, 3966. There is nothing strange in the fact that the legate received instructions concerning this area, while the bishops of Evreux and Senlis were given instructions for the whole kingdom. Eudes de Châteauroux must have been in the vicinity of Marseilles since he set sail with King Louis from Aigues-Mortes six weeks later.

[132] *Ibid.*, 3968.

[133] *Ibid.*, 3975-6.

[134] *Ibid.*, 3970.

same time to prepare to set out for the Holy Land.[135] In July of this
same year Eudes de Châteauroux again received instructions to
compel the resumption of the cross by all *crucesignati* in France.[136]
Since these letters were all issued on the eve of King Louis' departure
from France, it is easy to see why special precautions should have
been taken to avoid undue loss of personnel at the last minute; the
history of previous crusades would have lent substance to fears of
defections as the date for embarkation drew nearer. The papal letters
make it clear that it was not impossible for such defectors to make
use of the instruments of crusading policy to ensure their release
from crusading obligations.

It must not be assumed that duly authorised papal officials were
always responsible for misuse of the power of redeeming vows. It
is plain from the wording of many papal letters that frauds were
common, and that, as in the case of indulgences, *crucesignati* fell
victims to charlatans. Writing to the bishop of Troyes on 27 March,
1248, concerning the grant of a subsidy to Count Robert of Artois
from redemptions, among other sources, Innocent IV warned:

> Illos autem crucesignatos terrarum, castellaniarum et feudorum
> predictorum, qui se a votis suis dixerant absolutos, pro absolutis
> haberi nolumus, nisi tibi constiterit quod redemerint vota ipsa, et de
> redemptione hujusmodi satisfactum fuerit ab eisdem.[137]

Alexander IV, writing to the Franciscan crusade officials in Bohemia,
Poland and Austria, strictly forbade any redemptions of crusader vows
without special apostolic mandate, because of the frauds being
perpetrated by those who pretended to an apostolic power they did
not possess. This situation the pope described as of manifest danger to
crusade.[138] During the early preparations for King Louis' second
crusade Clement IV had to warn his legate, Aegidius, archbishop of
Tyre, to curb the immoderate behaviour of collectors[139] and to
inhibit the public or secret redemption of vows by magnates.[140]
Sometimes the redemption was not so much the result of imposture,

---

[135] Cf. p. 109, above.
[136] Innocent IV, *Register*, 4663.
[137] *Ibid.*, 3754; cf. also, 3730, 4038.
[138] Sbaralea, ii (Alexander IV), cccxl.
[139] *Register*, 1608.
[140] *Register*, 1676. Sternfeld points out that Clement on one and the same day
forbade redemptions in his letter to the archbishop of Tyre, and wrote to Alphonse
of Poitiers granting permission for the commutation of the vow of Barral des
Baux from the Holy Land to Sicily, (p. 13, and see Clement IV, *Register*, 1677).

or of attempts by reluctant *crucesignati* to be free of their obligations, as an effort by greedy officials to secure redemption money by force, whether the *crucesignati* were willing or not. Thus the bishop of Worcester, Walter de Cantilupe, was instructed by Innocent IV to protect the English *crucesignati* from being forced to redeem their vows.[141] Most of these difficulties would not have arisen with regard to able-bodied *crucesignati* had there not been a departure from the original method of redeeming vows, that is by substitution, for then redemptions could scarcely have had such a monetary appeal. Even so, the practice of substitution itself was not free from abuse since Innocent IV wrote to Walter de Cantilupe ordering a close inspection of the suitability of candidates for substitution. The pope remarked that he was taking these measures,

> Cum . . . super idoneitate bellatorum qui pro aliis mitti deberent in subsidium Terre Sancte sepe fuerit dubitatum . . .[142]

No extant record has been discovered of an actual case of fraudulent substitution, not even in the pages of Matthew Paris who was an extreme critic of crusade vow redemptions, so that the only evidence of abuses comes from official papal sources. It is unlikely that abuses in this direction reached the major proportions that more lucrative practices did.

Although substitution remained the official means of redeeming a vow, the question really became a matter of deciding for how much money a vow might be redeemed. Numerous papal letters attest official attempts to secure an adherence to a reasonable scale of values. Yet the nature of the whole transaction was such that full reliance had to be placed on the discretion and probity of the papal officials. The normal stipulation was that the vows should be redeemed by the *crucesignati* "secundum proprias facultates",[143] a practice strictly analogous to that of granting indulgences according to the amount contributed. Variations on the practice ranged from the contribution of an amount equivalent to the expenses which would have been incurred had the vow been fulfilled [144] to the payment of a sum fixed

---

[141] Innocent IV, *Register*, 2960.

[142] *Ibid.*, 2963.

[143] Urban IV, *Register*, 384, 468; Gregory X, *Register*, 497; cf. also Innocent IV, *Register*, 6285, 6419; Alexander IV, *Register*, 1104.

[144] Cf. *Royal and other historical letters illustrative of the reign of Henry III*, ed. W. W. Shirley, 2 vols, Rolls Series, London, 1862-66, ii, No. ccccxcvi. Robert Lucre took the cross on the Sunday before Ascension, 1252, vowing to set out

in advance at the time of taking the cross.[145] Granted the existence of a practice of redeeming vows for money, there is nothing intrinsically unjust in any of these methods of determining the payment. The real danger to crusade lay not so much in the possibility of demands by dishonest and greedy officials for exorbitant fees, as in the far more lucrative practice of allowing the faithful indiscriminately to take the cross, though few of them were likely to fulfil their vows. It was just as profitable to be able to lay hands on a large number of relatively small redemption fees as on a few large fees. It was to precisely this aspect of redemptions that Thomas de Cantimpré took exception, complaining bitterly that a *crucesignatus* could be free of his obligations for as little as a hundredth part of his moveable goods only, without any call upon his patrimony.[146] What Thomas, who was a Friar Preacher, had in mind was the injustice of allowing people to reap such a rich spiritual reward as a full indulgence for so little personal sacrifice, when religious paid so dearly for their salvation. It is strange that so many of the critics of papal policy with regard to redemptions took it for granted, as Thomas did, that the indulgence would be efficacious, even though papal statements insisted that the devotion of the recipient was a determining factor.

Such doubts as were cast on the validity of redemption-indulgences came mainly from non-theological sources, the only notable exception being Caesarius of Heisterbach who embodied his doubts in a dramatic narrative in which the fraudulent *crucesignatus* was borne off to hell.[147] The most interested of these sceptics was the Templar, Ricaut Bonomel, who wrote bitterly of the effect of the Sicilian affair, and papal avarice in allowing redemptions, on the Holy Land. His poem, "Ir' e dolors s'es a mon cors assezo", was written immediately after the loss of Caesarea and Arsuf to Baibars in 1265.[148] Other

---

with Henry III, or, if prevented by circumstances (forte casu) to give "tantum de suo in dictae terrae subsidium quantum esset expensurus". Cf. also Innocent IV, *Register*, 3975, for another example.

[145] Cf. Innocent IV, *Register*, 6419, "secundum consilium illorum a quibus sunt crucis caractere insigniti."

[146] *Bonum universale de apibus*, Lib. 2, Cap. III.

[147] *Dialogus Miraculorum Caesarii Heisterbacensis*, ed. J. Strange, 2 vols, Brussels, 1851, Distinctio Secunda, De Contritione, Cap. VII. It is interesting to note that, in the context, the monk-narrator is more concerned with the man *qua* usurer, and the fittingness of his punishment on that score. His being a fraudulent *crucesignatus* is, in a sense, incidental to the larger sin of serving Mammon.

[148] This poem is to be found in *Poesie Provenzali Storiche*, ed. V. de Bartholomaeis, 2 vols, Rome, 1931, ii, No. clx, pp. 222-4. It is to be noted that neither

lyricists who criticised the practice of redeeming crusader vows were not personally touched by the results of such a policy but were aware of the scandal given by the clergy responsible for implementing the policy.[149]

In his numerous references to the practice Matthew Paris indicated his firm belief that the fault lay always with the papacy. Once he even managed to have the pope directly involved in the traffic; the incident concerned a number of soldiers left behind by King Louis when he set off from Aigues-Mortes. These Matthew Paris represents as being mulcted by the pope and the curia of their "denarii" and their "viaticum" in return for redemptions.[150] The count of Poitiers is represented by Matthew Paris as blaming Innocent IV's greed for redemption money as ruining the former's crusade of assistance to King Louis in the Holy Land.[151] In judging the truth of this accusation one must take into account Paris' remarks about the unwillingness of King Louis' brothers to go on this crusade.[152] The usual plaint of the chronicler is, however, directed against the Mendicants, upstart favourites of the papacy employed in implementing its financial policies. Matthew Paris has two main complaints to make against the Friars. The first is that they inveigle all conditions of men and women into taking the cross,

> homines cujuscunque aetatis, sexus, vel conditionis, vel valoris, immo etiam valitudinarios vel valitudinarias, et aegrotantes et senio deficientes,

and then, with immoderate haste,

> in crastino et etiam incontinenti pro quantocunque pretio,

---

of these towns was a Templar holding; Arsuf was garrisoned by the Hospitallers; Caesarea was in the hands of the l'Aleman family by reason of the marriage of Margaret d'Ibelin, the heiress of John of Caesarea to Jean l'Aleman. Louis IX had taken much trouble over the refortification of Caesarea in 1251-2. One might have expected the Templar troubadour to save his laments for the loss of a Templar castle; this is perhaps the most striking evidence of the magnitude of the shock, that a Templar should bewail a Hospitaller defeat.

[149] This is the tenor of the poem of Austorc d'Aurillac lamenting (presumably) King Louis' defeat at Damietta, "Sanh Peire tenc la drecha via / Mas l'apostolis la'lh desvia / De fals clergues que ten en som poder / Que per deniers fan manh[s lo mal voler]" printed by A. Jeanroy in "Le troubadour Austorc d'Aurillac et son sirventés sur la septième Croisade" in *Mélanges Chabaneau, Festschrift Camille Chabaneau*, pp. 81-87.

[150] v, pp. 24-5.

[151] v, p. 188.

[152] See above, p. 77, and footnote 121.

have them purchase a redemption.[153] To round off his tale the old scandalmonger goes on the state that, on one occasion, Richard of Cornwall forced the collectors to hand the money over to him. This is patently untrue since evidence is to be found in the papal registers that the collectors were ordered by the pope to pay the money to Richard who had not yet received in full the subsidy which he had been granted when he went on crusade in 1240.[154]

The second main complaint which Matthew Paris lodged against the friars was that they frequented the houses of the dying in order to induce the latter to take the cross, and to redeem their vows by a legacy in their wills.[155] To give substance to this claim Matthew Paris put a similar accusation in the mouth of the dying Grosseteste,[156] though this is consistent neither with Grosseteste's known friendship for the Franciscans, nor with his general moderation. Rutebeuf shared Matthew Paris' hatred of the Mendicants, though for different reasons,[157] and he did not spare Louis IX a rebuke for favouring them.[158] Not only were they of no use in a war to save the Holy Land, but their greed for money constituted the major cause of the miserable state of that land.[159] Rutebeuf, too, accused the friars of extracting legacies from the dying.[160] It was because of the excesses of the friars who preached crusade that it was possible to say:

> Hom sermona por la croix prendre
> Que hom cuida paradix vendre
> Et livreir, de par l'apostole.
> Hom pot bien le sermon entendre
> Mais a la croix ne vout nuns tendre
> La main, por piteuze parole.[161]

Despite this conjunction of other evidence concerning redemptions,

---

[153] v, p. 73; cf. iv, p. 9.

[154] Innocent IV, *Register*, 3523, 4085. The papal letters disagree in date with Matthew Paris who placed the incident in 1249. The first of Innocent IV's letters was written on 31 December, 1247, and confirmed the grant made to Richard by Gregory IX. The second letter is dated 11 January, 1248.

[155] iv, p. 280.

[156] v, p. 405.

[157] Rutebeuf was a partisan of William de Saint-Amour; cf. *Onze poèmes de Rutebeuf concernant la croisade*, ed. J. Bastin & E. Faral, Paris, 1946, Introduction, p. 5, and E. B. Ham, "Rutebeuf and Louis IX", University of N. Carolina Studies in Romance Language & Literature, 42, 1962, *passim*.

[158] "La complainte de Constantinople" in *Onze poèmes*, No. ii.

[159] *Ibid.*, lines 61-120.

[160] *Ibid.*, lines 111-114.

[161] *Ibid.*, lines 97-102.

Matthew Paris has to be treated as a special case since he was always concerned rather with his partisan objectives than with the truth of a situation.

Perhaps the most significant development in the administration of redemption of crusader vows was that of allowing conditional vows. These seem to have been permitted first in the pontificate of Gregory IX,[162] but none is recorded in Innocent IV's early years. In October 1248 *crucesignati* in France and Poitou assumed the cross on the condition that if they were unwilling or unable to set out for the Holy Land, they should redeem their vows for a fixed sum of money. The treasurer of the church of St. Hilaire in Poitiers was ordered to collect the money accruing from the redemption of these vows, and to assign it to the count of Poitiers.[163] Five years later, when the count was organising his relief crusade Innocent IV wrote instructions of the same nature to Philippe, the treasurer of St. Hilaire, who was also the count's executor.[164] In this case the *crucesignati* had promised to pay either according to their means, or according to a sum fixed at the time of assuming the cross. There is also an implied reference to conditional vows in a letter of Innocent IV to Walter de Cantilupe in 1247. The pope, defending the principle that free service is most pleasing to God, reserved the right of the English *crucesignati* to contribute men or money according to their choice.[165] It is obvious that once crusading vows were permitted to all classes and conditions of people, there was an implicit distinction between the vows of those genuinely intending to set out, and those who were intent on gaining the indulgence through a money payment. The intention of the latter group was not expressed, but implied; the three letters quoted above show that in these cases the intention to redeem the vow was made explicit, and this is no more than the logical consequence of the practice of allowing anyone to take the cross.

---

[162] *Les Registres de Grégoire IX*, ed. L. Auvray, 4 vols, Paris, 1899-1955, 4626. This was a letter giving faculties to the bishops of Cambrai and Tournai to use their discretion in the redemption of vows taken by a certain Herbert and about twenty of his relatives and friends to go on crusade to the Holy Land, or Constantinople, or to redeem the vows according to their means.

[163] *Layettes*, iii, 3726. Throop, *Criticism of the Crusades*, p. 94, mistakenly asserts that Alphonse of Poitiers was one of the *crucesignati* who had taken a conditional vow. The letter quoted in the *Layettes* makes no mention of this, but orders the money to be paid to the count when he sets out.

[164] Innocent IV, *Register*, 6419, 6459.

[165] *Ibid.*, 2959.

Occasionally the popes had to issue warnings against *crucesignati* who had redeemed their vows for too small a sum. Gregory X, in dealing with one such group declared their indulgence defective and the *crucesignati* to be excommunicate. They could revive their indulgence, and receive absolution upon the payment of a suitable sum.[166] Such restitution was not always readily forthcoming, as can be seen from a letter of Martin IV written 25 October, 1281, concerning *crucesignati* who had assumed the cross in the time of Louis IX, had redeemed it for too small a payment, and had not yet made proper satisfaction.[167] Difficulties such as these in ensuring payment were not unrelated to the lack of efficacy of ecclesiastical censure,[168] and to papal inability to exercise a tight enough control over officials.[169] One case of great public scandal is recorded in the *Journal* of Eude Rigaud. Two official collectors each laid claim to the same territory. *Crucesignati* in the region were menaced by both parties with ecclesiastical censure should they seek redemption of their vows from the rival collector.[170] The appointment of the two collectors probably sprang from the same kind of mistake as Innocent IV was at pains to acknowledge, and correct, in several letters recorded in his register.[171]

The popes had also to ensure that *crucesignati* who had legitimately redeemed their vows, retained neither their subsidies, nor their privileges. The son of the duke of Burgundy took the cross to go on crusade with Louis IX, but presumably redeemed his vow, since Innocent IV ordered his subsidy to be recalled.[172] On another occasion Innocent IV directed his officials, the bishops of Evreux and Senlis to remind *crucesignati* that, by redeeming their vows, they fell liable to the payment of the tenth from which their vows exempted them.[173] John XXI likewise revoked the exemption of *crucesignati* who had failed to set out on crusade.[174] Roger de Leyburn was similarly reminded by Gregory X to repay the subsidy of two thousand marks sterling which he had been granted, but to which he was

---

[166] Gregory X, *Register*, 322. Letter dated 20 November, 1273.
[167] *Register*, 74.
[168] See below, Chapter 6, section (e), *passim*.
[169] Cf. Martin IV, *Register*, 356, for example.
[170] P. 733.
[171] *Register*, 2032-3, 6854. The pope usually inserted a clause saving the rights of any to whom monies collected may previously have been assigned. See the section on subsidies in Chapter Six, below.
[172] Innocent IV, *Register*, 2733.
[173] *Ibid.*, 3975-6.
[174] *Register*, 68; Potthast, 21201.

no longer entitled.[175] A case of a different sort is to be found in the cameral register of Urban IV. This is the grant of a redemption, and absolution from his vow, to a certain Gerard de Marbais-Marbisoux, lord of Bruco.[176] This man is described as a "consiliarius" of Henry, duke of Brabant, on whose behalf he had assumed the cross. The duke had assumed the cross *in extremis* and had died without fulfilling his vow; he had left four thousand pounds of Louvain for Gerard to make good his obligation. In 1263 Gerard had still not fulfilled his vow, and since there seemed little hope of a general passage in the immediate future, he feared for his own and the duke's salvation, should the vow remain any longer in abeyance. Gerard received permission to redeem the vow, the money left by the duke reverting to the general fund through the hands of the bishop of Troyes.

Although the papacy did make an effort to ensure the smooth and honest working of the system of redemptions, this system was inevitably compromised in the minds of the faithful by reason of the general distrust of papal financial dealings. This distrust of the curia is to be found summarised in a satiric dialogue between a petitioner just arriving in, and one just leaving Rome.[177] For those aware of the abuses in the financial aspects of crusade policy, there is a double irony, probably not intended by the author, in the following reference to crossing the sea.

Non te commoveat,   quod volo dicere!
Non est, qui valeat   Romanos fallere,
Quicunque studeat   posse divertere,
Si mare transeat   vel volet aere.[178]

Indeed crossing the sea was no proof against being mulcted by the papacy, any more than a vow to cross the sea was any proof of an intention to do so. By means of redemptions, crusading vows had become instruments of policies totally unrelated to crusade, and

---

[175] *Register*, 191. The letter does not specify that Roger de Leyburn had redeemed his vow, but if he had not done so, the pope would have commanded that he fulfil his vow, or redeem it, returning the subsidy only in the latter case. In the letter as it stands there is no question of Roger's fulfilling his vow. Cf, also, the more general direction of Gregory X to the patriarch of Jerusalem concerning the restitution of subsidies by *crucesignati* of England, Scotland and Ireland who had not set out. (*Register*, 967).

[176] Urban IV, *Register*, 125, and *Cameral Register*, 205.

[177] Printed in P. Herde, *Beiträge zum päpstlichen Kanzlei- und Urkundenwesen im dreizehnten Jahrhundert*, Kallmünz, 1961, pp. 181-5.

[178] *Ibid., loc. cit.*, lines 21-5.

frequently antipathetic to its interests. Whether it were kings and nobles who used crusading vows to enhance their reputations,[179] or their pockets, or officials who used them for their own worldly ends, the result for crusade was the same, a falling off of enthusiasm, and a prevention of effective action.

---

[179] Critical references to nobles who boasted in their cups of their crusading prowess, but who never came closer to crusade than taking the cross is to be found in such sources as the *Collectio de Scandalis Ecclesiae* § 21 and in "La Nouvelle Complainte d'Outre-mer" by Rutebeuf in *Onze Poèmes*, No. xi, lines 251-264.

SECTION C

THE PAPACY AND MATERIAL AID
TO *CRUCESIGNATI*

INTRODUCTORY REMARKS

Crusade was never so idealistic as to divorce itself from the notion of aiming at material, as well as spiritual, rewards to be won. In the early crusading period such material rewards lay in the East—lands and booty. Nur-ed-Din effectively curbed territorial expansion. Saladin drastically reduced the area held by the Franks. The only hope for the newcomer to the East from the late twelfth century was to marry an heiress, as Guy de Lusignan did, with dire results in this case for the Kingdom. The onus tended to fall more heavily on those in the West interested in promoting crusade, not only to make the way easy for crusaders to fulfil their vows, but to offer them positive inducements to do so. In practice this resulted in a more intense concentration on the type of material advantage which had been open to crusaders from the beginning but which had occupied a relatively unimportant position in the hierarchy of values. Of course, it would be taking far too simple a view to suppose that the only reason for the elaboration of those instruments of papal crusading policy aimed at effectively offering material inducements to the taking of the cross was the need to provide a substitute for the dwindling opportunities for rewards in the East. The cause of the elaboration, and the more intense use of these instruments, lay precisely in the development of a more efficient administrative machine for implementing papal policies. While *crucesignati* benefited by this improved efficiency, crusade ultimately fell victim to it. The instruments of papal crusading policy were set at variance with one another, each aiming at a short-term goal which could not but detract from a long term crusading policy. Because the material advantages offered to *crucesignati* were effective in the West, rather than in the East, there was a growing tendency in the thirteenth century to secure the maximum advantage from being *crucesignatus* while at the same time expending the minimum effort. As the status of being *crucesignatus* became more and more separable from actually going on crusade, and as the administration of those instruments of crusading policy which looked to the spiritual advantage of the *crucesignatus* tended less and less to demand actual crusading effort, this conspired with the administration of the instruments of material advantage, to produce a disproportionate number of *crucesignati* who never became crusaders, because spiritual and material rewards were theirs without the need for the ultimate effort.

The previous section has outlined the system of providing indulgences in return for crusading vows and the ultimately destructive impact of that system on crusade to the Holy Land, both because of the widening of the area of crusading endeavour, and because of the reduced demands for translating intention into act before receiving the fruits of the vow. The present section, dealing with the material advantages accruing to *crucesignati* in the latter half of the thirteenth century, will conveniently divide itself into three main fields of investigation and discussion.

(1) Subsidies, and other strictly financial benefits offered to *crucesignati*.
(2) Privileges, protections, and immunities extended to *crucesignati*, their families, and their officials.
(3) The use of excommunication and interdict to protect individual *crucesignati*, and to promote the success of a crusading venture.

CHAPTER SIX

MATERIAL ADVANTAGES OFFERED
TO *CRUCESIGNATI*

(a) PAPAL FINANCIAL POLICY

It would be unrealistic to attempt in a discussion of this length fully to cover all aspects of papal financial organisation on behalf of any crusading venture. While plenary indulgences and crusader vows sprang from, and were an integral part of, the notion of crusade, shaping this notion from within as well as deriving their own meaning from it, the papal arrangements for financing crusade were part of a system which went far beyond the limits of crusade, and whose service to that movement ended rather by absorbing crusade into the system, and shaping it from outside, not from within. Bearing this in mind it is possible to restrict one's discussion to those aspects of the financing of crusade which had a special impact on its development, or on public reaction, leaving aside what has been thoroughly explored elsewhere, that is, the basic organisation of the papal financial system.[1]

(i) *The crusading decrees*

The crusading decrees declared an ecclesiastical twentieth [2] for the general financing of crusade, without any precise details about the manner of collection,[3] or the mode of distribution. The pope himself, and the cardinals, were to pay a tenth.[4] Other funds were to be

---

[1] An excellent starting point for an examination of the nature and development of papal finance is to be found in the works of W. E. Lunt: (1) *Financial Relations of the Papacy with England to 1327*, Cambridge, Mass., 1939, and (2) *Papal Revenues in the Middle Ages*, Columbia Univ. Records of Civilisation, 2 vols, 1934, both with extensive bibliographies.

[2] The only one to declare a tenth from the outset was Gregory X's "Constitutiones pro zelo fidei". The twentieth declared in the earlier Council of Lyons was raised to a tenth when King Louis' crusade began to be preached.

[3] Gregory X issued separate, very detailed instructions, *Register*, 571, which it is not my intention to analyse. See Lunt, *Financial Relations*, pp. 314-17.

[4] This was exclusive of the special gift which Innocent III made, but which neither of the other popes was in a position to offer. Gregory X intended to go on the crusade himself, and reserved certain parts of the collection for his own expenses (*Register*, 1041).

raised by exhortation of the faithful who were impeded from personally setting out; these were to contribute to the upkeep of substitute warriors, or were to provide ships. It must also be taken into account when considering papal policy with regard to the financing of crusade, that a great deal of financial organisation was carried out by the *crucesignati* themselves, and was therefore only indirectly related to papal policy. This can be seen most clearly in the records which survive of Louis IX's preparations for this crusade,[5] and even better in the fuller records of his methodical younger brother, the count of Poitiers.[6]

Special financial privileges were granted to all *crucesignati*, whether clerics or laymen, to enjoy immunity from all taxes and levies. The decree of 1215 set a minimum period of service, namely anything in excess of one year, as a condition for this immunity; the decrees of 1245 and 1274 made no such stipulation.[7] Perhaps even more practical than this was the provision of the decrees for a ban on interest charged on loans made to *crucesignati*, and a moratorium on debts. Even if the *crucesignati* had pledged themselves on oath to pay interest to their creditors, they were to be held to be released from such oaths, and no interest was to be charged. If it were, the *crucesignati* could demand restitution, employing the secular arm to this end, if necessary. If the *crucesignati* had outstanding debts at the time of departure, the usurer was not permitted to charge interest, and was obliged to deduct from the capital debt gains accruing from the use of property pledged as security against the debt. Jews who failed to comply with this ruling were to be compelled by threat of ecclesiastical censure against any Christian who should communicate with them in any way.[8] Though there was no mention of lay subsidies in the decrees, there were special provisions for the financial benefit of clerical *crucesignati*. These were conceded the right to enjoy in full the revenues of their benefices, as if they were resident.[9] They were also given leave in case of necessity, to borrow money using their bene-

---

[5] Bibliographical details are to be found in such works as those of E. Berger, *St. Louis et Innocent IV* in *Les Registres d'Innocent IV*, ed. Berger, Vol. II, and J. R. Strayer, "Crusades of Louis IX" in *A History of the Crusades*, ed. K. Setton, 2 vols, Philadelphia, 1955-62, Vol. II.

[6] See especially the volumes of the *Layettes*, and *Correspondance administrative d'Alfonse de Poitiers*, ed. A. Molinier, 2 vols, Paris, 1894-1900.

[7] See Appendix A.

[8] See Appendix A, pp. 191-92.

[9] These remarks do not apply to the decree of 1274. See Chapter Two, p. 25.

fices as security. The absence from the decrees of any more detailed general financial provisions shows to what an extent papal financial arrangements for crusade were part of the ordinary system of finance. When this system developed more refined techniques of organisation later in the century, this was reflected in the greater detail of instruction given for the organisation of crusading finances. The Second Council of Lyons did not issue instructions within the crusading decree, but Gregory X's letters of appointment and instructions to collectors sprang from a far more sophisticated general system.[10]

(ii) *Clerical subsidies*

Provided that they had the permission of their ecclesiastical superiors,[11] and that there was no danger to souls by the absence of the priest, and the omission of divine services,[12] a cleric could set out for the Holy Land to fulfil his crusading vow, in the full enjoyment of the fruits of his benefice, except daily distributions.[13] If the cleric failed to obtain a licence his revenues were liable to sequestration.[14] Non-residence, except if it were for study or pilgrimage, or preeminently for crusade, was liable to heavy taxation such as that specifically levied by the Council of 1245 on behalf of the Latin Empire of Greece.[15] Some effort was made to see that the cleric did not, however, benefit as a *crucesignatus* from more than one benefice,[16] nor ordinarily from one with cure of souls.[17] In two recorded instances, canons *crucesignati* were protected against the depredations of their fellow canons on their revenues in their absence, when the exigency arose.[18] To raise money to pay expenses, clerics setting out on crusade were permitted to lease their vicarages,[19]

---

[10] *Register*. 571. This letter is echoed in the provisions made by Gregory's successors for collections. Cf. John XXI, *Register*, 13, for example.
[11] Cf. Hostiensis, *Summa Aurea*, III, tit. De voto § 6, 7 (Quis).
[12] For this reason parish priests were not normally eligible for a licence to go on crusade.
[13] Innocent IV, *Register*, 6469, for example. It was, in any case, normal practice to exempt daily distributions for such privileges even outside crusade.
[14] For an actual case of this see below, pp. 162-3.
[15] Canon 14.
[16] Cf. *Layettes*, iii, 4250, 4251, 4261.
[17] *Ibid.*, 4251. For an exception see the document concerning Stephan de Maulay in *C.P.L.*, I, p. 537.
[18] Innocent IV, *Register*, 4443, 5109.
[19] *The Register of Walter Gray*, Lord Archbishop of York, Surtees Society, London, Vol. LVI, 1870, Part I, xi.

or farm the produce of their benefice.[20] There is one case in the *Enquêtes* of Alphonse of Poitiers of a prior who farmed the revenues of his priory to provide for his crusade.[21] Many clerics, of course, went at the expense of lay *crucesignati* whose chaplains they were, or became.

Bishops could be awarded the fruits of vacant dignities and benefices in their dioceses so long as this did not result in danger to souls.[22] They were normally given a grant of a subsidy from the papal collections. Walter de Cantilupe, bishop of Worcester, and papal collector in England received a subsidy from redemptions, obventions and legacies to the Holy Land.[23] Henry, bishop of Liège, received a subsidy for taking the cross on behalf of William of Holland.[24] In Norway the bishop of Hamar was accorded an ordinary subsidy of a twentieth for setting out, presumably with Hakon.[25] Crusading officials were even better served, since they received the financial privileges of being *crucesignati* without the expenses attendant upon a venture overseas.[26] Their immunity from taxes covered the period during which they served as officials, but Martin IV was careful to restrict this immunity to the crusading tenth in the face of attempts by collectors in Ireland to extend their privilege further.[27] Collectors were allowed a stipulated amount for procurations,[28] which it was not impossible to have increased by the perennial plea of the rising cost of living.[29] It was not unknown for a crusading legate to be given faculties to provide his assistants to prebends, from which they were licensed to be absent,[30] even when these entailed cure of souls.[31]

---

[20] *The Register of Thomas de Cantilupe*, transcribed by R. G. Griffiths, Canterbury & York Society, London, 1907, pp. 6-7.

[21] *Enquêtes administrative d'Alfonse de Poitiers*, ed. P.-F. Fournier & P. Guebin, Paris, 1959, Pièce 128 (348), p. 331.

[22] Such a grant was made to Robert Burnell, the bishop of Bath and Wells. See *C.P.L.*, I, p. 510.

[23] Innocent IV, *Register*, 4873.

[24] *Ibid.*, 3842. See also Urban IV, *Register*, 2036-7.

[25] Innocent IV, *Register*, 3440. For another example see Urban IV, *Register*, 1986-7.

[26] Innocent IV, *Register*, 4671-2; Urban IV, *Cameral Register*, 314, 318; John XXI, *Register*, 13.

[27] *Register*, 31.

[28] This subject is discussed at length by W. E. Lunt in *Financial Relations*, Chapter XI. See especially sections 7-13.

[29] Martin IV, *Register*, 28.

[30] Innocent IV, *Register*, 4672; Urban IV, *Register*, 387; *Cameral Register*, 314; John XXI, *Register*, 129; Theiner, cclxvi.

[31] Urban IV, *Cameral Register*, 314.

(iii) *Lay subsidies*

Sources

The subsidisation of lay *crucesignati* was a complex affair, and did not fall wholly within the scope of papal policy, not all crusading monies being derived from ecclesiastical funds. The basic unit of payment so far as papal subsidies were concerned was the tenth, though the decrees of 1215 and 1245 both stipulated a twentieth. The second Council decreed a tenth from the beginning. The crusading tenth for King Louis' first crusade, and for other crusades up to 1274 was usually declared for three years in the first instance,[32] but was extended at the request of such high-ranking *crucesignati* as King Louis or Henry III,[33] though not with an equal degree of justification. The Lyons tenth of 1274 was levied for six years in the first instance. The tenth could, in fact, be collected over a much longer period, because of the need to make up arrears, and the Lyons tenth had a very extended period of collection.[34] As well as being extended in time, the tenth could be extended in scope, though some requests were refused. Both Louis IX and his mother sought to have the tenth extended to include daily distributions, but each was refused.[35] King Henry III, on the other hand, managed to gain papal approval of his demand that refractory bishops should be made to pay tenths on manors which they held by feudal tenure and which, on that account, they claimed to be exempt.[36]

The twentieth also remained a unit of crusading collections, though this seems to have been so for King Louis' first crusade only in those disputed dioceses on the borders of the Kingdom of France.[37] In the Scandinavian countries the basic unit remained the

---

[32] Examples are too numerous to mention. See, for example, Innocent IV, *Register*, 3057-8, 3318, 3432, 3719, 6214. See also Clement IV, *Register*, 464, 466, 508, 595, 1019. The grant made to the count of Vendôme by Clement IV in 1265 (*Register*, 80), was for two years. Sometimes the first grant was for five years (Innocent IV, *Register*, 3440). In this case the subsidy was a twentieth.

[33] Innocent IV, *Register*, 4928, 5106, 5154; cf. Clement IV, *Register*, 1019.

[34] Cf. W. E. Lunt, *Financial Relations*, Chap. VI, especially pp. 327-331; A. Gottlob, *Die päpstlichen Kreuzzugsteuern des XIII Jahrhunderts*, Heiligenstadt, 1892, pp. 94-134, shows how the Lyons tenth fused with the collections for the anti-Aragonese crusade. See also P. Guidi, *Rationes decimarum Italiae, nei secoli XIII e XIV*, Vatican, 1932, for a detailed examination of the collection in Tuscany.

[35] Innocent IV, *Register*, 5155; Clement IV, *Register*, 1374.

[36] Innocent IV, *Register*, 6400. The bishops urged the injury to their lay patrons, but this was over-ruled. See W. E. Lunt, *The Valuation of Norwich*, Oxford, 1926, Introduction, especially pp. 68 *et seq.*

[37] Innocent IV, *Register*, 3057, 3432. For King Louis' second crusade, cf. Clement IV, *Register*, 465.

twentieth.[38] The thirtieth which was to form part of Richard of Cornwall's long overdue subsidy was a tax of even earlier standing.[39] The redemption of crusading vows everywhere formed a major portion of the monies collected. It is difficult to judge just what proportion redemptions constituted of the total amount, except by inference from the attacks made on the practice, and already discussed at some length above.[40]

With reason Innocent IV might urge the Holy Land on the faithful as a major object of the pious work of almsdeeds.[41] From the beginning of the crusading era the Holy Land loomed large as a recipient of pious legacies. These seem to have been mainly "in subsidium Terrae Sanctae", and so easily interpreted as applicable to that species of help which was crusade. The papacy claimed jurisdiction over all legacies "in subsidium Terrae Sanctae", (as well as over all legacies left for indistinctly specified pious purposes) and it also claimed the right to dispose of these legacies as it judged best suited to the needs of the Holy Land.[42] The legacy was sometimes left by a *crucesignatus* who had failed to fulfil his vow, and who wished it fulfilled vicariously.[43] Not infrequently a *crucesignatus* inherited money to help him to fulfil his vow,[44] the testators no doubt thinking to participate more intimately in the venture by virtue of their kinship or friendship with the crusader. In either of these cases, the money had to be returned if the *crucesignatus* did not go to the Holy Land. Gerard de Marbais-Marbisoux, lord of Bruco repaid the £4,000 of Louvain which he had inherited from the duke of Brabant.[45] A later duke was given a Brabantine legacy for the Holy Land, because he was setting out.[46] Odo de Corpelay received a legacy for going on crusade to the Holy Land, but then commuted his vow

---

[38] Innocent IV, *Register*, 3439-40, for example.

[39] *Ibid.*, 3523. The thirtieth had been granted to Richard in 1238 by Gregory IX and had originally been intended for Constantinople; cf. Lunt, *Financial Relations*, pp. 194-6.

[40] pp. 126 *et seq.*

[41] *Register*, 3318.

[42] Cf. Lunt, *Papal Revenues*, i, p. 125, and *Financial Relations*, pp. 440-4.

[43] The duke of Brabant is a case in point. See above, p. 131. See also the wills mentioned in connection with the redemption of vows, p. 105 and footnote 27, above.

[44] Nicholas de'Offin, a follower of John de Montfort, inherited a sum of money left by Robert de'Offin, *crucesignatus*, (£ 100 *tournois*); see Innocent IV, *Register*, 2769.

[45] See above, p. 131.

[46] Gregory X, *Register*, 474.

to Sicily. He thus rendered himself ineligible for the legacy, until he again commuted his vow to the Holy Land.[47]

Often the legacies were, in fact, redemptions of vows, some of which had been taken even on the person's deathbed. It was this of which Matthew Paris complained when he denounced the friars for haunting the houses of the dying.[48] Undoubtedly there was pressure brought to bear on the faithful to leave legacies for the Holy Land, since there are papal mandates to the effect that the clergy were to represent the desirability of this course to the faithful by urging on them the needs of the Holy Land, and the compatibility of such a donation with their soul's salvation.[49] There can be no doubt that the most pertinent method of urging this course of action must have been to encourage the faithful to take the cross, and to make provision in their wills for the redemption of their vow. One wonders if it would be going too far to suggest that such people took vows conditionally on their being redeemable for a specified sum to be named in the person's will. This would ensure the dying person of a plenary indulgence at the moment of death.

Another type of legacy which found its way into crusading funds was that left for pious purposes not distinctly specified in the will: this was claimed by the papacy for distribution.[50] Indistinct or unspecified legacies frequently appear in the lists of sources from which subsidies were to be paid. Sometimes a *crucesignatus* would lay claim to such an indistinct legacy from the testament of a relative, and would be granted its use for his expenses. Such a case was that of Gibaud de Saint Verain who claimed £ 600 *tournois* left by his grandmother.[51] Alexander IV included among the indistinctly specified legacies to be devoted to the Sicilian crusade that part of the goods of an intestate clerk which was usually devoted to his soul's salvation.[52]

The remaining general source of crusading funds often listed in

---

[47] Clement IV, *Register*, 1508.
[48] Matthew Paris, iv, pp. 280, 604; v, p. 501.
[49] See, for example, Nicholas III, *Register*, 169, 173; Martin IV, *Register*, 79; and the "Constitutiones pro zelo fidei", Appendix A, p. 197.
[50] It was the custom to leave a sum to satisfy debtors, with the residue to be used for pious purposes. Martin IV set a limit of a year on claims to such money (*Register*, 76).
[51] Innocent IV, *Register*, 3317; cf. also, Urban IV, *Register*, 669, 696 for similar grants from legacies to Burchard, count of Vendôme.
[52] Rymer, i, p. 601.

the grants of subsidies was what might loosely be termed ill-gotten gains. This money fell into ecclesiastical hands either by confiscation, or as conscience money, and came from the proceeds of usury and theft.[53] It could be used for general purposes such as crusade only when there was no hope of discovering the legal claimant.[54] Once the donation had been conceded, the legal claimant ceased to have any right of appeal.[55] There is one record of instructions to the penitent himself to pay the conscience money to the crusading fund of William of Holland.[56]

Crusade was not the sole object of papal subsidisation, and all the sources of money indicated above except those peculiarly concerned with the Holy Land, or crusade thereto, were used for more general purposes such as the support of needy religious houses.[57] In these cases there was a specific exclusion of funds belonging to crusade. Gregory X also assigned to the general crusading fund all fines imposed on blasphemers.[58] This pecuniary penance had been decreed by Gregory IX,[59] but does not seem to have been much insisted upon except in France where, at the council of bishops called by King Louis in 1261 to discuss the levying of a tax in aid of the Holy Land, it was decided, among other compromise measures, to enforce this decree.[60] The decision seems to have been taken very seriously by the king, who was warned by Clement IV in 1268 not to be too harsh in his treatment of this variety of sinner.[61]

By using these miscellaneous sources of finance for crusade,

---

[53] Innocent IV, *Register*, 6661, for example.

[54] This was the normal ruling acted upon by confessors. See, for example, Urban IV, *Register*, 2087.

[55] *Layettes*, iii, 4405. This particular example refers to Louis IX's desire to convert monies to the use of the poor; the principle behind the ruling was general, however.

[56] Innocent IV, *Register*, 4760. The penitent in question was a relative of William, Otto II, count of Guelders.

[57] There are numerous examples. See, for instance, Innocent IV, *Register*, 6342; Honorius IV, *Register*, 300; J. Sbaralea, *Supplement* (Innocent IV) xvi, xxvi. In one case a religious house which had borrowed money left to the Holy Land by the bishop of Norwich, was given permission to omit repayment on account of its poverty. Innocent IV, *Register*, 6092.

[58] See Appendix A, p. 197.

[59] Gregory X states this in his *Constitutiones*; see Appendix A, p. 197.

[60] Cf. William of Nangis, *Chronicon*, ed. MM. Daunou & Naudet (*Recueil des Historiens des Galles et de la France*, Vol. XX), Paris, 1840, p. 558.

[61] Cf. Potthast, 20441. King Louis seems to have been extremely harsh in his treatment of blasphemers; cf. Joinville. cxxxviii, § 685-7, and William de Saint Pathus, *Vie de Saint Louis*, pp. 148-9.

the papacy was ostensibly concentrating all energies and resources on the project most pressing and urgent at that particular moment. On a different level it was absorbing crusade ever more deeply into the general pattern of papal finance, putting it alongside all the other temporary crises which beset Christendom and which called for a temporary financial adjustment. This made way for the development of a mind that could divert even specifically crusading funds, not simply for a papal struggle against the Hohenstaufen which, after all, was justifiable as the Church's own proper cause, but even in the struggle where papal partiality for one side constituted the primary reason for any aid at all.

Grants

Crusading monies from the above sources were collected, and stored at the pope's pleasure, or were marked out for payment to a particular *crucesignatus*, or group of *crucesignati*. The groups without mention of names consisted in the poor and the worthy.[62] The worthiness of the recipient could sometimes be taken into account since Clement IV saw fit to refuse a grant to James I of Aragon on account of his notorious sins, which included spoliation of the Church.[63] In the absence of more plentiful records it is difficult to tell what principles in fact governed the granting of papal subsidies for crusade. Kings, princes, and magnates are obvious recipients since these took the lesser *crucesignati* into their pay,[64] but there are examples of papal subsidies to lesser knights, just as there is evidence that princes and magnates were heavily subsdised by leaders.[65] Some lesser knights were granted papal subsidies at the request of

---

[62] Innocent IV, *Register*, 2961, 3727, for example.

[63] Clement IV, *Register*, 890, "cum sit indecens et indignum, quod spoliatori subsidium conferant spoliati".

[64] See pp. 52-3, above.

[65] Count Raymond of Toulouse was given a subsidy of £ 20,000 *parisis* by King Louis to provide himself with men and arms, and other necessities (*Layettes*, iii, 3672). Henry III promised a subsidy of ten thousand marks of Marseilles and a ship, as well as twenty war horses on his arrival in the Holy Land to Peter of Savoy, intending to accompany the English crusade (Rymer, i, pp. 488-9). The English king also promised a substantial subsidy to Gilbert de Clare as part of the settlement of the quarrel between the earl and the Lord Edward (Giffard, dccxliii). The sum of £ 70,000 *tournois* which Louis IX advanced to Edward to facilitate the latter's preparations to accompany the French crusade of 1270 was in the nature of a loan (Rymer, i, pp. 858-9; cf. also, J. P. Trabut-Cussac, "Le financement de la croisade anglaise de 1270", *Ecole des Chartes*, CXIX, 1961, p. 114).

important relatives, or patrons. Richard Giffard, a relative of the king of Scotland is an example of this. He is described as taking with him a certain number of knights at his own expense and the grant was extended to several of his kinsmen going with him at their own expense.[66] Another grant was made in England to Robert de Kenci, described as a kinsman of Simon de Montfort.[67] The nephews of the viscount of Châteaudun received a subsidy along with their uncle,[68] and Landry de Fleury, a retainer of Dreux de Mello, seigneur of Epoisses, was given a subsidy equal to one tenth part of that granted to his lord.[69] Thomas de Coucy-le-Château was granted a subsidy on the recommendation of the bishop of Tusculum and Peter Chambellan that his setting out would be greatly to the good of the Holy Land.[70]

The subsidy was normally granted from the funds collected within a man's own territories,[71] including the tenth; in the case of hereditary tenths there was a stipulation that they must revert to the Church within a year of the crusaders' return. The subsidy could also be paid from funds collected in the territories of a man's relatives [72] provided that these did not assume the cross,[73] in which case the grant of a subsidy in that area to someone else was revoked. The rights of vassals were also reserved,[74] as were those of prior

---

[66] Innocent IV, *Register*, 4814; cf. *C.P.L.*, I, p. 261 and Theiner, cxlii.

[67] Innocent IV, *Register*, 3475.

[68] *Ibid.*, 3318-20.

[69] *Ibid.*, 3450-1.

[70] Clement IV, *Register*, 1501; Potthast, 19736. The de Coucy family were inveterate crusaders; cf. J. Tardif, "Le procès d'Enguerran de Coucy", *Ecole des Chartes*, LXXIX, 1918, *passim*.

[71] The grants to the count of Joigny and Peter de Courtenay are typical; cf. Innocent IV, *Register*, 3311-16. The count, whose sister was married to Peter de Courtenay, received another grant, along with Peter, from the Scottish collection (Theiner, cxxviii).

[72] Peter de Courtenay received a grant of funds from the territories of his relative the count of Dreux (Innocent IV, *Register*, 3313). Walter de Châtillon was given a claim to the territories of the count of St. Pol, except the county itself (Innocent IV, *Register*, 4286). These are typical. John de Montfort sought and obtained a grant of monies in the territories of Simon de Nesle who was married to Alix de Montfort (Innocent IV, *Register*, 2765, 2766).

[73] Innocent IV, *Register*, 2765, 3475. Funds collected in the territory of the count d'Eu were assigned to Robert of Artois (*Ibid.*, 3754), but he did later assume the cross. There is no record of a grant to him until the crusade to be led by the count of Poitiers was being organised. He then received a subsidy of £ 6,000 *tournois* (*Ibid.*, 7991).

[74] Innocent IV, *Register*, 3475.

claimants by papal grant.[75] In England Henry III tried to claim the whole tenth once he had assumed the cross, but he was refused on the grounds that previous grants had to be honoured.[76] The subsidy, whether to the king or his followers, extended normally for three years. In some cases the grant was clearly of a specified sum,[77] in other cases one has to infer that a sum was specified. Several letters of Innocent IV instruct the collectors to make up the sum, which is not specified, from other sources if those mentioned do not yield a sufficient amount.[78] Some grants of subsidy contain the right to the reversion of monies assigned to other *crucesignati* who had died before fulfilling their vows.[79] In such a case the heirs of the *crucesignati* were constrained by the conditions of the grant to pay back all subsidies, unless they inherited the vow and actively undertook its fulfilment.[80] There is only one example in the papal registers of a subsidy to a woman *crucesignata*. This was to Alice, wife of the count of Blois, and her subsidy was to be a third part of monies from certain specified sources.[81]

The subsidy was made payable when the *crucesignatus* had set out,[82] or when he actually reached the Holy Land. This was an obvious measure against fraud. The English hierarchy in granting a subsidy to Henry III or Edward, whoever of the two set out, specified that the money was to be held until departure, and was not to be diverted to other purposes.[83] There were variations in this procedure since William Longespée seems to have been given a right to claim a *second* payment on departure.[84] This may have been because of the convincing hard luck story he told the pope during his interview

---

[75] It was normal for any grant to reserve the rights of prior claimants. See for example, Innocent IV, *Register*, 3317, 3730, 4929, 5127, 6247; Urban IV, *Register*, 694, 2177; Clement IV, *Register*, 1205.

[76] Innocent IV, *Register*, 4055, 4881.

[77] See, for example, Innocent IV, *Register*, 3723, 3730, 7815, 7991, etc.

[78] See, for example, Innocent IV, *Register*, 3065.

[79] Innocent IV, *Register*, 2016, 6419, 7058; cf. *Layettes*, iii, 3721. In the case of the duke of Brabant (*Ibid.*, 2016) the *crucesignati* were from his territories. For the count of Poitiers, the grant covered not simply the count's own territories, but the kingdom in general.

[80] See John XXI, *Register*, 11, 27; Martin IV, *Register*, 116; *Layettes*, iii, 4039.

[81] Urban IV, *Register*, 690.

[82] Innocent IV, *Register*, 2764, 2767, 3065, 5946; Urban IV, *Register*, 696, 2173; John XXI, *Register*, 11, 91; Nicholas III, *Register*, 547; *C.P.L.*, I, p. 255.

[83] Cf. *Northern Registers*, xvii.

[84] The English collectors were expressly directed to waive this condition in the case of William Longespée (*C.P.L.*, I, p. 444).

with Innocent.[85] Alphonse of Poitiers was paid all the monies collected up to the Easter Sunday before his scheduled departure.[86] This principle of payment in instalments was also operative in the case of subsidies granted by lay leaders since Louis IX promised the count of Toulouse £ 5,000 down and the rest when the count should have arrived in the Holy Land.[87] If one can judge by the case of Guy of Flanders, money from a subsidy could be advanced as a loan [88] presumably when it was to be used for purposes not directly connected with crusade preparations. All monies realised before departure had to be refunded, if the *crucesignatus* did not set out.[89]

The amount of the subsidy, so far as evidence exists, varied considerably from person to person, and from pontificate to pontificate. The largest amount specified in a grant by Innocent IV is £ 6,000 *tournois*,[90] whereas Guy of Flanders was accorded £ 20,000 *tournois*.[91] The subsidy was, no doubt, calculated on the number of armed followers accompanying the grantee. John XXI in making one grant specified that the *crucesignatus* was to receive no further subsidy for his followers over and above what had already been granted and that any further monies were to go towards the support of mercenaries.[92] In this connection it is interesting to note that Alphonse of Poitiers' calculations of the cost of paying knights to follow him on King Louis' second crusade were upset by the scarcity of such men. The cost, therefore, rose considerably above the count's original estimate.[93]

---

[85] Matthew Paris, iv, pp. 629-30.

[86] Innocent IV, *Register*, 4295.

[87] *Layettes*, iii, 3672.

[88] Clement IV, *Register*, 2173.

[89] Roger de Leyburn received two thousand marks sterling and failed to set out; the money had to be restored. See Gregory X, *Register*, 191. Restitution was demanded also from the son of Hugh IV of Burgundy (Innocent IV, *Register*, 2733), and from the bishop of Skaar (Nicholas III, *Register*, 547). These are typical cases. The penalty, expressed in the case of Roger de Leyburn, was excommunication and interdict (*C.P.L.*, I, p. 444; the amount is wrongly stated here as one thousand marks).

[90] These were grants to the sons of John de Brienne, the counts de Montfort and d'Eu. See Innocent IV, *Register*, 7815, 7991.

[91] Clement IV, *Register*, 351. On this Guy actually borrowed £ 40,000 *tournois*; cf. Honorius IV, *Register*, 425.

[92] *Register*, 11. The insistence in the pope's letter on the need to maintain the sworn number of followers for the whole time suggests that frauds were practised in this respect. This letter throws further light on the terms under which Barral des Baux agreed to serve Alphonse of Poitiers in the Holy Land. In his case simple defect of numbers was not to constitute an invalidation of his service. See p. 53, above.

[93] Cf. *Correspondance administrative*, I, 167-9.

Innocent IV ordered Walter de Cantilupe during his period as collector, to distribute monies to the English *crucesignati*,[94] and other collectors received similar orders, thus indicating that much of the papal subsidisation was carried out at the local level, and at the discretion of the local collectors. All grants of papal subsidies, at whatever level, were conditional upon the fulfilment of the vow, and the papacy reserved the right to withdraw, and re-allocate the monies should neither the *crucesignatus* nor his heirs go on crusade.[95] Should payment have been received, the *crucesignati* were obliged to make restitution, as shown above, but, on the other hand, if monies which had been granted to a crusader who actually fulfilled his vow, had not been paid, efforts were made to secure a full payment for him [96] or for his heirs.[97]

(iv) *Difficulties and diversions of funds*

Difficulties over the collection of taxes are not only expected, but follow a calculable pattern no matter how different the attendant circumstances:

(a) objections on the part of those paying, with attempted frauds and obstructions;
(b) the problem of exemptions;
(c) the problems of administration and keeping accurate records;
(d) frauds on the part of collecting officials;
(e) diversions of the funds by the taxing body from the cause stated to be the object of the levy.

Basically all objections to taxation spring from the conviction that the amount is too great, or that the object is unworthy. No clerical objection to crusading collections ever suggested the latter as the cause of reluctance; almost invariably the reason was one which went beyond the question of a particular tax to a general dissatisfaction with the amount and frequency of the demands. The French

---

[94] Cf. Innocent IV, *Register*, 2961; *C.P.L.*, I, p. 263.
[95] Such conditions are to be found expressed in various grants. See John XXI, *Register*, 11, and Martin IV, *Register*, 116.
[96] Prolonged efforts on behalf of Richard of Cornwall are typical. See Innocent IV, *Register*, 3523, 4085. Cf. also E. W. Lunt, *Financial Relations*, pp. 194-6. Similar action, though not so prolonged, was taken on behalf of Robert Tiptoft and Payn de Chaourse (Gregory X, *Register*, 232), and the count of Vendôme (Clement IV, *Register*, 80-1). Robert Tiptoft and Payn de Chaourse were among the witnesses to Edward I's will made at Acre; cf. Rymer, i, p. 885.
[97] Innocent IV ordered the payment of an overdue subsidy to the heirs of Amalric de Montfort (*Register*, 345).

clergy in 1262 included among their reasons for unwillingness the lack of urgent need in the Holy Land,[98] but even then their primary objection was more general in import. In the latter part of the period under examination clerical objections did take into account suspicions that the monies were not reaching the Holy Land anyway.[99]

Clerical resentment reached such proportions that Clement IV promised that there would be a general exemption from crusading tithes for ten years after the expiry of the current imposition.[100] The tardy payment of the Lyons tenth, and the obstructions met with by collectors show how excessive taxation had killed all sense of the crusading tenth as an almsdeed meritorious of eternal salvation. Recalcitrance on the part of the clergy was answered by threats of ecclesiastical censure, but objections continued to be raised. During the collection for King Louis' first crusade, apart from the ordinary failures to pay and attempts at fraud, there was one interesting attempt at an evasion on a point of principle, namely that the clergy were consenting parties to a tax. The archbishop of Narbonne and his suffragans, the bishops of Saintes and Angoulême refused payment of the tenth for King Louis on the grounds that they had not been present at the meeting which ratified the tax, and were, therefore, not consenting parties. Innocent IV at first upheld their protest [101] but after some delay they were ordered to pay.[102] A year later the argument was still in progress.[103] On another occasion French bishops insisted that they would not pay unless the collectors could produce letters which nominated them individually. The pope pointed out that it would be impossible to cope with such a demand.[104]

Called upon in 1254 to grant a subsidy to Louis IX while he was still delaying in Syria, the French hierarchy consented to the payment of a twelfth which was to be paid in two instalments, the second of which was to be waived should the king come home in the meantime; it was not to be enforced by the secular arm.[105] In August/September, 1262, a council was called in Paris by the bishop of Agen [106] to discuss the raising of a hundredth for the recovery

[98] *Journal des visites*, p. 440.
[99] See below, pp. 153 ff.
[100] *Register*, 508.
[101] Innocent IV, *Register*, 2492.
[102] *Ibid.*, 3055.
[103] *Ibid.*, 3980.
[104] *Ibid.*, 6067.
[105] *Journal des visites*, pp. 754-5. The archbishop of Rouen was official collector.
[106] *Ibid.*, p. 440. The bishop of Agen was legate.

of Constantinople; by implication this tax was also to be applied
to the saving of Achaia and the Holy Land. The archbishop of
Tours, speaking for the hierarchy, dwelt on the long oppressions
of the French clergy by papal taxes for the Holy Land, as well as
by special subventions for other purposes. The hierarchy in a letter
of protest formulated the following day objected on other grounds
besides, namely recent crop failures, and consequent hardship at
home, as well as the lack of any sign of an imminent general passage,
or of a leader to organise it; they also pointed out that the subsidy
was rendered unnecessary by the current truce between Saracens
and Christians in the Holy Land.[107] Quite unintentionally the hierarchy thus perfectly epitomised the basic indifference of the West to
the Crusader East, while cloaking that indifference under a guise of
concern for more urgent needs at home. This indifference is manifest
also in the sheer ignorance underlying the estimated value of the
truce to the Crusader States if they were left to depend on their
own resources. After the Council of Lyons in 1274 some of the
German hierarchy went even further in forbidding their clergy to
pay the tenth under pain of censure.[108]

The practice of exemptions, though of far wider implications
than simply crusading policy, created specifically crusading problems.
Basically they had an effect on the amount collected, and caused
resentment not only on the part of the non-exempt, but also on the
part of the *crucesignatus* to whom the collection had been promised.
Letters concerning payment of the crusading tenth in Sicily by the
exempt, their possible reactions, and the precautions to be taken
against the further reactions of Charles of Anjou show to what
turns the papacy could be put to cope with all exigencies, and placate
all parties.[109] By way of contrast King Louis was careful to secure
exemptions from his crusading tenth for poor religious houses
with a yearly income of less then £ 15 *tournois*.[110] Attempts at waiving

---

[107] Urban IV replied tersely that he knew the state of the Holy Land from
personal experience, and held the bishops' pretexts frivolous, and the tax was,
therefore, levied the following year (*Register*, 373-4).

[108] This is made clear by a letter of Martin IV to the collector in Cologne,
Bremen and Magdeburg, denouncing the hierarchy for their conduct and threatening them with ecclesiastical censure, *Register*, 152.

[109] Clement IV, *Register*, 1436, 1451.

[110] Innocent IV, *Register*, 4292; cf. 3056. Louis IX continued to have a tender
conscience on this score. See his letter to Eude Rigaud in *Journal des visites*, pp.
797-8.

all exemptions in favour of crusading funds met with opposition, and ultimate failure. Gregory X's "Constitutiones pro zelo fidei" show him determined to allow no exceptions,[111] but his registers tell a different tale.[112] Gregory made provision, of course, for poor religious houses, and those religious orders engaged in social work.[113]

Some of the difficulties were, in fact, purely administrative ones which arose from attempts to suit the grant of subsidies to all the vagaries of feudal rights and tenures. The inevitable result was a certain amount of crossing and overlapping. Numerous papal letters attest the efforts made to sort out the double grants; many simply reserved the prior rights of any other *crucesignatus*,[114] others dealt with specific cases of error. Typical of these are the efforts made by Innocent IV to find a suitable source of funds for a subsidy to Henri Clément, marshal of France. The grant was of £ 1,000 *tournois*, and was first ordered to be paid from redemptions and legacies in the diocese of Sens. This proved to be a violation of the prior rights of Hugh IV of Burgundy; a second grant in the diocese of Rouen cut across earlier grants to King Louis, and others. A third grant ordered the money to be paid from the collection in the diocese of Rouen, but specified less distinctly crusading sources, such as ill gotten gains, unspecified pious legacies, and redemptions of vows not to the Holy Land.[115] Such muddles sometimes resulted in acrimonious exchanges, and sometimes in outright scandal as when two rival collectors resorted to threats and menaces.[116] Double collections could also result from the attempts of officials of a lay *crucesignatus* to whom a subsidy had been promised, to secure the money at all possible speed. This is the import of a reproof delivered by William Wickwane to the prior of St Oswald's, Nostell, for his negligence in collecting the tenth. The king had already rebuked the archbishop and had ordered his sheriff to levy the tax if the collector continued to be tardy.[117] A more notorious example is to be found in a case cited in a letter by Innocent IV.[118] The pope ordered strong measures to be taken against the procurators of the duke of Burgundy who

---

[111] See Appendix A, p. 197.
[112] Gregory X, *Register*, 384, 399, 409, 1048, 1056, 1069.
[113] See his instructions to collectors (*Register*, 571).
[114] See above, pp. 146-47, and footnote 75.
[115] Innocent IV, *Register*, 6661.
[116] For an example see above, p. 130.
[117] Wickwane, No. 709.
[118] *Register*, 6207.

were resorting to manifold abuses and extortionate practices to secure the duke's subsidies. These abuses included usurpation of ecclesiastical rights with regard to judging questions related to legacies, extorting money by threats, subverting wills and even resorting to violence.[119] False collectors, like false pardoners, were also rife.[120]

It is not surprising to find that some people entertained a great reluctance to act as temporary guardians of the crusading monies as they were collected. The increasing use of Italian banking houses made such problems less urgent, but there was still grave danger of theft and misappropriation. Some found the task of keeping the money safe under threat of censure far too onerous, and pleaded to be spared.[121] There is evidence for their fears in the record of the Dominican priory in Utrecht which was violently entered and the money carried off at the instigation of John of Nassau, bishop-elect of Utrecht.[122] In this case the friars were not held responsible. In another case a Templar ran away with the proceeds of the collection which was in the safe keeping of his community. The Master of the house was held responsible, but given time in which to pay.[123]

A major reason for the growing reluctance to pay crusading tithes was the grave, and not unjustified, suspicions which were rife about the diversion of crusading monies from the Holy Land, and their use for papal purposes. Alexander IV saw nothing inconsistent in the commutation of all Henry III's English subsidy to the Sicilian crusade. Clement IV who even more determinedly diverted crusading funds to Sicily, not stopping short of trying to persuade King Louis that he had a duty to support his brother financially,[124] denied the justice of any suspicions of a diversion of money from the Holy Land.[125] Clement IV also diverted much money into the English royal purse in the struggle against the barons.[126]

---

[119] There are other examples of legacies to the Holy Land subverted by executors, not by collectors. Cf. Sbaralea, iii (Clement IV) xviii.

[120] Clement IV warned against them, *Register*, 1608. Oliver Scholasticus did the same (Letter 10, p. 316). John Peckham recorded an actual case of forged letters of credence which were uncovered by the English hierarchy who had met to discuss the (unrelated) case of Amaury de Montfort. The collectors at the time were Arditio and John of Darlington; Peckham, i, ccxxxv.

[121] See, for example, Honorius IV, *Register*, 428-9 and Peckham, ii, ccccxcvi.

[122] Nicholas III, *Register*, 126.

[123] Martin IV, *Register*, 204.

[124] See above, p. 85.

[125] Letter to the bishop of Lismore, collector, quoted in *C.P.L.* I, p. 349.

[126] *C.P.L.*, I, pp. 432-3. This was not a strictly crusading tenth even though the pope saw the struggle as a crusade-equivalent, but it served to heighten

The German clergy were rebuked by Nicholas III for their negligence in paying the tenth, his letter making clear that they had objected on the grounds that the collection "pro maiori parte in usus alios est conversa." [127] The same pope also had cause to remonstrate with the Swedish hierarchy for their neglect in making the collection. The bishops of Ripa and Skaar he accused of prevarication.[128] The latter bishop, St. Brynjolf Algotsson, seems to have refused to pay because he was a *crucesignatus*,[129] but it is not clear why, in this case, he should have been accused of lying. Perhaps the pope's rebuke was not unrelated to the theft of money collected for the tenth by the citizens of Skaar from the church where it was stored.[130] Nicholas III ordered its restitution.

Martin IV, more active than any in the French cause in Sicily, was supremely guilty of sacrificing the needs of the Holy Land, despite his assurance to the German clergy that money intended for the Holy Land was not being diverted into French hands.[131] Martin argued plausibly that the money collected in Germany was not safe, and ordered its removal, despite local protests.[132] The scandal which he gave by his fierce partisanship in the French-Aragonese quarrel is clear in the pages of Muntaner.[133]

Martin IV's complaisance in regard to the demands of the French monarchy for the diversion of crusading funds was not without precedent even if it were without parallel. Innocent IV had transferred the crusading tenth in Germany from King Louis' crusade to that of William of Holland.[134] A slightly later attempt to widen the area of diversion led to retaliation on the part of Queen Blanche.[135] Innocent IV and his successors allowed crusading funds to be used

---

ecclesiastical discontent with taxation, and to form another precedent for taxes imposed by the pope for the benefit of a lay ruler. On the growing dangers of the practice in the later thirteenth century, see J. R. Strayer, "The Laicization of French and English Society in the 13th century", *Speculum*, XV, 1940, pp. 76-86.

[127] F. Kaltenbrunner, *Actenstücke zur Geschichte des Deutschen Reiches*, Vienna, 1889, No. 107.

[128] Nicholas III, *Register*, 549.

[129] P. Riant, *Expéditions et pèlerinages*, p. 367.

[130] Nicholas III, *Register*, 553.

[131] *Register*, 244. Compare his denial with the implications of such letters as 271-4, 549, 583-91, for example.

[132] Kaltenbrunner, No. 250.

[133] Muntaner, *Chronicle*, especially LVI *et seq.*

[134] See above, pp. 74 ff.

[135] See above, pp. 78-9.

for the northern campaigns against pagans;[136] in Spain the money was needed for campaigns against the Moors. The major diversion of crusading funds was, however, for the Sicilian campaigns, and this bedevilled crusading finances from the final years of Innocent IV's reign onwards. Louis IX held aloof,[137] and did all he could to raise funds for the Holy Land, until he should be free to embark on another crusade.[138] What Philip III sent to the Holy Land by way of subsidy at the instigation of Gregory X was consumed by 1273.[139] Gregory X shared Louis IX's urgent concern for the Holy Land, but was hampered from either organising a crusade or sending adequate financial aid. Gregory's successors saw themselves as involved in the Franco-Aragonese struggle as his predecessors had been in the anti-Hohenstaufen campaigns in Sicily.

The dangerous precedent set by the popes in diverting crusading monies, and in allowing themselves to be manoeuvred by circumstance, or their own partisan spirit, into consenting to the diversion of those monies by lay rulers, was inevitably destructive of both the means of financing crusade, and any lingering desire on the part of the faithful to make a real effort. The Military Orders sought, and obtained, the right to put crusading funds to their own purposes. They whose *raison d'être* depended on an ideal of chivalric poverty of spirit had lost the spiritual capacity for aspiring to that ideal. Where once their Western possessions were sought and held as strictly ancillary to their whole purpose which lay in the East, possession of wealth had led them into dangerous paths of seeking to increase those possessions as an end in themselves, and as a means to more power. Letters from the Templars and Hospitallers in Syria in the last years of the Crusader States speak of their great financial needs there [140] while in France the Templars were wealthy enough

---

[136] See above, pp. 88 ff. This was even more notable in the case of the Teutonic Knights. Monetary grants on their behalf are too numerous to quote. The collection of documents related to the Teutonic Order made by E. Strehlke, *Tabulae Ordinis Theutonici*, Berlin, 1869, gives some idea of their extent.

[137] See above, pp. 77, 85.

[138] He subsidised crusaders (*Regesta Regni Hierosolymitani* 1339, 1343, 1351-2), and paid for the upkeep of a force under Geoffrey of Sargines, for example.

[139] *Regesta Regni Hierosolymitani*, 1387, and p. 350, note 1.

[140] Notification of many such letters is to be found in *Regesta Regni Hierosolymitani*, Nos 1387, 1404, 1446, 1470. Supporting evidence, which can have left the West in very little doubt about the state in the Frankish East is to be found in Nos 1348, 1405, 1410, 1436 and in *Additamentum* 1291a. See also the letter of Thomas, bishop of Bethlehem, given in full in *Menkonis Chronicon* (*M.G.H.*

to excite the greed of Philip IV.[141] The Teutons, a later foundation, retained all their privileged status, even when they had diverted their energies to north eastern Europe. There they stood unrivalled in their hunger for land and the means of acquiring ever more wealth and power.

Edward I, devout *crucesignatus* as he was, shared in the general greed for crusading funds. Not only did he set a bad example by quarrelling with his brother Edmund over the division of the subsidy granted by Gregory X after the crusade of 1270,[142] but later he appropriated the proceeds of the Lyons tenth by main force,[143] intending to use them for his domestic wars. There can be no doubt that Edward was far more interested in laying his hands on the money collected, than in laying his hand to the sword in actual crusade.[144] His actions drew on him papal rebuke [145] but he continued to employ every effort to gain access to the funds. The king of Scotland followed Edward's example and laid violent hands on officials trying to take the collection out of the country. The representatives of the Italian banking houses complained to the pope who rebuked the king, and demanded restitution.[146] The local collector for Scotland pleaded the king's prohibition as an excuse for his own misappropriation of the collection.[147] Even John Peckham was nothing loath to raise a loan from the crusading funds to tide him over financial difficulties.[148] The king of Norway proved obstructive about the removal of the money collected from his territories,

---

SS. XXIII, pp. 547-9), that of Hugh Revel to Guy de Dampierre printed in "Six lettres relatives aux croisades", ed. P. Riant, *Archives de l'Orient latin*, I, 1881, pp. 390-391 and the "Lettre des Chrétiens de Terre Sainte à Charles d'Anjou", ed. H. F. Delaborde, *Revue de l'Orient latin*, II, 1894, pp. 206-215.

[141] This is not the place to enter into a discussion of the motives which led to Philip IV's destruction of the Templars, but their wealth was a not negligible factor.

[142] Gregory X, *Register*, 328-30.

[143] He had first forbidden its removal from England. Rymer, ii, pp. 250-1.

[144] The history of Edward's frustrated attempts to secure crusading funds is well summarised in Lunt, *Financial Relations*, Chap. VI, and need not be repeated in detail here.

[145] *C.P.L.*, I, p. 476. Martin IV refused to accept Edmund as a substitute for his brother (*Register*, 286).

[146] Honorius IV, *Register*, 66. Cf. Theiner, ccxcv.

[147] Martin IV, *Register*, 356.

[148] Peckham, i, xv; the significance of this lies in the manner in which the crusading funds were beginning to be regarded as convenient for such emergencies.

issuing an edict prohibiting the sale of bullion to clerics.[149] Earlier Nicholas III had ordered stern measures to be taken against the king of Aragon for appropriating crusading funds.[150] This pope also had difficulties with the king of Sweden over the collection and transfer of crusading money from his country.[151] The reasons for such behaviour are not far to seek—the rulers wished to put the money to their own use, and they distrusted the ultimate object of the funds once these were in papal hands.

In these circumstances crusading ventures can scarcely be expected to have flourished, despite the promise of subsidies, and despite papal attempts to ensure adequate finances to make good those subsidies. Financial benefits were not, however, the only material advantage held out to *crucesignati* as an inducement to take the cross. The next section will deal with the privileges, protections and immunities which were offered to those taking the cross.

(b) Privileges

Because those interested in promoting crusade were ever alive to the possibilities of a new inducement to take the cross, and because *crucesignati* were nothing loath to make use of their status to obtain what they wanted, the assumption of the cross was frequently urged as a reason for granting certain privileges to laymen and clerics. In discussing crusader privileges, however, it is as well to bear in mind the relation of this topic to the far larger one of the growing impatience of secular authorities with the claims of ecclesiastical authorities, manifesting itself more urgently than ever before in the latter half of the thirteenth century. This tended to absorb crusader privileges into the more general struggle, in a way not possible to take into account here.[152]

While the financial assistance accorded to *crucesignati* aimed at being directly auxiliary to the fulfilment of crusading vows, other privileges which were granted to *crucesignati* as such did not pretend to a direct

---

[149] Martin IV, *Register*, 120-1.

[150] Nicholas III, *Register*, 199.

[151] Nicholas III, *Register*, 544. The pope spoke of the king's action in carrying off the money under cloak of necessity as having been "non sine vehementis admirationis causa".

[152] For the specific effects of this tendency on crusader privileges see E. Bridrey, *La condition juridique des croisés et le privilège de Croix*, Paris, 1900, especially Chap. V, where there is a discussion of the renunciation of their privileges by *crucesignati* because of the pressures imposed by changes in social organisation.

connection with crusade, nor with the fulfilling of a vow. These privileges were by no means reserved for *crucesignati* either in fact, or in the minds of the faithful, and were just as readily accorded to non-crusaders. What scandals there were concerning abuse of these privileges whether by *crucesignati* or not, tended to redound to the discredit of crusade, but it would be false to claim anything exclusively crusading about crusader privileges.

Perhaps the most generally useful of these privileges was that of having the right not to be cited for legal proceedings outside those dioceses in which one's person or one's property lay.[153] It was a common practice to have a defendant cited to appear in a far distant court, on pain of default should he not arrive in time to answer proceedings. A doubly ruinous method was to have him cited to appear in far separated courts simultaneously.[154] There had been legislation against this malpractice at the Fourth Lateran Council, not merely with reference to *crucesignati*, but for general application.[155] The frequency with which *crucesignati* were specially awarded this privilege suggests that the ruling of 1215 had not been effectively enforced, though there is an entry in the registers of John Peckham which shows that individual bishops still made an effort to secure this right for the general faithful in their dioceses.[156] Papal mandates in favour of specific *crucesignati* such as Alphonse of Poitiers,[157] or John de Montfort,[158] for example, or of the general body of crusaders,[159] seem to have been aimed at reiterating an already existing prohibition. In this way *crucesignati* would have to hand recent documentary proof of the privilege, and its specific relation to them by the pope.

On setting out, the crusaders had perforce to leave their business

---

[153] Cf. Urban IV, *Register*, 2906, for example.

[154] Innocent IV, *Register*, 4665.

[155] Canon 37. See Brundage, *op. cit.*, pp. 174-175.

[156] No. ccciii dated 28 July, 1282. The archbishop expressly states that the ordination constitutes part of his effort to deal with "illo demoniaco monacho Pontineacensi . . . qui in nostros subditos grassatur et ad ipsorum enervationem insurgere nititur quantum potest".

[157] Cf. Innocent IV, *Register*, 6469.

[158] *Ibid.*, 7978; cf. also, 8005, 8007 granting the same privilege to Count Alphonse d'Eu and his wife. John of Ibelin was given similar privileges as *bailli* of Jerusalem (*ibid.*, 6457), as were Opizon Fieschi, patriarch of Antioch, and his household (*ibid.*, 7910).

[159] Innocent IV, *Register*, 6469; Urban IV, *Register*, 392, 470, 2906; *C.P.L.*, I, p. 394.

in the hands of their officials. Judging from the actions of Alphonse of Poitiers, and others, in obtaining this same legal privilege for their officials,[160] it would seem that there was considered to be a danger of some advantage being taken of the crusader's absence, to cite his officials to distant courts. The charges would, of course, be only nominally against the official, and the absent crusader stood in danger of heavy financial loss.

In the absence of any extensive records of actual cases, it is difficult to tell how effective the privilege was in the thirteenth century. Matthew Paris does give an account of a case in which Innocent IV gave judgment concerning an appeal by a certain Stephen, rector of Cotenham, *crucesignatus*, against being cited by G., rector of Hayes in Kent, also *crucesignatus*, to appear before the prior of Rochester, this being more than two days' journey outside Stephen's diocese. Stephen's appeal was upheld, but this ruling was not accepted by the rector of Hayes who urged his own status as *crucesignatus*. The pope, on a second appeal, stated that since the case did not touch on matters in which the rector of Hayes could urge crusader privilege, his former ruling should stand.[161] The register of Thomas Cantilupe contains mention of another case between the prior and convent of Wrokestone and William de Lages, *crucesignatus*, described as exempted by the Second Council of Lyons from answering proceedings in courts outside his diocese. The nature of the appellant's cause is not mentioned, but the privilege was upheld.[162] In a characteristic letter Robert Grosseteste urged the crusader privileges of Richard Syward to the king to secure the former's release from prison.[163] This privilege of not being cited beyond the diocese was also conceded to deputies appointed by papal crusading officials.[164]

There were a number of privileges granted to *crucesignati* to ensure their spiritual welfare, but none of these was exclusively reserved to crusaders. These privileges were usually granted at the request of the leading *crucesignati* to the clerics who were to act as chaplains

---

[160] Innocent IV, *Register*, 4623, 4641; cf. Urban IV, *Register*, 2181. The condition of course was that the *crucesignati* and their officials must be willing to appear before the ordinary.

[161] Matthew Paris, *Additimenta*, p. 170.

[162] Cantilupe, pp. 74-5.

[163] *Roberti Grosseteste Episcopi Quondam Lincolniensis, Epistolae*, ed. H. R. Luard, Rolls Series, London, 1861, Letter xxix.

[164] Clement IV, *Register*, 732.

and special confessors.[165] The clerics thus marked out were raised
to a privileged status in the crusading forces, for their faculties
extended to the generality of the army, as well as to the magnate
and his immediate circle. The special faculties accorded to these
confessors included power to absolve from excommunication of
whatsoever kind that may hinder the crusader from Christian burial.[166]
King Louis, writing to the cardinals in conclave concerning his
coming second crusade, urged on them the necessity to have a
legate for his army, to provide all the necessary spiritual consolation
and strength for such a venture.[167] Joinville, too, insisted on the
consolations which he derived from the ministrations of his chaplain.[168] It was no mere pious show to make provision for clerical
crucesignati who should have all the requisite powers to comfort and
absolve. However, it was usual for these same privileges to be granted
to the courts and households of kings and magnates at home, and,
going on crusade, such men were merely granted a continuation
of these same privileges.[169] If the chosen confessor happened to be a
mendicant, he was granted a dispensation from the rule which
forbade friars to be on horseback.[170] A friar seems also to have been
allowed to choose a *socius* from his order to accompany him.[171]

A series of letters from Innocent IV to Ferdinand III of Castille
and Leon, and the members of his family including Alfonso, concerning the establishment of a bishopric in an area conquered by
Alfonso seems to indicate that leaders of a crusade were likely to be
granted the privilege of having the patronage of such foundations; [172]
in the same way missionaries were allowed to establish new episcopal

---

[165] Innocent IV, *Register*, 2714; Potthast, 12820 (both to Alfonso X of Castille
and Leon); Innocent IV, *Register*, 6414 (to Alphonse of Poitiers); Urban IV,
Register, 2092 (to Henry, bishop of Liège).

[166] Cf. Potthast, 12820. Cf. also, Sbaralea, i, (Innocent IV) cdxxxv.

[167] Cf. Sternfeld, p. 328. The underlying theme of the letter is rather the
dangers of the long interregnum, than the more ostensible complaint about the
lack of a legate.

[168] lx, § 299-300.

[169] This is borne out by the reiterated, and numerous grants of special privileges
to the French royal family in the persons of their chosen confessors. There is
another interesting variation to be found in the *C.P.L.*, I, p. 321, of a grant
to William of Valence, earl of Pembroke, who was described as *crucesignatus*,
but whose privileges were granted in consideration of the merits of his brother,
Henry III.

[170] Cf. Sbaralea, i (Innocent IV) ccl and cccxxv.

[171] *Ibid., loc. cit.*, ccl.

[172] *Ibid., loc. cit.*, ccxciv-ccxcvii.

sees, though the leader of crusade would have had in mind the material advantages of being able to nominate to these new sees. Certainly Hakon of Norway was specifically given rights of patronage in conquered areas.[173] To crusading leaders also came the privilege of public prayers for the success of the venture.[174]

The question of lawful and valid marriages being such an abnormally vexed one in the middle ages, on account of the over-refinements of the canonists on the subject of contracts, it is no wonder that being a *crucesignatus* was made a pretext for securing matrimonial dispensations. Couples were dispensed in retrospect because the husband was a *crucesignatus*,[175] because the case was urged by a *crucesignatus*,[176] or because such a dispensation would rally support for a crusade.[177] Most of the recorded dispensations of this nature— for a prohibited degree of either consanguinity, or affinity—were connected with supporters of William of Holland.[178] Joinville used the services of King Louis IX, Thibault V of Navarre, and Eudes de Châteauroux to obtain matrimonial dispensations for himself,[179] and for his brother, Simon.[180] Charles of Anjou, with his propensity for securing maximum benefits from his crusader status, was accorded a dispensation for his infant daughter,[181] and for his unborn child.[182] King Edward I was also granted by Honorius IV just such a politically convenient dispensation for his children, provided that they did not contract a marriage with an enemy of the Church.[183] Edward's eldest daughter Eleanor, was, in fact, betrothed to Alfonso, the eldest son of Peter of Aragon, a marriage to which Honorius objected in the light of the anti-Aragonese crusade supported by the papacy.

On the same level of importance for the cleric as matrimonial

---

[173] *Diplomatarium Norvegicum*, ed. C. A. Lange & C. R. Unger, 5 vols, Christiania, 1849-60, i, 37.

[174] Innocent IV, *Register*, 6035-6.

[175] *Ibid.*, 1833-4, 4168, 4177; Alexander IV, *Register*, 2838; Nicholas III, *Register*, 493-4.

[176] Alexander IV, *Register*, 571.

[177] Innocent IV, *Register*, 4302; Alexander IV, *Register*, 450.

[178] Innocent IV, *Register*, 4168, 4177, 4302, 7327; Alexander IV, *Register*, 450, 966; cf. Sbaralea, i (Innocent IV) dxxi.

[179] Alexander IV, *Register*, 2838. The lady was Joinville's second wife, and was related to him in the fourth degree of consanguinity. She was Alice de Reynel, the daughter of Gautier de Reynel. Joinville, xci, § 466.

[180] Alexander IV, *Register*, 571.

[181] Innocent IV, *Register*, 7024.

[182] *Ibid.*, 7025.

[183] Honorius IV, *Register*, 932-3, 944; Potthast, 22460, 22461.

dispensations for the layman, were licences for non-residence. Clerical absenteeism was one of the major social problems of the middle ages since it led to so many evils through neglect of souls. The most recent attempt to legislate about it had been at the first Council of Lyons where the intentions to study, or to go on pilgrimage, were specified as the most acceptable reasons for granting licences of non-residence.[184] A cleric could assume the cross provided that he had obtained the permission of his ecclesiastical superiors.[185] His licence normally came from his ordinary,[186] though it could come directly from Rome.[187] It was granted for a specified period—extant records showing a variation of from two to five years.[188]

It is apparent from cases reported in episcopal records that absence on crusade could lead to gross neglect of souls at home. Eude Rigaud presumably was aware of such neglect when he granted the licence for a two year absence, mentioned above,[189] compelling the recipient to take an oath that he would return within two years, or resign all further claim to his benefice. On another occasion the archbishop reported his visitation of a certain priory in Neufmarché, a cell of St. Evroult, which was poverty stricken and deficient in monks, and where services were wanting in the parish because of the absence of the priest in the Holy Land.[190] From the registers of John le Romeyn, archbishop of York, comes another case of a vicar, Adam de Radeford, who had gone to the Holy Land despite an oath to reside in his own vicarage of Hucknall Torkard. This man was guilty of both perjury, and visiting the Holy Places without

---

[184] Canon 14. The canon sought to curb the abuse by imposing a heavy tax on all non-residents of more than six months absence. The tax was to take the form of a moiety of their ecclesiastical revenues to be paid as a subsidy for the Latin Empire of Constantinople.

[185] Cf. Hostiensis, *Summa Aurea*, III, tit. De voto § 6-7 (Quis).

[186] Giffard, No. ccxxxviii, licence to John de Selleston, vicar of Rothwell to be absent for five years.
Cantilupe, p. 290, licence to Reginald, vicar of Lydney, to be absent for three years.
Ibid., pp. 6-7, licence to Canturmus, rector of Eastnor, to be absent for five years.
Wickwane, No. 294, licence to Edmund de Everley, rector of a moiety of the church of Treswell to be absent for three years.
Rigaud, *Journal des visites*, licence for two years' leave of absence to Sylvester, rector of Warungierville.

[187] Innocent IV, *Register*, 2304-5; Urban IV, *Register*, 667.

[188] See note 186, above.

[189] See note 186, above.

[190] *Journal des visites*, p. 499.

licence, as well as of neglect of souls. The archbishop issued a mandate to his official to sequestrate the fruits of the vicarage.[191] The vicar of Rothwell mentioned above,[192] was given his licence with the proviso that his church should not be deprived of services in his absence. Clerics used crusade as a pretext for non-residence, and so clerical *crucesignati*, whether they were sincerely intent on fulfilling their vows, or not, added to the problem of absenteeism, and neglect of souls.

Just as the crusading indulgence was extended to those engaged in the business of crusade, though they were not intending to take part in the crusade itself, so also the privilege of non-residence was granted to these officials.[193] The Dominican, John of Darlington, is a case in point. He was appointed collector in England by Gregory X.[194] In 1279 he was promoted by Nicholas III to the see of Dublin.[195] Instead of taking up residence in his see, the new archbishop continued to perform his duties as collector for another four years. He then resigned his collectorship on the plea that his diocese was in a very bad way,[196] but he died the following year, presumably without effecting much reform in the diocese.[197]

Clerics who were hindered from major orders by illegitimacy were granted dispensations if they assumed the cross.[198] The faculty to grant such dispensations was ordinarily included among those conceded to crusading legates.[199] The cleric remained ineligible for major orders, however, if he were the product of an adulterous or incestuous union, if his father were a regular, or if he showed a tendency to moral irregularities himself.[200] These dispensations for *defectus natalium* by no means always required the assumption of the cross and were obtainable on much easier terms than going on crusade.

---

[191] John le Romeyn, i, No. 870.

[192] See above, p. 162, footnote 186.

[193] Clement IV, *Register*, 732.

[194] *C.P.L.*, I, p. 449.

[195] There had been an election dispute in progress since the death of the previous archbishop, and Nicholas III settled it by appointing John of Darlington; cf. *C.P.L.*, I, pp. 458-9.

[196] Martin IV, *Register*, 385. Evidence of the state of affairs in the diocese is to be found in the same *Register*, 423.

[197] John died in 1284.

[198] Urban IV, *Register*, 380.

[199] It was enjoyed, for example, by Aegidius, archbishop of Tyre; cf. Urban IV, *Register*, 380.

[200] *Ibid., loc. cit.*

Like almost all the other crusader privileges, taking the cross was not a *sine qua non* for a grant, but merely another convincing pretext.

(c) PAPAL PROTECTIONS

A wider group of people than *crucesignati* came under the special protection of the Holy See; these protections were extended in such a way as to assure the recipient that the whole weight of ecclesiastical censure would fall on any who should presume to attack him in any way that violated the privileges of his status. All calls to crusade, modelled on the decrees of 1215 and 1245, declared *crucesignati* to be under the protection of the Holy See in all that pertained to their status.[201] The onus of the protection fell on special conservators appointed by the pope, or chosen by his delegate.[202] A papal protection was extended to *crucesignati*, not only in the general call to crusade, but more specifically as followers of a certain magnate, or leader, who himself obtained a special grant of protection.[203] This lasted for the duration of the crusade, from the setting out, until the crusader returned, or his death was known for certain.[204]

Individual *crucesignati*, especially the more powerful, seem to have considered it worthwhile to seek a personal grant of protection.[205] At its widest this covered not only the *crucesignatus* and his followers,[206] but also his wife and family,[207] as well as his officials.[208] In England Henry III's protection was extended by name to Queen Eleanor and the Lord Edward; it included also the rest of the king's children, his household, his realm, and his moveable property.[209] It was, in fact, usual for the protection to cover family, household, lands and moveable goods,[210] and in the case of a king, to cover his realm. A

---

[201] It would be impossible to cite every example. Urban IV, *Cameral Register*, 320, presents a typical grant. See Brundage, *op. cit.*, pp. 160 *et seq.*

[202] Cf. Innocent IV, *Register*, 2962.

[203] *Ibid.*, 7946, offers one example.

[204] The normal form in papal letters is similar to that in the decrees, "donec de ipsorum reditu vel obitu certissime cognoscatur integra maneant et quieta".

[205] See, for example, Innocent IV, *Register*, 6039, 6072, 6985 for protections granted to Henry III, and *Diplomatica Norvegica*, i, 24, 33, 47-8, concerning protections accorded to Hakon of Norway. Individual grants are too frequent to enumerate.

[206] Innocent IV, *Register*, 7946.

[207] *Ibid.*, 2218, 4664, 5437-8, 6147-8, 6469, 6985. See Brundage, *op. cit.*, pp. 165 *et seq.*

[208] Innocent IV, *Register*, 6440, for example.

[209] *Ibid.*, 6985.

[210] *Ibid.*, 6147 and del Giudice, i, xciv, for example.

protection conceded to Louis IX for his second venture extended to his kingdom, and the lands of all those accompanying him overseas.[211] Henry III, too, was granted special protection in each part of his realm—England, Ireland, Wales and Gascony,[212] and also in Bordeaux and Auch.[213] In the northern kingdoms crusading protection was granted in turn to the kings of Dacia,[214] Lithuania,[215] and Norway. Hakon was eager to pay any price for papal protection, his claim on the throne being shaky. He first assumed the cross in 1237 [216] and received the desired protection; when Hakon felt he could commute the vow without jeopardising his chances of retaining this protection, he did so, in 1241.[217] Later Hakon felt called upon once more to assume the cross for the Holy Land at the time of King Louis' first crusade and to receive a reiteration of the papal protection.[218] This vow in turn was commuted at the earliest safe opportunity, and once more Hakon retained his papal protection; [219] so, too, did Henry III after he had commuted his vow to Sicily. The papacy, was, in fact, lavish with protections to Charles of Anjou and his followers in the Sicilian venture. The territories which they should conquer were included in advance in the grant.[220]

The *crucesignati* were to be protected most specifically against being molested by creditors, or oppressed by usurers.[221] There were also measures taken by secular authorities to ensure that *crucesignati* were not molested for debt. St. Louis was particularly exigent in asserting his authority on this score.[222] The count of Poitiers also issued explicit instructions for the protection of poor *crucesignati* in his territories.[223] Matthew Paris more than hints that Henry III's

---

[211] Clement IV, *Register*, 467.

[212] Innocent IV, *Register*, 6985.

[213] *Ibid.*, 6072.

[214] *Ibid.*, 1089.

[215] *Ibid.*, 5437-8.

[216] Cf. P. Riant, *Expéditions et pèlerinages*, p. 343.

[217] *Diplomatica Norvegica*, i, No. 24; cf. Potthast, 11045.

[218] *Diplomatica Norvegica*, i, Nos 33; 35-36 (to the queen); 47-8.

[219] The case of Hakon presents a slight problem since he still seems to have been considered obliged by his vow in 1254 when Alexander IV offered him a commutation if he should go to the aid of Henry III in Sicily. Rymer, i, p. 549.

[220] del Giudice, i, xv.

[221] These are the two protections specified in the crusading decrees of 1215 and 1245. See Appendix A.

[222] Cf. *Les Établissements de St. Louis*, ed. P. Viollet, 4 vols, Paris, 1881-86, Vol IV, p. 32, and G. J. Campbell, "*The Attitude of the Monarchy towards the use of ecclesiastical censures*", *Speculum*, XXXV, 1960, p. 544.

[223] *Correspondance administrative*, Vol. II, 1639.

object in taking the cross was to save his financial situation which was far from promising.[224] Since many *crucesignati* had to borrow money to finance their venture overseas, it was not practicable to rule out their having recourse to Jews; the normal threat of ecclesiastical censure against those molesting *crucesignati* was of no avail against non-Christians. To overcome this, threats were issued against any Christian who should have any sort of intercourse with a Jew found guilty of extorting money from a *crucesignatus*.[225]

The protection included the prevention of forcible redemption, or commutation, of vows,[226] as well as any other sort of inhibition attempted against the fulfilment of vows.[227] How effective this last form of protection was in practice can be judged, perhaps, by the apparent willingness with which Innocent IV agreed to Henry III's request for a forcible deferment of the vows of English *crucesignati*. On the other hand Innocent IV did not allow Henry III to encroach on the prior rights of *crucesignati* who had been granted subsidies before the king assumed the cross but protected their rights unequivocally.[228] Yet another form of protection was that which assured the *crucesignatus* not only of the privilege of answering legal charges within his own diocese, but also of having revoked any judgments contrary to his privileges as a *crucesignatus*. This protection was indicated in general terms to Walter de Cantilupe in a letter from Innocent IV.[229] Later in the same year, 1247, the pope ordered the revocation of a judgment made against the viscount of Châteaudun, contrary to his privileges as a *crucesignatus*.[230] In 1254 Innocent IV also charged the bishop and chapter of Cambrai to inhibit sentences passed against crusaders who were reported to be dead, and whose protection had been claimed on that account to have expired.[231]

Certain cases recorded by the inquisitors of the count of Poitiers give some notion of the ways in which crusaders did actually sustain injuries, which involved troublesome litigation either when they returned, or on the part of their heirs. Arnold de Belvedere, a clerical

---

[224] v, p. 102. Matthew Paris purports to be stating what people thought.
[225] These were the ordinary regulations contained in any call to crusade from the Fourth Lateran Council onwards.
[226] Innocent IV, *Register*, 2644, 2960.
[227] *Ibid.*, 3384.
[228] Cf. *C.P.L.*, I, p. 264.
[229] Innocent IV, *Register*, 2959.
[230] *Ibid.*, 2871.
[231] *Ibid.*, 7348.

crucesignatus, was despoiled of his church by a fellow cleric, Hector, the son of Guy IV de Séverac, who, to that end, used lay force, and arms.[232] It is not altogether clear if Arnold was on crusade at the time of the spoliation, but his being a *crucesignatus* made the attack doubly reprehensible. Another enquiry was concerned with the claims of the heir of a crusader killed at Mansourah. This crusader's lands had been seized and held for £ 550 by the seneschal of Poitou. Peter d'Aleman, the nephew and heir, claimed that the land had come to his family as a grant of Richard I of England, free of all but military service.[233]

Conversely, not all papal letters about protections of *crucesignati* dealt with the need for enforcing the protection. A considerable number were devoted to stressing the invalidity of these protections in certain stated circumstances. Quite early during the preparations for King Louis' crusade, Innocent IV issued a warning to the legate, Eudes de Châteauroux, and the French hierarchy, not to allow *crucesignati* make their privileged status an excuse for committing crimes, for which they thought not to be prosecuted—"furta, homicidia, raptus mulierum, et alia detestanda".[234] Papal protection was not to be allowed to extend to the sheltering of such criminals from the full rigours of the law, though one gathers from the tone of the pope's letter that the *crucesignati* in question had been claiming immunity from criminal prosecution. Philippe de Beaumanoir states quite explicitly that the *crucesignatus* was not considered to be under ecclesiastical jurisdiction in all that pertained to prosecution for criminal behaviour.[235]

Recanted heretics who, after they had assumed the cross, lapsed once more into heresy, likewise invalidated the protection extended to them.[236] The journal of Eude Rigaud contains a record of a letter from Alexander IV concerning the usurpation by ecclesiastical authorities of matters pertaining to the secular jurisdiction of lay *crucesignati*. The ecclesiastical authorities had no power to impede the prosecution of such *crucesignati* for capital crimes.[237] This denial of papal protection extended also to scandalous cases of married

---

[232] *Enquêtes administrative*, Pièce 128 (428), p. 342.

[233] *Ibid.*, Pièce 23 (29), p. 99.

[234] Innocent IV, *Register*, 2230; cf. also, Potthast, 12342 and *Layettes*, iii, 3923.

[235] Cf. P. de Beaumanoir, *Les coutumes du Beauvoisis*, ed. Le Comte Beugnot, 2 vols, Paris, 1842, i, p. 160. See also, Brundage, *op. cit.*, pp. 171-172.

[236] Innocent IV, *Register*, 3866-8.

[237] *Journal des visites*, pp. 758-9.

clergy, including those guilty of bigamy.[238] There were further papal declarations on the score of criminous *crucesignati* by Gregory X,[239] Nicholas III,[240] and Martin IV.[241]

The lay authorities in France asserted their right to prosecute certain *crucesignati* for crimes committed prior to their taking the cross, and to obtain absolution from which they may even have been encouraged to assume the crusading cross. Martin IV granted this revocation of the protection extended to such *crucesignati*, and in addition he ordered that anyone who impeded their prosecution should be struck with ecclesiastical censure. One may justifiably question the wisdom of attracting recruits to crusading forces by this method, or even its ultimate efficacy in swelling numbers, while at the same time having some measure of sympathy for the dilemma in which both ecclesiastical and lay authorities found themselves on this score. Philip IV was still pursuing this subject in 1286 for he included a clause to this effect in the minute of instructions to his ambassador going to Rome to congratulate Honorius IV on his election. The wording of the minute is instructive.

> Item quod laici crucesignati ante tempus arrepti itineris nullatenus gaudeant privilegiis Apostolice Sedis aut legatorum ejus, vel immunitate sive privilegio fori, quod eis competere quidam dicunt, ex longa consuetudine vel usu, sed diffiniatur certum tempus, a die itineris arrepti, quo gaudeant privilegio vel indulgentia tali, contraria consuetudine non obstante.[242]

Another protection to which *crucesignati* seem mistakenly to have laid claim from their assumption of the cross, was that of not being forced to pay the imposts of secular authorities. John XXI made it clear that all such exemptions were invalid if the *crucesignatus* failed to set out in the general passage.[243] Nicholas III also had occasion to remind ecclesiastical authorities of the same thing.[244] Honorius IV was even more explicit in stating that protection against these secular imposts was not valid until the crusader had actually set off.[245] There

---

[238] It is to be remembered that bigamy included marriage with widows, and that, in any case, bigamous clerics lost their benefit of clergy.

[239] *Register*, 1017.

[240] *Register*, 171.

[241] *Register*, 51-2.

[242] G. Digard, *Philippe le Bel et le Saint-Siège*, 2 vols, Paris, 1936, Vol. II, Pièces justificatives ii, p. 219.

[243] *Register*, 68.

[244] *Register*, 172.

[245] *Register*, 398.

can be no doubt at all that *crucesignati*, like all tax payers, tried every means of evading payments, and claiming crusader privilege was as good a pretext as any other.

As might be expected, papal protection was accorded to crusading officials, both collectors and preachers. The unpopularity of papal collectors was as proverbial as that of any tax collector, and extant letters from those concerned with collecting crusade monies relating the hazards to which they were exposed in the course of their duties are numerous. Aliro, collector in the diocese of Salzburg, affords an example of the kind of physical dangers which might beset a collector or his officials.[246] Preaching also had its perils, as the *Collectio de Scandalis Ecclesiae* bears witness.[247] Caesarius of Heisterbach provides some tales of the sort of dangers encountered by crusade preachers, ranging from mere interruption [248] to attempted murder.[249]

It must not be supposed that protection of the rights and properties of *crucesignati* was undertaken only by ecclesiastical authorities. The *crucesignati* received safe conducts, and legal protection from secular authorities as well.[250] Some paid for their lands to be protected in their absence by a lay official.[251] The prior of la Peyrouse, Aveyron, having farmed out the revenues of his priory to raise money to go overseas, sought protection of the seneschal of Rodez for those who purchased the farm.[252] It would seem likely that these were typical cases. On the whole, however, it could still be assumed that the threat of ecclesiastical censure constituted a surer, and more universally recognised form of protection than that extended by lay authorities. As an inducement to taking the cross, and fulfilling a vow, papal protection participated in all the fluctuating confidence in the papacy's ability to formulate, and impose its system of sanctions against offenders. These sanctions, and the method of imposing them, will be discussed below.

(d) IMMUNITIES

The crusading decrees of 1215 and 1245 declared that all *crucesignati* should be deemed to enjoy immunity from all levies and tallages

---

[246] Honorius IV, *Register*, 5.
[247] § 6.
[248] *Dialogus Miraculorum*, Dist. IV, De Tentatione Cap. XI.
[249] *Ibid.*, Dist. XII, De Praemio Mortuorum Cap. XXIII.
[250] *Rymer*, i, pp. 447, 861-2, and *Correspondance administrative*, Vol. II, 1218.
[251] *Enquêtes administratives*, Pièce 4 (66), pp. 51-2.
[252] *Ibid.*, Pièce 128 (348), p. 331.

while they were in the service of the cross.[253] This immunity applied
to ecclesiastical levies and taxes, and must have been a cause of
embarrassment to collectors of crusading monies in a district where
there were a lot of *crucesignati*. It applied also to lay imposts, as can be
seen from the papal letters discussed above, setting the limit of this
immunity from the time of setting off.[254] Immunity from money
exactions was extended also to crusading officials, for the length of
their service. The more elaborate letters of appointment of papal
collectors from the time of Gregory X specified exemption from
the crusading tenth for the collector, and his deputies.[255] Preachers
were granted immunities such as those enjoyed by *crucesignati*,[256]
and this presumably excluded all but specifically crusading exactions,
since otherwise officials would have enjoyed a far more valuable
immunity than *crucesignati* who were not exempt from lay impositions
until they had set out.

In addition to immunity from money exactions, *crucesignati* also
enjoyed immunity from being struck by ecclesiastical censure. This
was not the same as the absolution which a man might receive on
assuming the cross, nor stand to receive for minor excommunication
incurred in the course of the venture.[257] The more important *crucesignatus* usually sought to be granted an immunity from being touched
by general letters of ecclesiastical censure which did not mention
him by name,[258] at least within his own territories.[259] Whether inside
or outside his own territory he could seek to avoid the effects of an
interdict by petitioning the pope to be allowed to have services in
his own private chapel.[260] There were special regulations governing
interdict during the time a crusade was being preached. The legate

---

[253] The actual phrase is, "... crucesignati, a collectis, vel a taliis, aliisque
gravaminibus sint immunes ..." See Appendix A. Such immunities were not
peculiar to crusading policy. Exemption was a particularly strong political
weapon used by the papacy throughout the feudal period to cultivate loyalty
to itself, and to strengthen its own power. There was also a well established
practice of feudal immunities. Gregory X's decree does not mention immunities.

[254] See above, pp. 168-9.

[255] *Register*, 571.

[256] Gregory X, *Register*, 913.

[257] Innocent IV, *Register*, 6414.

[258] See, for example, Innocent IV, *Register*, 7977.

[259] *Ibid.*, 8006.

[260] Jean de Joinville enjoyed such a privilege from Alexander IV, but this
was after he had returned from the Holy Land (Alexander IV, *Register*, 572).
This was a commonly sought privilege of the French royal family, and undoubtedly of many other important people.

and those deputised by him to preach, were permitted to suspend the interdict on a church where they chose to preach,[261] provided that they did not allow excommunicates to be present.[262]

It is impossible to assess the value of these immunities without first examining the instruments used to ensure their effective administration, and control. As in the case of protections, to which immunities were closely related, one must examine the sanctions which were invoked, and the way these sanctions were enforced before estimating the efficacy of the inducement to crusade.

(e) ECCLESIASTICAL CENSURE

(i) *Background*

As was the case with the financing of crusade, to contain the subject of ecclesiastical censure within the limits of a discussion of crusading policy is to leave aside, without ignoring, the greater part of the complex subject. By the thirteenth century such power of censure had long been used as an argument for, as well as a practical demonstration of, papal supremacy. Once incorporated as a political weapon into that long struggle, the system of ecclesiastical censure was open to all the disintegrating and corrupting influences to which the controversy gave rise. Thundering anathemas against a Henry IV, and bringing him to heel at Canossa, was a very different thing from the more modestly enunciated anathema which began the history of ecclesiastical censure in the Christian Church, and fell with such startling results on the heads of Ananias and his wife.[263]

The thirteenth century Church had moved beyond the more primitive notions implicit in the term *anathema*, and Gregory IX produced a settled formula with a distinction between major and minor excommunication.[264] While the latter involved deprivation of the rights to participate in acts of worship, and to administer or receive the sacraments, the former involved a total separation from the Church, and the body of the faithful. Bracton described this in terms of the legal disabilities which resulted at least as far as ecclesiastical courts were concerned.[265] Though an excommunicate

---

[261] Urban IV, *Register*, 385; Gregory X, *Register*, 522.

[262] Urban IV, *Register*, 385.

[263] *Acts*, v.

[264] *Decretum*, lib. V, tit. xxxix, De sententia excommunicationis Cap. LIX.

[265] Henrici de Bracton: *Legibus et consuetudinibus Angliae*, ed. Sir T. Twiss, 6 vols, Rolls Series, London, 1878-83, vi, f. 426 b.

could be brought to court, he could not sue, nor could he issue legally valid documents.[266] It was unlawful for anyone, even his relations, to pray, eat, or speak with him, either openly or in secret. It was thus by implication also unlawful to deal with an excommunicate in way of business.[267]

Interdict, the other chief form of ecclesiastical censure, while it deprived individuals, or localities, of the use of things spiritual, did not cut them off from communion with the Church, nor from the body of the faithful. Interdict did not extend to the last rites. It was not, therefore, considered so harsh a sentence as that of major excommunication,[268] nor did it produce the same drastic legal and social disabilities. Individual persons could be placed under interdict, but this was akin to minor excommunication.[269] It was much more common to proclaim an interdict on a certain region, or country. If the interdict were general, everyone was included, even visitors and non-residents, except by special dispensation. Sometimes the interdict was partial, and applied only to specified churches within an area. In some cases interdict was accompanied by a concurrent excommunication of specified persons. The whole notion of interdict, however, rested on a concept not expressly formulated before Innocent IV produced his *Apparatus*, namely that of the *persona ficta*.[270] Only so could individual moral responsibility be reconciled with corporate punishment. The specific form of interdict imposed on clerics, namely suspension, had a long history of development prior to the formulation given to it by Innocent III.[271] This sanction was more relevant to crusading policy than the severer clerical punishments of deposition and deprivation.[272]

---

[266] In practice, an example during the period under discussion was the nullification of the acts of Ezzelino di Romano (Innocent IV, *Register*, 7788). Letters of Pedro III of Aragon were also declared null; cf. Potthast, 22031.

[267] To mitigate the severity of this ruling on those innocent people who could not avoid communication with the guilty person, especially his wife and infant children, some necessary exceptions were made. See Innocent IV, *Apparatus*, V, tit. De sententia excommunicationis Cap. V in VI (Romano Ecclesia); cf. also St. Thomas, *S. T. Supp.*, Q 23 a 1-3.

[268] *Ibid.*, Q 22 a 5 ad 2.

[269] Cf. G. le Bras, *Institutions ecclésiastiques de la Chrétienté médiévale*, Première partie, Livres II à VI, Tournai, 1964 (Vol. 12 of *Histoire de l'Eglise*, ed. Fliche & Martin), p. 246, note 11.

[270] Cf. W. S. Holdsworth, *A History of English Law*, 16 vols, London, 1922-1966, Vol. III (5th ed.), p. 470, quoting O. Gierke, *Political Theories of the Middle Ages*.

[271] Cf. G. le Bras, *Institutions ecclésiastiques*, p. 249.

[272] There is one recorded example in the period under discussion of the de-

By the First Council of Lyons there were a number of fairly major obstacles to the general efficiency of ecclesiastical censure as a deterrent. In a unified, and delimited Christendom, it constituted the most possible form of universally valid, inter-national sanction. Like all instruments of government it depended on the probity and discretion of the officials responsible for administering it, and on the measure of co-operation elicited from those governed, but it depended also on a unanimous acceptance of the claims of the ruler to such supreme authority. On all scores ecclesiastical censure was beset by problems and weaknesses, and these affected the attempted uses of it in favour of crusade and its organisation.

On an administrative level the problem was twofold—a question of authority to impose, and a question of ultimate appeal in the face of resistance. The question of authority was again one involving definition of the power of the keys. In effect all ranks of ecclesiastics down to the level of parish priest claimed the power to excommunicate.[273] Aquinas clearly disagreed with this, but felt that the weight of practice allowed him to do no more than to suggest what he considered a more reasonable conclusion, namely that the power to excommunicate was enjoyed *ex officio* only by bishops and higher prelates; all others held the power by delegation from the law itself, or from an ecclesiastical superior.[274] This included officials such as legates, who, even if they were not priests, held jurisdiction.[275] Aquinas' solution here is consistent with his teaching about the power to grant indulgences.[276] The danger of a too subjective and light use of ecclesiastical censure arising from too widespread a power of imposition was by no means avoided. The Councils of 1215, 1245 and 1274 all enacted canons which give evidence of this.[277] These canons were meant to curb abuses which were destructive

---

position of a bishop for injuries done to *crucesignati*. This was the bishop of Trèves who was an opponent of William of Holland; cf. Ripoll, i, (Innocent IV) cclxxiii and cclxxiv, and Raynaldus, § 18, for the year 1252.

[273] Cf. Hostiensis, *Summa Aurea*, V, tit. De Sententia excommunicationis § 5 (Ne dum autem).

[274] *S. T. Supp.*, Q 22 a 1.

[275] *Ibid.*, Q 22 a 2.

[276] *Ibid.*, Q 26 a 1-3.

[277] (i) Canon 47 of the Fourth Lateran Council;
    (ii) Canon 12 of the first Council of Lyons (an expanded version of this canon issued later by Innocent IV is printed in Hefele-Leclercq, v, 2, pp. 1672-6);
    (iii) Canon 29 of the Second Council of Lyons.

of the efficacy of the Church's sanctions. The popes themselves were not without blame in this matter of being too ready to impose maximum penalties for what were often partisan motives.

Papal preoccupation with the need to win a victory over the Hohenstaufen, and then to consolidate the supposed gains of that victory, led to a fatally partisan spirit in the direction of ecclesiastical sanctions against all opponents of papal aims in this matter. Whereas appeal to the secular arm had always been the ultimate resort against those who resisted the moral force of censure, the thirteenth century saw the use of crusade as the last resort against papal enemies. Crusade became for Innocent IV and for many of his successors, the Church's own form of physical coercion, hallowed by connections with the Holy Land. Though at first indeliberate, this combination of partisan sanctions and partisan crusade effectively reduced the whole idea of crusade to the level of party politics, and just as effectively reduced the strength of ecclesiastical censure as a weapon against offenders. In this respect the pontificate of Martin IV marks the extreme development of a movement which, in its immediate effects, was fatal to the Crusader States. The registers of Martin IV are full of evidence of an almost pathological determination to turn all the instruments of papal policy to the benefit of the French party. Besides numerous letters concerned with sanctions against the Aragonese,[278] there is evidence of a constant diversion of crusading monies into the coffers of the anti-Aragonese faction.[279]

In addition to the damage thus done by the popes themselves, the canonists of the thirteenth century succeeded in further destroying the broad effectiveness of the system of ecclesiastical sanctions by postulating what is to us a ludicrously refined list of possible infractions of the law, all resulting in automatic excommunication.[280] When it is patently impossible for a man to know whether he has unwittingly infringed the law, then the law itself suffers a loss of credence; as it did here. Moreover, too refined and inflexible a system demands a compensatory code of dispensation from the rigours of the law. This in turn served to diminish the effectiveness of the system under discussion, the more especially since immunities from censure were as partisan a weapon as sanctions themselves.

---

[278] Martin IV, *Register*, 284, 309-10, 460-1, 467-70, 482-4, 490; Potthast, 22031-2, 22077, 22123, 22141.

[279] See Martin IV, *Register*, 457-8, and above, note 131, for example.

[280] Cf. Hostiensis, *Summa Aurea*, V, tit. De Sententia excommunicationis § 3 (Quis possit excommunicare).

(ii) *Applied to crucesignati*

Crucesignati were at once protected, and constrained, by ecclesiastical censure. They enjoyed all privileges and immunities under pain of censure against any who should molest them.[281] Where it was a question of preserving their immunity against the exactions of Jews, censure had to be applied obliquely. All Christians who should in any way communicate with Jews guilty of extorting money from *crucesignati* were liable to the penalty of excommunication.[282] The Jews themselves could be constrained only by the secular arm. There is a clause in the crusading decrees which gives some clue as to the nature of the real problem in imposing censures. This clause threatened with severe punishment all prelates who should have been found negligent in seeing justice done to *crucesignati* and their families.[283] Presumably this refers to prelates who were officially appointed to maintain crusading privileges and immunities, and presumably the severe punishment which threatened them was the same censure which they were negligent in imposing. Short of resorting to forms of coercion forbidden to ecclesiastics, there was no means of avoiding this kind of circularity. The specifically acceptable form of coercion in the thirteenth century, apart from invoking the secular arm, was to wage a crusade. Thus, for example, Innocent IV called for the preaching of a crusade not simply against an opponent like Frederick II but also against such as the duke of Bavaria who had ignored the excommunication imposed on him as a follower of Frederick II.[284] How dangerous this sort of use of crusade as a coercive force within Christendom was to the cause of crusade to the Holy Land has been clear throughout this discussion.

Besides being protected by ecclesiastical censure, *crucesignati* were constrained by it to fulfil their vows in the manner they had vowed to do. Their crusading immunity from ecclesiastical censure did not extend to breaches of crusading vows. *Crucesignati* who failed to set out at the appointed time automatically incurred (minor) excommunication. This applied to those who set out before the appointed time, as well as to those who were laggards;[285] it applied to those who

---

[281] Walter Giffard pronounced major excommunication against those who molested or impeded *crucesignati*, dccxxix.

[282] Appendix A, p. 192.

[283] See Appendix A, *loc. cit.*

[284] Innocent IV, *Register*, 4333. The duke was to take the cross against Frederick, as a sign of his repentance.

[285] See above, pp. 123-4, for example.

failed to redeem their vows [286] and to those who redeemed them for too little.[287] Laggards were absolved provided that they set out in the next general passage,[288] and defaulters in the matter of redemptions could obtain absolution by paying the deficit, and so making satisfaction.[289] It is as well to note in passing here that threats of deprivation of all privileges of both clerics and laymen were relatively common in the crusade against Frederick, in Germany,[290] in Sicily,[291] as well as in Italy and the Holy Land.[292] The Military Orders were similarly threatened.[293] One other offence committed by *crucesignati* called for excommunication, and that was participation in tourneys. This was not only contrary to the general prohibition, but it also placed the *crucesignatus* in imminent danger of being unable to fulfil his vow. The penalty entailed not a simple excommunication, but a prohibition of Christian burial, and of suffrages for the dead should the *crucesignatus* be killed.[294]

(iii) *Applied to officials*

Legates enjoyed all crusading immunities,[295] as well as the faculties to impose or lift ecclesiastical censure where this should seem in the best interest of the crusading venture.[296] Both the immunity, and the faculty to impose censure could be delegated to the legate's deputies.[297] These could, in fact, be co-opted under pain of censure.[298] Censure fell on all who placed obstacles in the way of preachers, or collectors.[299] The preacher could command an audience by threat of censure,[300] and he could raise an interdict on a church where he

---

[286] See above, Chapter Five, Section (d), pp. 118 ff.

[287] See above, *loc. cit.*

[288] See above, *loc. cit.*

[289] See above, *loc. cit.*

[290] Innocent IV, *Register*, 4572.

[291] *Ibid.*, 4681.

[292] *Ibid.*, 4107.

[293] *Ibid.*, 4107, 4711.

[294] Peckham, iii, dlxiv. Letter to the bishop of Bangor dated 3 July, 1284.

[295] See pp. 169-71, above.

[296] Typical of the faculties granted to legates were those enjoyed by Simon de Brie (see Urban IV, *Register*, 813-15, 818-36) and Aegidius, archbishop of Tyre (*Ibid.*, 373-392).

[297] *Ibid.*, 381, for example.

[298] *Ibid.*, 382, 386.

[299] This is the general concession in letters of instruction to preachers and collectors; see Innocent IV, *Register*, 6469; Gregory X, *Register*, 571.

[300] Innocent IV, *Register*, 6469; *Northern Registers*, xxxiii.

wished to preach,[301] provided that he did not admit excommunicates to the assembly.[302] Collectors stood in need of strong protection against bodily attack, or coercion exercised by rulers who were loath to allow the crusading collection out of their country.[303] There is something faintly pathetic about Nicholas III's grant to his collector for Hungary and Poland, Gerard of Modena, of the faculty to compel protection from local ecclesiastics and members of the Military Orders while he was conveying monies collected to Zagreb.[304] This constant resort to threat—and there are many more petty examples than Gerard of Modena, harrassed by wars and violence in the region through which he was travelling—shows clearly the extent to which the instrument had been devalued by over-use.

Collectors all too frequently had recourse to their powers of censure in dealing with defaults of payment. The normal threat was excommunication,[305] but they could have recourse to the secular arm.[306] Not uncommonly collectors too readily imposed sanctions, and merited a rebuke from higher authority. John of Darlington, working in conjunction with Master Arditio, caused something of a stir in England by his uncompromising methods with defaulters. The result was a complaint to Rome, and an investigation, after which the collectors were warned to be more moderate.[307] There is an entertaining sidelight on this affair in the register of John Peckham where the archbishop is seen at his most fussy, comforting and advising the prior of Canterbury, when the latter had incurred excommunication because of a delay granted by a deputy collector whose power to grant such a delay was denied by Arditio and John of Darlington.[308] Collectors themselves felt the weight of censure when they were detected in some fraud concerned with handing over the money they had collected. A collector for Scotland had managed to establish a lucrative business lending out the money at interest.[309] One gains the impression that payments were still haphazard enough

---

[301] Urban IV, *Register*, 385.

[302] *Ibid.*, 385.

[303] See above, pp. 156-7.

[304] *Register*, 131.

[305] See, for example, Gregory X, *Register*, 571; John XXI, *Register*, 13; and Martin IV, *Register*, 152-5, 157, 436.

[306] Martin IV, *Register*, 436, for example.

[307] *C.P.L.*, I, pp. 452-3.

[308] Peckham, i, xxii, li-lii.

[309] Martin IV, *Register*, 356.

for it to have been difficult to keep an exact account of the returns of any collector.[310]

(iv) *Other applications of sanctions*

To ensure a prevailingly peaceful atmosphere in the West, the crusading decrees reiterated the ban on tournaments, under pain of excommunication. This applied not only to *crucesignati*, but to everyone else as well. Lay authorities co-operated in this matter when it suited their purposes—Henry III feared the political implications of tourneys during his troubles with the barons, but Philip III of France certainly gave his sanction to a tournament for which Robert of Artois was fined £ 500 *tournois* in 1280,[311] since he had issued an edict in direct opposition to the pope's ban.[312] It is notable that Robert of Artois' fine was not made payable "in subsidium Terrae Sanctae".

One group of people who constituted a grave threat to the success of any crusade were designated by the crusading decrees as subject to censure should they jeopardise the crusade. They were the completely lawless crews of pirates and corsairs who ranged the Mediterranean menacing all ships. Because these pirates constituted such a danger, many *crucesignati* were deterred from setting out. To preclude this loss of personnel the Councils decreed that ecclesiastical censure should fall on the pirates, and anyone who should aid and abet them. One can scarcely believe that such measures would have been effective against these pirates.

More important for the success of the crusade were the efforts made by the popes to enforce a general peace during the time of the general passage. This desire for peace sprang partly from purely spiritual motives that the crusade might thereby be blessed, and partly from a realisation of the need to relieve men of the fear of what might happen in their absence from their own domains. Peace by coercion has never succeeded, more especially when the proposed coercion is moral rather than physical. Though the popes consistently pursued a policy of peace-making, and were untiring in their efforts, they had set too bad an example to be really convincing in their pleas for peace as their heartfelt concern. There was plenty of evidence pouring into Europe in the last twenty years before the fall of Acre

---

[310] Cf. W. E. Lunt, *Financial Relations*, especially Chapters VI, VIII and XII.
[311] Nicholas III, *Register*, 621.
[312] *Ibid.*, 301, 746.

of the disastrous situation in the Holy Land,[313] but one cannot be wholly convinced that the major consideration behind all the papal pleas for peace was the detrimental effect of Western quarrels on crusade to the Holy Land.[314] This was indeed the constant refrain in papal letters calling for peace between France and Aragon, and threatening each side with the strongest censures, but the argument seems to be stereotyped, and to lack any vital consciousness of the urgent needs of the East. Ecclesiastical censure and crusade alike suffered great loss of prestige from their partial, and largely unsuccessful, application by the papacy to the last mentioned quarrel. Christendom had, as it were, supped full of the horrors of diverted crusade in the years immediately preceding the fall of Acre, so that what should have been the greatest disaster of the century, left their withers quite unwrung.

The popes also endeavoured to bring moral pressure to bear on the merchants who carried on trade with the Saracens. These merchants, the majority of whom were Italians, supplied the Saracens with much of their most necessary war equipment: ships, or the materials for building them, and arms, or material for their manufacture. All such trade with the enemy was prohibited for a period of four years from the time of the general passage under pain of censure.[315] Any who ignored the prohibition were to be publicly anathematised in the churches of the maritime cities on Sundays and feast days. If they were captured, they were to be reduced to slavery, their goods confiscated and they were to be sentenced to pay a heavy fine in aid of the Holy Land. All Christians were similarly forbidden to send, or go in, ships to Saracen ports for four years. This was a double measure to prevent the Moslems from having the use of such ships either by trade or capture, against the crusaders, and to ensure a plentiful supply of ships for transporting the Christians going on crusade.

---

[313] See above, p. 155, footnote 140.

[314] Examples are too numerous to quote. Every papal letter which touched on the prolonged quarrels between France and Spain pleaded the Holy Land as a prime reason for peace, just as papal control of Sicily was urged as desirable on account of the strategic benefit to crusade.

[315] See Appendix A. This same prohibition was placed on trade in materials of war with the northern pagans (Innocent IV, *Register*, 4619) and with the Greeks (*Ibid.*, 73). One might add that these merchants also supplied the Saracens with slaves, not stopping at selling Christians to the infidel (Innocent IV, *Register*, 2122). The prohibition was extended to six years by the Council of 1274.

Even a cursory study of the history of the commercial relations between the Italian city states and the non-Christian East will show how supremely unlikely ecclesiastical censure was to take effect in these circumstances.[316] The subject is far from being a simple one, and cannot be given a detailed treatment here, since to do so would be to go beyond the scope of the discussion. Ideally, from the point of view of crusading policy, there needed to be a permanent ban on all such trade, but the popes had to be realistic about tolerating trade in times when there was no general passage. This was so, not only because of the close connections between papal finances and the merchants of the city states, but because the Crusader States themselves depended to a considerable extent on good trade relations with the Moslems. To some extent Innocent IV showed his realisation of this by granting dispensations for trade with the Moslems,[317] and even by revoking the prohibition placed by Eudes de Châteauroux on such trade in the period immediately following Louis IX's crusade. He merely added the proviso that nothing must be done inimical to the faith.[318] Trading ties were too strong to be suspended by threat of ecclesiastical censure, and, in any case, the city states were somewhat inured to the rigours of excommunication and interdict by reason of the too frequent imposition of such punishments.[319]

The situation in the Crusader States was a complex one so far as the rivalries of the Italian merchants were concerned, and the use of ecclesiastical censures had failed to produce any amelioration of the quarrels. The war of St. Saba, and its aftermath of even more bitter quarrels, as well as the history of independent treaties between the Italian cities and the Moslems, especially in the final years of the Crusader Kingdom,[320] display with painful clarity the futility of threatening these single-minded merchants with moral force. As well might the papacy, like Cnut, have threatened the advancing waves

---

[316] The subject is treated at length in such works as W. Heyd, *Histoire du Commerce du Levant au Moyen-Age*, 2 vols, Amsterdam, 1959 (Repr.), especially Vol. I, Deuxième période.

[317] Cf. *Register*, 621, 3731, 6586, for example.

[318] *Register*, 6586.

[319] Cf. G. le Bras, *Institutions ecclésiastiques*, p. 248, note 30.

[320] Typical of such treaties was that made by the Genoese with the Sultan of Egypt on the very eve of the fall of Acre in May, 1290, and notified in Röhricht, *Regesta*, No. 1503. See also Nos 1218, 1222. A number are also to be found in L. de Mas Latrie, *Traités de paix et de commerce et documents divers concernant les relations des Chrétiens avec les Arabes*, Paris, 1866, *passim*.

though, unlike Cnut, the popes had no notion that these waves were not theirs to command.

The system of ecclesiastical censure had begun seriously to break down in the thirteenth century. It is not surprising, perhaps, that the popes themselves were slow to recognise this fact.[321] How far the papacy failed to grasp the significance, not only of the growing secularisation within Christendom but of the increasing size, and impact of the non-Christian world on the West, is best to be seen in the tone which the popes adopted in their dealings with non-Christian rulers. Though Innocent IV insisted on the rights of pagan rulers within their own territories unless they engaged in offensive warfare against Christians,[322] he could yet threaten the king of Morocco with the same kind of oblique censure as was practised against the Jews within Christendom. If he did not meet Christian demands the king was to be deprived of the services of Christians.[323] Elsewhere in his correspondence Innocent IV attempted to exercise the same sort of moral authority over the Tartars and even over the Moslems. Inability such as this to distinguish between the possible and the impossible left the papacy incapable of meeting the growing crisis of authority with a vigorous rethinking of the forms and methods of ecclesiastical censure.[324] This in turn reacted unfavourably on crusade since the imposition of sanctions played such an increasingly integral part in the organisation and conduct of crusade in inverse proportion to the decreasing spontaneity of the movement.

---

[321] Cf. for example, G. J. Campbell, "The Attitude of the Monarchy towards the use of ecclesiastical censures in the reign of Saint Louis", *Speculum*, XXXV, 1960, pp. 535-555; J. R. Strayer, "The Laicization of French and English Society in the thirteenth century", *Speculum*, XV, 1940, pp. 76-86; and the more discursive work of G. de Lagarde, *La Naissance de l'esprit laïque au déclin du moyen âge*, 6 vols in 4, Vienna, 1934, and Paris, 1942-1946.

[322] Innocent IV, *Apparatus*, III, tit. De voto Cap. VIII (Quod super).

[323] Innocent IV, *Register*, 5173.

[324] There is an obvious parallel in the crisis of authority in the post-Vatican II Church.

CONCLUSIONS

Mystical notion and military venture: in this polarity lies the explanation of the disintegration of crusade in the thirteenth century, and the failure of the West to come adequately to the aid of the Crusader States in their last crisis before the fall of Acre. Papal crusading policy as it had evolved by the Fourth Lateran Council was aimed at meeting the practical demands of military organisation, but had taken its essential shape from the notion of crusade as the most meritorious of all works of penance, worthy of an uniquely valuable reward. What was seen as characteristic of crusade was not the engagement in war, but the assumption of the cross which bespoke the holiness of that war. This wearing of the cross was the outward symbol of the more profound spiritual realities—the crusading vow and the plenary indulgence.

Papal crusading policy in the thirteenth century, however, failed to come to terms with two major developments which closely concerned its proper functioning. The one was doctrinal, and related to the use of indulgences as an instrument of that policy; the other was the rapid increase in the tendency of the papacy to use crusade for causes other than that of the Holy Land. The first of these affected the coherence of crusading policy by setting up inner tensions between the spiritual purpose of the instrument and its practical application in the context of crusade. Divergence of crusading goal created an external pressure which largely contributed to the disintegration of the whole framework of traditional crusading policy.

Hugh of St. Cher's formulation of the notion of the treasury of the Church freed indulgence from the restraint imposed by the belief that satisfaction had to be supplied by the ranks of the Church militant. Though plenary indulgence was thus released from the necessity of a close tie with as arduous a work of penance as crusade, no corresponding adjustment was made in the official practice of requiring plenary indulgences to be associated with crusade to the Holy Land, by being dependent on the penitent's having taken a crusading vow. Adjustments therefore, when they took place, did so within the framework of crusading policy itself, thus threatening its integrity from inside. A plenary indulgence still depended on a crusading vow, but the vow no longer bespoke a positive intention of going on crusade to the Holy Land.

From this the logical development within the framework of the traditional policy was the introduction of conditional vows, and the multiplication of commutations and redemption of crusading vows. In terms of the desirability of making such a powerful means of salvation accessible to all the faithful instead of to the few capable of actually going on crusade this was justifiable; so also was it justifiable in terms of the resultant increase in financial support for crusade. What constituted its destructive force was the strain which it imposed on the credibility of the traditional notion of crusade, since little or no distinction was made in practice in the spiritual reward meted out to the *crucesignatus* who actually fulfilled his vow, and the one who had never intended to do so.

The extension of plenary indulgence to those who contributed to crusade other than by personal service set up a tension between the two chief practical aims of crusading policy, recruitment and financial support. The elimination of personal service as a *sine qua non* of full remission of sins, while it opened up fresh channels of financial aid, militated against effective recruitment. Moreover there was an obvious danger which the thirteenth century papacy did not avoid. The desire to raise money, being of more immediate concern than the general aim of saving souls, often caused a simple but destructive inversion in the practical application of the redemption of crusading vows. The indulgence tended to become a reward directly granted for a monetary contribution instead of being the reward for a crusading vow which (incidentally) had been redeemed by a monetary contribution. Critics were quick to attack this appearance of simony in the seemingly direct use of vows and indulgences for financial ends. Recruitment suffered from a devaluation of the actual effort of going on crusade by its simple equation with a direct financial contribution.

Diversionary crusades were not new in the thirteenth century; what was new was the intensity of papal involvement. Crusades such as those against the Slavs were largely a matter of self help by gaining papal countenance for the manipulation of the conveniently justificatory instruments of crusading policy. Crusades against the Hohenstaufen, or in support of the Angevin cause in Sicily, had more than papal countenance, they had active and enthusiastic papal support and encouragement.

The organisational forms of traditional crusade were not only well developed and relatively efficient, but they lent a frequently spurious justification to papal preoccupation with its own political struggles, and blinded even the popes to the disintegration which would inevitably result from a persistent turning aside of those forms from their acknowledged goal. It was fatal to the credibility of crusade to the Holy Land to involve the instruments connected with it in partisan struggles. This was the more total a destruction because spiritual instruments such as vows and indulgences were seen to be subordinated not simply to the material ends of the papacy, but to the desires of papal allies who themselves used the papacy to their own ends.

Though there is no exact parallel between the subordination of the spiritual instruments of crusading policy to the desire to ensure maximum financial support, and the gradual diminution in effectiveness of the measures to secure the material wellbeing of *crucesignati* by privileges, protections and immunities, it is not by coincidence that these trends were contemporaneous. Loss of the credibility of crusade was only one aspect of the transformation of society which was in train in the latter part of the thirteenth century, and which was characterised by attitudes inimical to that species of papal supremacy which the popes had prostituted crusade to assert.

While it is true to conclude that traditional crusade lost its credibility as a Christian endeavour by reason of the diversionary uses made of the instruments of papal crusading policy, and that these diversionary uses were made all the more easy by developments in the doctrine of indulgence which allowed a more flexible application of this instrument of policy, one must not lose sight of the fact that traditional crusade was no longer the answer to the problems of the Crusader States. In its final years of existence, what the mainland Kingdom needed above all was financial support, and a permanent, tractable and dependable mercenary army. Only so could the Eastern Franks be sure of help which would not act independently, and in ignorance of the local political and military problems. Thoughtful contemporaries recognised this fact, and in recognising it, tacitly accepted the abandonment of traditional forms of crusade. Though the popes were capable of diverting the instruments of crusading policy from the Holy Land, they were incapable of divorcing crusade from the mystique which had grown to surround it.

In the West the spiritual forms in crusading policy had been subordinated to the material needs of political crusade, and had then been made to subserve the purposes of secular rulers. When looking at the East, the West was prevented by the mystical in the concept of crusade from a proper recognition of the most practical needs. The fall of Acre found the traditional forms of crusade incapable of inspiring the effort that was needed to meet the challenge, while the very tradition of those forms prevented the evolution of a new type of crusade. Thus in the West military venture reduced crusade to political expediency, in the East mystical notion reduced it to military impracticality.

Because the decrees of 1215 and 1245 so closely resemble one another, it has been possible to present them as parallel texts. The decree of 1274 presents far more problems than its predecessors, though it is heavily reliant upon them. These problems have been discussed by H. Finke to whom we owe the discovery and publication of the unique extant version of what is generally known as the "Constitutiones pro zelo fidei", and is generally accepted as being in substance the crusading decree issued by the second Council of Lyons.[1] The "Constitutiones pro zelo fidei", because it contains so many differing clauses from the earlier decrees will be included, not as a parallel text, but as a separate entity. Those clauses which bear striking resemblance to the earlier decrees are shown within square brackets.

Ad liberandum (Fourth Lateran Council, 1215)
Afflicti corde (First Council of Lyons, 1245)
Zelus fidei (Second Council of Lyons, 1274)

CRUSADING DECREES OF 1215 AND 1245

IV Lateran Council, 1215 [2(a)]
Ad liberandam terram sanctam de manibus impiorum ardenti desiderio aspirantes,

de prudentum virorum consilio, qui plene noverant circumstantias temporum et locorum,
sacro approbante concilio, diffinimus:
ut ita Cruce signati se præparent, quod in Kalendas Junii sequentis post proximum, omnes qui disposuerunt transire per mare,

conveniant in regnum Siciliæ: alii, sicut oportuerit et decuerit, apud Brundusium, et alii apud Messanam, et partes utrobique vicinas:

First Council of Lyons, 1245 [2(b)]
Afflicti corde pro deplorandis Terræ Sanctæ periculis, sed pro istis præcipue, quæ constitutis in ipsa fidelibus noscuntur noviter accidisse, ad liberandam ipsam, Deo propitio, de manibus impiorum totis affectibus aspiramus;

diffinientes sacro approbante concilio,
ut ita crucesignati se præparent, quod oportuno tempore universis insinuando fidelibus per prædicatores nostrosque nuntios speciales, omnes qui disposuerint transfretare, in locis idoneis ad hoc conveniant,

---

[1] See H. Finke: *Konzilienstudien zur Geschichte des 13 Jahrhunderts*, Münster, 1891, pp. 1-15. The text is printed on pp. 113-117.

[2] The texts are taken from (a) Mansi, Vol. XXII, cols 1058-67 and (b) Matthew Paris, iv, pp. 456-62. Words italicised in these texts, and in that taken from Finke, are dubious readings which, however, follow the printed sources. They may, therefore, be scribal or printing errors, but, with one exception (*interdum/ interdictum*) do not alter the sense.

ubi et nos personaliter, Domino annuente, disposuimus tunc adesse, quatenus nostro consilio et auxilio, exercitus Christianus salubriter ordinetur, cum benedictione Divina et apostolica profecturus.

Ad eumdem quoque terminum se studeant praeparare qui proposuerunt per terram proficisci: significaturi hoc interim nobis, ut eis ad consilium et auxilium legatum idoneum de nostro latere concedamus.

de quibus in ejusdem terrae subsidium cum divina et Apostolica benedictione procedant.

Sacerdotes autem, et alii clerici, qui fuerint in exercitu Christiano, tam subditi quam praelati, orationi et exhortationi diligenter insistant:
docentes eos verbo pariter et exemplo, ut timorem et amorem semper habeant Divinum ante oculos, ne quid dicant aut faciant quod Divinam majestatem offendat.

Et si aliquando lapsi fuerint in peccatum, per veram poenitentiam mox resurgant, gerentes humilitatem cordis et corporis,
et tam in victu, quam in vestitu mediocritatem servantes,
dissensiones et aemulationes omnino vitando, rancore ac livore a se penitus relegatis:
ut sic spiritalibus et materialibus armis muniti, adversus hostes fidei securius praelientur;
non de sua praesumentes potentia, sed de Divina virtute sperantes.

Sacerdotes autem et alii clerici, qui fuerint in exercitu Christiano, tam subditi quam praelati, orationi ac exhortationi diligenter insistant;
docentes eos verbo pariter et exemplo, ut timorem et amorem Domini semper habeant ante oculos, ne quid dicant aut faciant, quod aeterni Regis majestatem offendat.

Et si aliquando lapsi fuerint in peccatum, per veram poenitentiam mox resurgant; gerentes humilitatem cordis et corporis,
et tam in victu quam in vestitu mediocritatem servantes,
dissensiones et aemulationes omnino vitando, rancore ac livore a se penitus relegatis;
ut sic spiritualibus et materialibus armis muniti adversus hostes fidei securius praelientur,
non de sua praesumentes potentia, sed divina virtute sperantes.

Nobilis quidem et potentes exercitus ac omnes divitiis abundantes piis praelatorum monitis inducantur ut intuitu Crucifixi, pro Quo crucis signaculum assumpserunt, ab expensis inutilibus et superfluis, sed ab illis praecipue quae fiunt in comessationibus et conviviis, abstinentes, eas convertant in personarum illarum subsidium, per quas Dei negotium valeat prosperari;
et eis propter hoc juxta praelatorum ipsorum providentiam peccatorum suorum indulgentia tribuatur.

Ipsis autem clericis indulgemus, ut
beneficia sua integra percipiant per
triennium, ac si essent in ecclesiis
residentes;
et, si necesse fuerit, ea per idem
tempus pignori valeant obligare.
Ne igitur hoc sanctum propositum
impediri vel retardari contingat,
universis ecclesiarum prælatis
districte præcipimus, ut singuli per
loca sua illos qui signum crucis
disposuerunt resumere,
ac tam ipsos, quam alios cruce-
signatos, et quos adhuc signare
contigerit, ad reddendum vota sua
Domino diligenter moneant et inducant,
et, si necesse fuerit, per excommunicationis in personas,
et interdicti sententias in terras
eorum,
omni tergiversatione cessante,
compellant:
illis dumtaxat exceptis, quibus tale
impedimentum occurrerit, propter
quod, secundum sedis apostolicæ
providentiam, votum eorum com-
mutari debeat merito vel differri.
Ad hæc, ne quid in negotio Jesu
Christi de contingentibus omittatur:
volumus et mandamus ut patriarchæ, archiepiscopi, episcopi,
abbates, et alii qui curam obtinent
animarum, studiose proponant sibi
commissis verbum crucis,
obsecrantes per Patrem, et Filium,
et Spiritum sanctum, unum solum
verum æternum Deum,
reges, duces, principes, marchiones,
comites, et barones, aliosque magnates,
necnon communiones civitatum,
villarum, oppidorum,
ut qui personaliter non accesserint
in subsidium terræ sanctæ,
competentem conferant numerum
bellatorum, cum expensis ad

Prædictis autem clericis indulgemus,
ut beneficia sua integre percipiant
per triennium, ac si essent in
ecclesiis residentes.
Et si necesse fuerit, ea per idem
tempus pignori valeant obligare.
Ne igitur hoc sanctum propositum
impediri vel retardari contingat,
universis ecclesiarum prælatis
districte præcipimus, ut singuli per
loca sua illos qui signum crucis
deposuerunt resumere,
ac tam ipsos quam alios cruce-
signatos et quos adhuc signari
contigerit ad reddendum Domino
vota sua dilligenter moneant ac
inducant;
et si necesse fuerit, per excommunicationis in personas
et interdicti sententias in terras
ipsorum,
omni tergiversatione cessante,
compellant.

Ad hæc, ne quid in negotio Jesu
Christi de contingentibus omittatur,
volumus et mandamus, ut patriarchæ, archiepiscopi, episcopi,
abbates, et alii qui curam optinent
animarum, studiose proponant commissis sibi populis verbum crucis;
obsecrantes per Patrem et Filium
et Spiritum Sanctum, unum solum
verum æternum Deum,
reges, duces, principes, marchiones,
comites et barones, aliosque magnates,
necnon communia civitatum, villarum, et oppidorum,
ut qui personaliter non accesserint,
in subsidium Terræ Sanctæ
competentem conferant numerum
bellatorum cum expensis ad

triennium necessariis, secundum
proprias facultates,
in remissionem peccatorum suorum,

prout in generalibus litteris est
expressum, et ad majorem cautelam
etiam inferius exprimetur.

Hujus remissionis volumus esse
participes, non solum eos qui naves
proprias exhibebunt,
sed etiam illos qui propter hoc
opus naves studuerint fabricare.
Renuentibus autem, si qui forte tam
ingrati fuerint Domino Deo nostro,
ex parte apostolica firmiter protes-
tentur, ut sciant se super hoc nobis
in novissimo districti examinis die
coram tremendo judice respon-
suros: prius tamen considerantes,
qua conscientia, quave securitate
comparere poterunt coram unigenito Dei Filio Jesu Christo, cui
omnia Pater dedit in manus, si ei pro
peccatoribus crucifixo servire renuerint in hoc negotio quasi proprie
sibi proprio, cujus munere vivunt, cujus beneficio sustentantur,
quinetiam cujus sanguine sunt redempti.
Ne vero in humeros hominum onera
gravia et importabilia imponere
videamur, quæ digito nostro movere
nolimus, similis illis qui dicunt
utique, sed non faciunt: ecce nos
de his, quæ ultra necessaria, et
moderatas expensas potuimus reser-
vare, triginta millia librarum in hoc
opus concedimus et donamus:
præter navigium, quod crucesignatis de Urbe, atque vicinis partibus
conferimus: assignaturi nihilo minus
ad hoc ipsum tria millia marcarum
argenti, quæ apud nos de quo-
rundam fidelium eleemosynis
remanserunt: aliis in necessitates
et utilitates prædictæ terræ, per manus
felicis memoriæ Alberici Hierosolymitani patriarchæ, ac magis-

triennium necessariis, secundum
proprias facultates,
in remissionem suorum peccaminum;
prout in generalibus literis, quas
pridem per orbem terræ miserimus,
est expressum, et ad majorem
cautelam inferius exprimetur.
Hujus igitur remissionis volumus
esse participes non solum eos qui
ad hoc naves proprias exhibebunt,
sed illos etiam qui propter hoc
opus naves studuerint fabricare.
Renuentibus autem, si qui forte tam
ingrati fuerint Domino Deo nostro,
ex parte Apostolica firmiter protes-
tentur, ut se sciant super hoc nobis
in novissimo districti examinis die
coram tremendo Judice respon-
suros; prius tamen considerantes,
qua conscientia quave securitate
comparere potuerunt coram Dei
Filio unigenito Jesu Christo, Cui
omnia dedit Pater in manus, si Ei
pro peccatoribus crucifixo servire
renuerint in hoc negotio; quasi
proprie sibi proprio, Cujus munere
vivunt, Cujus beneficio sustentantur, quinetiam Cujus sanguine sunt
redempti.

trorum templi et hospitalis fideliter distributis.	
Cupientes autem alios ecclesiarum prælatos, nec non clerico universos, et in merito et in præmio habere participes et consortes:	Cæterum
ex communi concilii approbatione statuimus, ut omnes omnino clerici, tam subditi, quam prælati, vigesimam partem ecclesiasticorum proventuum usque ad triennium conferant in subsidium terræ sanctæ,	ex communi concilii approbatione statuimus, ut omnes omnino clerici, tam subditi quam prælati, vicesimam ecclesiasticorum proventuum usque ad triennium integre conferant ad subsidium Terræ Sanctæ,
per manus eorum qui ad hoc apostolica fuerint providentia ordinati:	per manus eorum, qui ad hoc Apostolica fuerint providentia ordinati;
quibusdam dumtaxat religiosis exceptis,	quibusdam tamen religiosis exceptis,
ab hac prætaxatione merito eximendis,	ab hac præstatione merito eximendis,
illis similiter qui assumpto vel assumendo crucis signaculo sunt personaliter profecturi.	illisque similiter qui, assumpto vel assumendo crucis signaculo, sint personaliter profecturi.
Nos autem, et fratres nostri sanctæ Romanæ ecclesiæ cardinales, plenarie decimam persolvemus:	Nos autem et fratres nostri sanctæ Romanæ ecclesiæ cardinales plenarie decimam persolvemus.
sciantque se omnes ad hoc fideliter observandum per excommunicationis sententiam obligatos:	Sciantque omnes, se ad hoc fideliter observandum per excommunicationis sententiam obligatos;
ita quod illi, qui super hoc fraudem scienter commiserint, sententiam excommunicationis incurrant.	ita quod illi qui fraudem super hoc scienter commiserint, sententiam excommunicationis incurrant.
Sane quia justo judicio, cœlestis imperatoris obsequiis inhærentes speciali decet prærogativa gaudere, cum tempus proficiscendi annum excedat in modico,	Sane quia justo judicio cælestis Imperatoris obsequiis inhærentes speciali decet prærogativa gaudere,
crucesignati, a collectis, vel a talliis, aliisque gravaminibus sint immunes,	crucesignati a collectis et talliis aliisque gravaminibus sint immunes;
quorum personas et bona post crucem assumptam, sub beati Petri et nostra protectione suscepimus:	quorum personas et bona post crucem assumptam sub beati Petri et nostra protectione suscipimus;
statuentes, ut sub archiepiscoporum, episcoporum, ac omnium prælatorum ecclesiæ defensione consistant:	statuentes, ut sub archiepiscoporum et episcoporum ac omnium prælatorum ecclesiæ Dei defensione consistant,
propriis nihilo minus protectoribus ad hoc specialiter deputandis,	propriis nihilominus protectoribus ad hoc specialiter deputandis,
ita ut, donec de ipsorum obitu vel	ita ut donec de ipsorum reditu vel

reditu certissime cognoscatur, integra maneant et quieta:

et si quisquam contra præsumpserit, per censuram ecclesiasticam compescatur.

Si qui vero proficiscentium illuc ad præstandas usuras juramento tenentur adstricti: creditores eorum, ut remittant eis præstitum juramentum, et ab usurarum exactione desistant,

eadem præcipimus districtione compelli.

Quod si quisquam creditorem eos ad solutionem coegerit usurarum: eum ad restitutionem earum simili cogi animadversione mandamus.

Judæos vero ad remittendas usuras per sæcularem compelli præcipimus potestatem:

et donec illas remiserint, ab universis Christi fidelibus per excommunicationis sententiam eis omnino communio denegetur.

His autem, qui Judæis debita solvere nequeunt in præsenti, sic principes sæculares utili dilatione provideant:

quod post iter arreptum, usquequo de ipsorum obitu vel reditu certissime cognoscatur, usurarum incommoda non incurrant:

compulsis Judæis proventus pignorum, quos interim ipsi perceperint, in sortem, expensis deductis necessariis, computare:

cum hujusmodi beneficium non multum videatur habere dispendii, quod solutionem sic prorogat, quod debitum non absorbet.

Porro ecclesiarum prælati, qui in exhibenda justitia crucesignatis et eorum familiis negligentes extiterint, sciant se graviter puniendos.

Ceterum quia cursarii et piratæ *ninium* impediunt subsidium terræ sanctæ, capiendo et expoliando

obitu certissime cognoscatur, integra maneant et quieta.

Et si quisquam contra præsumpserit, censura ecclesiastica compescatur.

Si qui vero proficiscentium illuc ad præstandas usuras juramento teneantur astricti, creditores eorum, ut remittant eis præstitum juramentum et ab usurarum exactione desistant,

eadem præcipimus districtione compelli.

Quod si quisquam creditorum eos coegerit ad solutionem usurarum, eum ad restitutionem earum simili cogi animadversione mandamus.

Judæos vero ad remittendas usuras per sæcularem compelli præcipimus potestatem;

et donec illas remiserint, ab universis Christi fidelibus per excommunicationis sententiam eis omnino communio denegetur.

His qui Judæis debita solvere nequeunt in præsenti, sic principes sæculares utili dilatione provideant,

quod post iter arreptum, usquequo de ipsorum reditu vel obitu certissime cognoscatur, usurarum incommoda non incurrant,

compulsis Judæis proventus pignorum, quos interim ipsi perceperint, in sortem, expensis deductis necessariis, computare;

cum hujusmodi beneficium non multum videatur habere dispendii, quia sic solutionem prorogat, quod debitum non absorbet.

Porro ecclesiarum prælati, qui in exhibenda justitia crucesignatis et eorum familiis negligentes extiterint, sciant se graviter puniendos.

Cæterum quia cursarii et piratæ nimis impediunt subsidium Terræ Sanctæ, capiendo et spoliando

transeuntes ad illam, et redeuntes ab ipsa:
nos speciales adjutores et fautores eorum excommunicationis vinculo innodamus, sub interminatione anathematis inhibentes, ne quis cum eis scienter communicet aliquo venditionis vel emptionis contractu;

et injungentes rectoribus civitatum et locorum suorum, ut eos ab hac iniquitate revocent et compescant:

alioquin, quia nolle perturbare perversos, nihil aliud est quam fovere, nec caret scurpulo societatis occultæ, qui manifesto facinori desinit obviare: in persona et terras eorum per ecclesiarum prælatos severitatem ecclesiasticam volumus et præcipimus exerceri.
Excommunicamus præterea et anathematizamus illos falsos et impios Christianos, qui contra ipsum Christum et populum Christianum Saracenis arma, ferrum, et lignamina deferunt galearum:

eos etiam qui galeas eis vendunt, vel naves, quique in piraticis Saracenorum navibus curam gubernationis exercent,
vel in machinis
aut quibuslibet aliis aliquod eis impendunt consilium vel auxilium, in dispendium terræ sanctæ,
ipsarum rerum suarum privatione mulctari,
et capientium servos fore censemus.
Præcipientes ut per omnes urbes maritimas, diebus Dominicis et festivis hujusmodi sententia innovetur,
et talibus gremium non aperiatur ecclesiæ, nisi totum, quod ex substantia tam damnata perceperint,

transeuntes ad illam et redeuntes ab ipsa,
nos eos et principales adjutores et fautores eorum excommunicationis vinculo innodamus, sub interminatione anathematis inhibentes, ne quis cum eis scienter communicet in aliquo venditionis vel emptionis contractu,
et injungentes rectoribus civitatum et locorum suorum, ut eos ab hac inquietatione revocent et compescant;

alioquin, quia nolle perturbare perversos nihil aliud est quam fovere, nec caret scrupulo societatis occultæ qui manifesto facinori desinit obviare, in personas et terras eorum per ecclesiarum prælatos severitatem ecclesiasticam volumus et præcipimus exerceri.
Excommunicamus præterea et anathematizamus illos falsos et impios Christianos, qui contra ipsum Christum et populum Christianum Sarracenis arma, ferrum, et lignamina deferunt galearum;

eos etiam, qui eis galeas vendunt vel naves; quique in piraticis Sarracenorum navibus curam gubernationis exercent
vel in machinis
[aut] quibuslibet aliis aliquid eis impendunt consilium vel auxilium, in dispendium Terræ Sanctæ
Ipsosque rerum suarum privatione mulctari
et capientium fore servos censemus;
præcipientes ut per omnes urbes maritimas diebus Dominicis et festivis hujusmodi sententia publice innovetur,
et talibus gremium non aperiatur ecclesiæ; nisi totum quod commercio tam dampnato percepe-

et tantumdem de sua in subsidium prædictæ terræ transmiserunt:

ut æquo judicio, in quo deliquerint, puniantur.
Quod si forte solvendo non fuerint, alias sic reatus talium castigetur, quod in pœna ipsorum aliis interdicatur audacia similia præsumendi.
Prohibemus insuper omnibus Christianis, et sub anathemate interdicimus, ne in terras Saracenorum, qui partes orientales inhabitant, usque ad quadriennium transmittant aut transeant naves suas:
ut per hoc volentibus transfretare in subsidium terræ sanctæ major navigii copia præparetur,
et Saracenis prædictis subtrahatur auxilium, quod eis consuevit ex hoc non modicum provenire.
Licet autem torneamenta sint in diversis conciliis sub certa pœna generaliter interdicta: quia tamen hoc tempore, crucis negotium per ea plurimum impeditur, nos illa sub pœna excommunicationis firmiter prohibemus usque ad triennium exerceri.
Quia vero ad hoc negotium exequendum est permaxime necessarium ut principes populi Christiani adinvicem pacem observent: sancta universali synodo suadente statuimus, ut saltem per quadriennium in toto orbe Christiano servetur pax generaliter,
ita quod per ecclesiarum prælatos, discordantes reducantur ad plenam pacem aut firmam treugam inviolabiliter observandam:
et qui acquiescere forte contempserint, per excommunicationem in personas,
et *interdum* in terras arctissime compellantur:
nisi tanta fuerit injuriarum malitia,

rint, et tantundem de suo, in subsidium Terræ Sanctæ transmiserunt;
ut æquo judicio, in quo deliquerint, puniantur.
Quod si forte solvendo non fuerint, sic alias reatus talium castigetur, quod in pœna ipsorum interdicatur audacia similia præsumendi.
Prohibemus insuper omnibus Christianis et sub anathemate interdicimus, ne in terram Sarracenorum, qui partes orientales inhabitant, usque ad quadriennium transmittant aut transvehant naves suas;
ut per has transfretare volentibus in subsidium Terræ Sanctæ major navigii copia præparetur,
et Sarracenis prædictis subtrahatur auxilium, quod eis consuevit ex hoc non modicum provenire.
Licet autem torneamenta sint in diversis conciliis sub certa pœna generaliter interdicta, quia tamen hoc tempore crucis negotium per ea plurimum impeditur, nos illa sub pœna excommunicationis firmiter prohibemus usque ad triennium exerceri.
Quia vero ad hoc negotium exequendum permaxime necessarium est, ut principes et populi Christiani ad invicem pacem observent, sancta universali sinodo suadente, statuimus, ut saltem per quadriennium in toto orbe Christiano pax generaliter observetur;
ita ut per ecclesiarum prælatos discordantes reducantur ad plenam pacem aut firmam treugam, inviolabiliter observandam.
Et qui forte adquiescere contempserint, per excommunicationem in personas
et interdictum in terras arctissime compellantur;
nisi tanta fuerit injuriarum malitia,

quod ipsi tali non debeant pace gaudere.

Quod si forte censuram ecclesiasticam vilipenderint, potuerunt non immerito formidare, ne per authoritatem ecclesiæ, circa eos, tanquam perturbatores negotii crucifixi, sæcularis potentia inducatur.

Nos igitur omnipotentis Dei misericordia, et beatorum apostolorum Petri et Pauli authoritate confisi, ex illa, quam nobis, licet indignis, Deus ligandi atque solvendi contulit, potestate,

omnibus qui laborem propriis personis subierint et expensis, plenam suorum peccaminum, de quibus veraciter fuerint corde contriti et ore confessi, veniam indulgemus,

et in retributione justorum salutis æternæ pollicemur augmentum.

Eis autem qui non in personis propriis illuc accesserint, sed in suis dumtaxat expensis juxta facultatem et qualitatem suam viros idoneos destinarint;

et illis similiter, qui licet in alienis expensis, in propriis tamen personis accesserint,

plenam suorum concedimus veniam peccatorum.

Hujus quoque remissionis volumus et concedimus esse participes, juxta qualitatem subsidii,

et devotionis affectum,

omnes qui ad subventionem ipsius terræ de bonis suis congrue ministrabunt,

aut consilium et auxilium impenderint opportunum.

Omnibus etiam pie proficiscentibus in hoc opere in communi universalis Synodus omnium beneficiorum suorum suffragium impartitur, ut eis digne proficiat ad salutem.

Amen.

quod ipsi tali non debeant pace gaudere.

Quod si forte censuram ecclesiasticam vilipendant, poterunt non immerito formidare, ne per auctoritatem ecclesiæ contra eos, tanquam perturbatores Crucifixi negotii, sæcularis potentia inducatur.

Nos ergo, de omnipotentis Dei misericordia et beatorum Apostolorum Petri et Pauli auctoritate confisi, ex illa, quam nobis, licet indignis, Deus ligandi atque solvendi contulit potestate,

omnibus, qui laborem istum in propriis personis subierint et expensis, plenam suorum peccaminum, de quibus fuerint veraciter corde contriti et ore confessi, veniam indulgemus,

et in retributione justorum salutis æternæ pollicemur augmentum.

Eis autem qui non in personis propriis illuc accesserint, sed in suis duntaxat expensis juxta facultatem et qualitatem suam viros idoneos destinaverint,

et illis similiter, qui licet in alienis expensis, in propriis tamen personis accesserint,

plenam suorum concedimus veniam peccatorum.

Hujus quoque remissionis volumus et concedimus esse participes, juxta quantitatem subsidii

et devotionis affectum,

omnes qui ad subventionem illius terræ de bonis suis congrue ministrabunt,

aut circa praedicta consilium aut auxilium impenderint oportunum.

Omnibus etiam pie proficientibus in hoc opere, sancta et universalis sinodus orationum et beneficiorum suorum suffragium impertitur, ut eis digne proficiat ad salutem.

Amen.

CONSTITUTIONES PRO ZELO FIDEI

Incipiunt constitutiones concilii Lugdunensis edita a Gregorio papa anno domini Mo. CCo. LXXIIIIo.

Zelus fidei, fervor devotionis et compassionis pietas excitare debent corda fidelium, ut omnes, qui christiano nomine gloriantur, de sui contumelia redemptoris tacti dolore cordis intrinsecus potenter et patenter exurgant ad Terre Sancte presidium et adiutorium cause Dei. Quis vere fidei luce perfusus pia mente revolvens eximia beneficia, que salvator noster in Terra Sancta humano generi contulit, devotione non ferveat et karitate non ardeat et illi Terre Sancte, que funiculus est hereditatis dominice, ex intimis visceribus et toto mentis non compatiatur affectu? Cuius cor non emolliet ad compassionem ipsius, a creatore nostro in terra ipsa tot iudicia caritatis ostensa? Set heu proh dolor! ipsa terra, in qua dominus salutem nostram dignatus est operari et quam, ut hominem commertio mortis sue redimeret, proprio sanguine consecravit, per nefandissimos hostes nominis christiani plasfemos et perfidos Sarracenos audacia secuta occupata diutius et temere detinetur et intrepide devastatur. Trucidatur in ea inhumaniter populus christianus et ad maiorem contumeliam creatoris et iniuriam et dolorem omnium, qui fidem catholicam profitentur: ubi sit Deus Christianorum? improperant multis opprobriis christicolas insultantes. Ista et alia, que circa hoc nec animus sufficit plene concipere vel lingua referre, accenderunt cor nostrum et excitaverunt animum, ut nos, qui in transmarinis partibus premissa non tantum audivimus set oculis nostris aspeximus et manus nostre contractaverunt, exurgentes, quantum se possibilitatis nostre conatus extendit, ad vindicandam iniuriam crucifixi, illorum interveniente auxilio, quos ad hoc zelus fidei et devotionis accendet. Et quia prefate terre liberatio tangere debet omnes, qui fidem katholicam profitentur, concilium mandavimus evocari, ut deliberatione habita in eodem cum prelatis, regibus et principibus et aliis prudentibus viris illa statueremus et ordinaremus in Christo, per que dicte terre liberatio proveniret, et nichilominus reducerentur Grecorum populi ad ecclesie unitatem, qui superba cervice nitentes scindere quodammodo inconsutilem domini tunicam se a sedis apostolice devotione ac obedientia subtraxerunt, et reformarentur mores, qui sunt peccatis exigentibus in clero et populo quam plurimum deformati, illo in premissis omnibus nostros actus et consilia dirigente, cui nichil est inpossibile, set, cum vult, res difficiles faciles facit et aspera sua virtute complanans prava dirigit in directa. Sane ut premissa perduci possent liberius ad effectum, attendentes guerrarum pericula et viarum discrimina, que subire poterant illi, quos ad idem concilium duximus evocandos, nobis et nostris fratribus non parcentes set appetentes labores spontaneos, ut quietem aliis preparare possemus, ad civitatem Lugdunensem, in qua credebamus ad concilium evocatos minori honere laborum et expensarum convenire, accessimus cum fratribus nostris et curia nostra periculis variis ac diversis incommoditatibus et multis discriminibus pregravati, ubi convenientibus tam per se quam per procuratores ydoneos universis ad ipsum concilium evocatis frequenter de prefate terre subsidio deliberavimus cum eisdem, ut, quod debuerint, ad vindictam iniurie

salvatoris accensi pro ipsius terre succursu vias excogitantes laudabiles
probata dederunt consilia et discreta. Nos autem auditis eorum consiliis,
ipsorum voluntates et affectus laudabiles, quos ostendunt de terre liberatione
predicte merito conmendamus. [Set ne in humeros hominum onera gravia
et importabilia imponere videamur, que digito nostro movere nolimus,]
incipientes a nobis ipsis, qui profitemur nos omnia, que habemus, possidere
[ab unigenito Dei filio Ihesu Christo, cuius munere vivimus, cuius beneficio
sustentamur, quin etiam cuius sanguine redempti sumus, nos et fratres
nostri sancte Romane ecclesie cardinales plenarie] usque ad VI annos
continuos [de omnibus reditibus, fructibus et proventibus nostris ecclesiasticis pro predicte terre subsidio decimam persolvemus, ap(p)robante
hoc sacro concilio, statuentes et ordinantes] quod usque ad predictos VI
annos ab instanti festo nativitatis beati Johannis Baptiste proximo continue
numerandos [ab omnibus personis ecclesiasticis, quacunque dignitate
prefulgeant] seu cuiuscunque pre(e)minentie, conditionis vel ordinis aut
status religionis vel ordinis, quibus et eorum alicui nulla *priviligia* vel
indulgentias sub quacunque verborum forma vel expressione concessa
volumus suffragari set ea, que ad hoc penitus revocamus, de omnibus
reditibus, fructibus et proventibus ecclesiasticis anni cuiuslibet terminis
infra scriptis, medietas scilicet in festo nativitatis domini et alia medietas
in festo beati Johannis Baptiste integre sine diminutione qualibet decima
persolvatur. Ut ei, cuius negotium agitur, reverentia debita in se ac sanctis
suis et precipue in virgine gloriosa, quorum in his et aliis suffragio utimur,
servetur attentius, cuiusque plenior terre subventio predicte, constitutionem
felicis recordationis Gregorii pape predecessoris nostri contra plasfemos
editam precipimus inviolabiliter observari, penamque pecuniariam in ipsa
statutam per potestates locorum, in quibus plasfemia committitur, ceteros-
que, qui inibi iurisdictionem temporalem exercent coactione, si necesse
fuerit, per diocesanos et aliorum locorum ordinarios ad exhibenda inte-
graliter exigi et dicti subsidii collectoribus assignari in idem subsidium
convertenda. Confessoribus insuper ex parte ordinaria vel ex privilegio
confessiones audientibus districte mandamus, ut confitentibus sibi suggerant
et iniungant, quod de pecunia predicta eidem terre plenariam satisfactionem
inpendant. Inducant etiam confitentes ultimas voluntates, quod in testa-
mentis suis pro modo facultatum suarum aliquid de bonis suis pro subsidio
Terre Sancte relinquant. In singulis nichilominus ecclesiis truncum con-
cavum poni precipimus tribus clavibus consignatum, prima penes 'epi-
scopum, secunda penes ecclesie sacerdotem, tertia penes aliquem religiosum
laicum conservandis, et in eo fideles quilibet, iuxta quod dominus eorum
mentibus inspiraverit, suas elemosinas ponere in remissionem suorum
peccaminum moneantur et in ipsis ecclesiis semel in ebdomade pro remis-
sione huiusmodi peccatorum et presertim offerentium elemosinas certa
die, quam tum sacerdos pronunciet populo, missa publice decantetur.
Preter hec ut Terre Sancte plenius succurratur, exortamur et suadere inten-
dimus monitis et exortationibus reges et principes, marchiones, comites
et barones, potestates, capitaneos et alios quoscunque terrarum duces,
ut ordinetur in terris suis cuiuslibet iurisdictioni eorum subiectis, quod a
singulis fidelibus unus denarius ad valorem Turonensis vel unius Sterlingi

iuxta consuetudinem vel condictionem regionis et alia modica sine cuiuscunque gravamine in remissionem peccaminum iniungentes annis singulis
in ipsius terre subsidium persolvatur, ut, sicut nullus excusare se potest,
quin teneatur compati statui miserabili Terre Sancte, sic nec aliquis excutia-
tur subsidio nec a merito excludatur. Etiam ne, quod provide ordinatum
est de predicte terre subsidio, impediri contingat fraude vel malicia vel
ingenio alicuius excommunicamus et anathematizamus omnes et singulos,
qui scienter impedimentum prestiterint directe vel indirecte, publice vel
occulte, quominus prestentur decime, sicut superius est expressum, in
predicte terre subsidium. [Ceterum quia cursarii et pirate nimium impediunt
capiendo et spoliando transeuntes ad illam et redeuntes de illa, nos eos
et principales adiutores et fautores eorum excommunicationis vinculo
innodamus, sub interminatione anathematis inhibentes, ne quis cum eis
communicet scienter in aliquo contractu venditionis vel emptionis. Iniun-
gimus etiam rectoribus civitatum et locorum, ut eos ab iniquitate revocent
et compescant, alioquin in terra ipsorum per ecclesiarum prelatos severitatem ecclesiasticam volumus exerceri. Excommunicamus preterea et
anathematizamus eos falsos et impios Christianos, qui contra Christum et
populum christianum Sarracenis arma et ferrum, quibus Christianos
inpugnant, et lignamina galearum et aliorum vasorum navigalium deferunt,
et eos etiam qui galeas eis vendunt vel naves, per que in piraticis Sarracenorum navibus curam gubernationis exercent, vel in machinis aut
quibuslibet aliis aliquod eis impendunt consilium vel auxilium in Christianorum dispendium, specialiter Terre Sancte, ipsos rerum suarum privatione
mulctari et capientium servos fieri censemus. Precipientes, ut per omnes
urbes maritimas diebus dominicis et festivis huiusmodi sententia publice
innovetur et talibus ecclesie gremium non aperiatur nisi totum, quod de
commercio tam dampnato perceperunt et tantumdem de suo in subsidium
Terre Sancte transmittant, ut equo iudicio, in quo delinquunt, puniantur.
Quod si forte solvendo non fuerint, sic alias reatus talium castigetur,
quod in pena ipsorum aliis interdicatur audacia similia presumendi. Prohibemus insuper omnibus Christianis et sub anathemate interdicimus,
ne in terris Sarracenorum, qui partes orientales inhabitant, usque ad VI
annos transmeant aut transvehant naves suas, ut per hoc volentibus transfretare in subsidium Terre Sancte maior copia navigii preparetur et Sarracenis subtrahatur auxilium, quod eis consuevit ex hoc non modicum
provenire. Et quia ad hoc negotium prosequendum permaxime est necessarium, ut principes et populi christiani ad invicem pacem observent,
hac sancta universali synodo approbante statuimus, ut in toto orbe inter
christianos pax generaliter observetur, ita quod per ecclesiarum prelatos
discordantes ducantur ad plenam concordiam sive pacem (aut) ad firmam
treugam per VI annos inviolabiliter observandam. Et qui acquiescere forte
contempserint, per excommunicationis sententiam in personas et interdictum in terras arctissime compellantur, nisi tanta fuerit iniuriatorum
malicia, quod tali non debeant pace gaudere. *Qud* si forte censuram ecclesiasticam vilipenderint, poterunt non inmerito formidare, ne per auctoritatem ecclesie contra eos tamquam perturbatores negotii crucifixi secularis
potencia inducatur. Nos igitur de omnipotentis Dei misericordia et bea-

torum Petri et Pauli auctoritate confisi ex illa, quam nobis licet *indingnis* Deus ligandi atque solvendi contulit, potestate, omnibus, qui transfretandi pro subsidio Terre Sancte in propriis personis laborem subierint et in expensis, plenam suorum peccaminum, de quibus veraciter fuerint corde contriti et ore confessi, veniam indulgemus et retributionem iustorum, salutis eterne pollicemur augmentum. Eis autem, qui non in propriis personis illic accesserint, set in suis dumtaxat expensis iuxta facultatem et qualitatem suam viros ydoneos destinaverint et illis similiter, qui licet in alienis expensis, in propriis tamen personis accesserint, plenam suorum concedimus veniam peccatorum. *Hiiusmodi* quoque remissionis volumus et concedimus esse participes iuxta qualitatem subsidii et devotionis affectum omnes, qui ad subventionem ipsius terre de bonis suis congrue ministrabunt, aut circa predicta consilium et auxilium inpenderint oportunum nec non omnes illos, qui pro subsidio Terre Sancte naves proprias exhibebunt aut eos, qui propter hoc opus naves studuerint fabricare; omnibus etiam pie profitentibus in hoc opere pia et sancta universalis synodus orationum et beneficiorum suffragium impertitur, ut eis digne proficiat ad salutem.]

Non nobis set damus gloriam domino et honorem et ipsi gratias reddimus, quod ad tam sacrum concilium patriarcharum, archiepiscoporum, episcoporum, primatum, abbatum, priorum, prepositorum, decanorum, archidiaconorum et aliorum ecclesiarum prelatorum tam per se quam per procuratores ydoneos nec non capitulorum, collegiorum, conventuum, procuratorum, advocatorum copiosa multitudo convenit. Sane licet pro felici prosecutione tanti negotii esset eorum consilium oportunum et ipsorum tamquam filiorum dilectorum presencia delectemur et quodammodo spirituali gaudio affluamus circa illos, tamen eorum propter varia incommoda, que ipsorum multitudo et copiositas ingerit, ne pre turba nimia se diucius conprimant et eorum absencia ipsis et ipsorum ecclesiis posset esse dampnosa, quadam prouida pietate commoti de fratrum nostrorum consilio super hoc salubriter providere decrevimus, ut sic gravaminibus occurratur, quod prosecutio huius negotii, quod ferventi spiritu et sollicitudine indefessa persequimur, nullatenus derogetur. Omnes igitur patriarchas, primates, archiepiscopos, episcopos, abbates, priores, per nos nominatim et specialiter evocatos, sic remanere decrevimus, ut ante diffinitum concilium absque nostra speciali licentia non discedant. Ceteris vero abbatibus et prioribus non mitratis et aliis abbatibus et prioribus, qui per nos non fuerant nominati et specialiter evocati, nec non prepositis, decanis, archidiaconis et aliis ecclesiarum prelatis ac quorumlibet prelatorum, capitulorum, collegiorum et conventuum procuratoribus, recedendi Dei gratia et benedictione nostra clementer licentiam impertimur, mandantes, ut omnes taliter recedentes primitus, prout infra scribitur, procuratores sufficientes dimittant ad suscipienda nostra mandata et ea, que in presencia nostra concilio ordinata sunt et in futurum actore Domino contigeri(n)t ordinari. Mandamus scilicet, (ut) de regno Francie taliter recedentes IIII, de regno Alamanie IIII, de regnis Yspaniarum IIII, de regno Anglie IIII, de regno Scotie unum, de regno Datie unum, de regno Boemie unum etc, de ducatu Polonie unum, procuratores sufficientes dimittant.

APPENDIX B

LITURGICAL CEREMONY OF CONFERRING THE CROSS

The interest in this ceremonial lies precisely in the fact that the concentration was on the assumption of the external symbol, the cross. There was no public emission of vows as in the ceremony of religious profession. There the emission of the vow was the externalisation of the inward intention of dedication to God; the wearing of symbolic garb was purely secondary to the emission of the vow. For the crusader the *votum itineris* was never publicly expressed in words which made it specific, but solely in the action of assuming the cross, a symbolic and not a specifying action in the manner of a religious vow. Thus, while the religious vow was an expressed and specified intention, the *votum itineris* of the crusader remained an unspecified inward intention. The prayers assume the intention of the recipient, but this is nowhere solemnly expressed. What might also be noted is that the modern liturgical ceremony of conferring a cross is concerned with missionaries.

De b[e]n[e]dictione et i[m]positione crucis profiscentibus in subsidiu[m] et defensionem fidei christiane seu recuperatione[m] terre sa[n]cte.[1]

Profecturus in subsidium et defensionem fidei christiane seu recuperatione[m] terre sancte genuflectit ante pontifice[m]: coram quo unus ministrorum tenet cruce[m] benedicendam illi i[m]ponenda[m]. Tu[m] po[n]tifex stans sine mitra dicit sup[er] crucem.
V. Adiutoriu[m] n[ost]r[u]m in no[m]i[n]e d[omi]ni.
R. Qui fecit celu[m] et terra[m].
V. D[omi]n[u]s vobiscum.
R. Et cum spiritu tuo.
Oremus.

Omnipote[n]s deus: q[ui] crucis signu[m] p[re]cioso filii tui sanguine dedicasti quiq[u]e p[er] eande[m] cruce[m] filii tui d[omi]ni nostri iesu christi mundum redimere voluisti: et p[er] virtutem eiusdem venerabilis crucis: humanu[m] genus ab antiqui hostis cyrographo liberasti: te suppliciter exoramus: vt digneris ha[n]c cruce[m] paterna pietate bene+dicere: et celeste[m] ei virtute[m] et gr[ati]am i[m]partiri: vt q[ui]cu[m]q[ue] eam in passionis et crucis vnigeniti tui signu[m] ad tutelam corp[or]is et a[n]i[m]e sup[er] se gestauerit: celestis gratie plenitudine in ea et munimen: valeat tue b[e]n[e]dictionis accipere: et que[m]admodu[m] virga[m] aaro[n] ad rebelliu[m] p[er]fidia[m] repellenda[m] b[e]n[e]dixisti: ita et hoc signu[m] tua dextera b[e]n[e]+dic: et co[n]tra o[mn]es diabolicas fraudes: virtute[m] ei tue defensionis i[m]pendas: vt portantibus illud a[n]i[m]e pariter et

---

[1] The text is taken from *Pontificale secundum Ritum sacrosancte Romano ecclesie,* 1520.

corporis prosperitate[m] co[n]ferat salutarem: et sp[irit]ualia in eis dona multiplicet. Per eunde[m] christum d[omi]n[u]m n[ost]r[u]m. R. Ame[n].

(Marginal rubric) Pontifex aspergit cruce[m] aqua b[e]n[e]dicta et eum q[ui] ea[m] recipit et dicit orationem

Deinde po[n]tifex asp[er]git cruce[m] ipsa[m] aq[ua] b[e]n[e]dicta et sup[er] receptur[um] ipsam dicit
Orem[us] Domine iesu christe fili dei viui: q[ui] es verus et o[mn]ipote[n]s deus: sple[n]dor et imago p[at]ris et vita eterna: qui tuis discipulis asseruisti: vt q[ui]cunq[ue] vult post te venire semetipsu[m] abneget: et suam cruce[m] tolle[n]s: te sequat[ur]: qu[ae]sum[us] i[m]me[n]sam cleme[n]tia[m] tua[m] vt hu[n]c famulum tuu[m] qui iuxta verbu[m] tuu[m] seip[su]m abnegare: sua[m]q[ue] cruce[m] tollere: et te sequi: ac co[n]tra inimicos n[ost]ros pro salute populi tui electi properare et pugnare desiderat: semp[er] et vbiq[ue] protegas: ac a periculis o[mn]ibus eruas: et a vi[n]culo peccator[um] absoluas: acceptu[m]q[ue] votu[m] ad effectum deducas optatum. Tu d[omi]ne qui es via: veritas et vita: et in te sp[er]antiu[m] fortitudo: ei[us] iter bene disponas: et prospera cu[n]cta concedas: vt inter presentis seculi angustias: tuo semp[er] auxilio gubernetur. Mitte ei d[omi]ne angelu[m] tuu[m] raphaelem: qui thobie comes fuit in itinere suo: eiusq[ue] patre[m] a corp[or]is cecitate liberauit: et in eundo et redeu[n]do fit ei defensor[um] co[n]tra o[mn]es visibiles et invisibiles hostis insidias: et omne[m] me[n]tis et corp[or]is ab eo cecitate[m] repellat: qui cu[m] deo p[at]re et sp[irit]u sa[n]cto viuis et regnas deus: per o[mn]ia secula seculor[um]. R. Ame[n].

(Marginal rubric) Po[n]tifex impo[n]it illi cruce[m] dice[n]s Accipe etc.

Tum po[n]tifex‹sedens accepta mitra:›[2] imponit illi crucem dicens. Accipe signu[m] crucis. In no[m]i[n]e patris et filii et sp[irit]us sancti in figura[m] crucis passionis et mortis christi: ad tui corporis et a[n]i[m]e defensione[m]: vt diuine bonitatis gr[ati]a post iter expletu[m] saluus et eme[n]dat[us] ad nos [3] valeas remeare. Per christum dominu[m] nostru[m]

(Marginal rubric) Po[n]tifex asp[er]git signatu[m] aq[ua] b[e]n[e]dicta q[ui] genuflexus osculat[ur] manum pontificis.

Demu[m] pontifex aspergit crucesignatum aqua benedicta. Qui genuflexus osculatur manum pontificis et discedit.

---

[2] These three words have been supplied from J. Gretser, *De Cruce Christi*, 3 vols, Ingolstadt, 1600-05, Vol. III, Book 2, pp. 6-7.
[3] Gretser reads, more probably, *tuos*.

BIBLIOGRAPHY

(i) MISCELLANEOUS COLLECTIONS

Acta imperii inedita Saeculi XIII, ed. E. Winkelmann, 2 vols, Innsbruck, 1880-85.

Actenstücke zur Geschichte des Deutschen Reiches unter den Königen Rudolf I und Albricht I, ed. F. Kaltenbrunner, Vienna, 1889.

Bullarium Franciscanum Romanorum Pontificum, ed. J. H. Sbaralea, 3 vols, Rome, 1759-65; *Supplementum*, Rome, 1780.

Bullarium Ordinis FF. Praedicatorum, Tomus primus 1215-1280, ed. T. Ripoll, Rome, 1729.

Calendar of Entries in the Papal Registers relating to Great Britain and Ireland, Papal Letters, Vol. I, A.D. 1198-1304, ed. W. H. Bliss, London, 1893.

Chansons. *Les chansons de croisade avec leur mélodies*, ed. J. Bédier (and P. Aubry), Paris, 1909.

Corpus Iuris Canonici, Pars Secunda, Decretalium Collectiones, ed. A. Friedberg. Editio Lipsiensis Secunda post Aemilio Ludovici Richteri, Leipzig, 1879-81.

Diplomatarium Norvegicum, ed. C. A. Lange & C. R. Unger, 5 vols, Christiania, 1849-60.

Diplomatarium Suecanum, ed. J. G. Liljegren (& others), 6 vols, Stockholm, 1829-1946, Vol. I, 817-1285, Vol. II, 1286-1310. Appendix, *Acta Pontificum Svecica*, ed. L. M. Bååth, 2 vols, Stockholm, 1936-42, Vol. I, *Acta Cameralia*, 1062-1370.

Foedera, Conventiones, Literae, ex cujuscunque generis Acta Publica, inter reges Anglia et alios etc., ed. T. Rymer, 16 vols, London, 1704-15.

Gesta Dei per Francos, sive Orientalium Expeditionum et Regni Francorum Hierosolimitani Historia, ed. J. Bongars, 2 vols in 1, Hanover, 1611.

Histoire des ducs et des comtes de Champagne, ed. H. d'Arbois de Jubainville, 7 vols in 8; Vol. IV, 1181-1285, Vols V and VI, Catalogue des actes des comtes de Champagne, Paris, 1859-69.

Historical Papers and Letters from the Northern Registers, ed. J. Raine, Rolls Series, London, 1873.

Layettes du Trésor des Chartes, ed. J. Teulet & J. de Laborde, 3 vols, Paris, 1863-75.

Monumenta Germaniae Historica, ed. G. H. Pertz, 32 vols, Hanover [Vols 30/2: Leipzig; Vol. 32 Hanover and Leipzig], 1826-1934.

Olim, *Les Olim ou Registres des arrêts rendus par la cour du roi sous les règnes de Saint Louis, de Philippe le Hardi, de Philippe le Bel, de Louis le Hutin et de Philippe le Long*, ed. Le Comte Beugnot, 2 vols (Collection de Documents inédits sur l'histoire de France), Paris, 1839-44.

Poesie Provenzali Storiche relative all'Italia, ed. V. de Bartholomaeis, 2 vols (Fonti per la Storia d'Italia), Rome, 1931.

Privilèges accordés à la couronne de France par le Saint-Siège, ed. A. Tardif (Collection de Documents inèdits sur l'histoire de France, 1ière série, histoire politique), Paris, 1855.

Recueil des historiens des croisades, ed. Académie des Inscriptions et Belles-Lettres, Paris, 1841-1906.
   Historiens occidentaux, 5 vols;

Historiens orientaux, 5 vols;
Documents arméniens, 2 vols;
Lois. Les Assises de Jérusalem, 2 vols.
Recueil des historiens des Galles et de la France, Vol. XX, *La Première livraison des monuments des règnes de Saint Louis, de Philippe le Hardi, de Philippe le Bel, de Louis X, de Philippe V et de Charles V, 1226-1328*, ed. MM. Daunou et Naudet, Paris, 1840.
Vol. XXI, *La deuxième livraison...*, ed. MM. Guigniaut et de Wailly, Paris, 1855.
Regesta Imperii V, 1198-1272, ed. J. F. Böhmer, J. Ficker & E. Winkelmann, 2 vols, Innsbruck, 1879-92.
Regesta Imperii VI, 1246-1313, ed. J. F. Böhmer & O. Redlich, 2 vols, Stuttgart, 1844 and Innsbruck, 1898.
Regesta pontificum Romanorum, 1195-1303, ed. A. Potthast, 2 vols, Berlin, 1873-5.
Regesta Regni Hierosolymitani, 1097-1291, ed. R. Röhricht, Innsbruck, 1893; *Additamentum*, Innsbruck, 1904.
Regesten. *Die Regesten der Erzbischöfe und des Domkapitels von Salzburg, 1247-1343*, ed. F. Martin, 2 vols in 1, Salzburg, 1926-1934.
Sacrorum Conciliorum nova, et amplissima collectio, 31 vols, ed. J. D. Mansi, Florence & Venice, 1759-98.
Sinica Franciscana, ed. A. van den Wyngaert, O.F.M., Vol. I, Itinera et relationes fratrum Minorum Saeculi XIII et XIV, Florence, 1929.
Tabulae Ordinis Theutonici, ed. E. Strehlke, Berlin, 1869.
Urkunden zur Alteren Handels- und Staatsgeschichte der Republik Venedig, ed. G. L. F. Tafel & G. M. Thomas, 3 vols (Vols XII-XIV of Fontes Rerum Austriacarum — *Diplomataria et Acta*), Vol. III, 1256-1299, Vienna, 1857.
Vetera Monumenta hibernorum et Scotorum Historiam Illustrantia, ed. A. Theiner, Rome, 1864.

(ii) INDIVIDUAL SOURCES

Albéric de Trois Fontaines, *Chronicon*, ed. MM. Guigniaut et de Wailly (*Recueil des historiens des Galles et de la France*, XXI), Paris, 1855.
Albert, St., *Opera Omnia*, ed. A. Borgnet, 38 vols, Paris, 1890-99, Vols 29-30, *Commentarii in IV Sententiarum*.
Alexander IV, *Les Registres d'Alexandre IV*, ed. C. Bourel de la Roncière, J. de Loye, & A. Coulon, 3 vols (Bibliothèque des Ecoles françaises d'Athènes et de Rome), Paris, 1895-1953.
Alexander of Hales, *Glossa in Quatuor Libros Sententiarum Petri Lombardi*, ed. PP. Collegii S. Bonaventurae, 4 vols (Vols XII-XV of Bibliotheca Franciscana Scholastica Medii Aevi), Florence, 1951-57.
Alphonse of Poitiers, *Correspondance administrative d'Alfonse de Poitiers*, ed. A. Molinier, 2 vols (Collection de Documents inédits sur l'histoire de France), Paris, 1894-1900.
——, *Enquêtes Administratives d'Alfonse de Poitiers*, Arrêts de son Parlement tenu à Toulouse et textes annexés 1249-1271, ed. P.-F. Fournier & P. Guebin (Collection de Documents inédits sur l'histoire de France), Paris, 1959.
Annales de Terre Sainte, ed. R. Röhricht, *Archives de l'Orient latin*, Vol. II, Paris, 1884.
Annales Ianuenses, ed. G. Pertz (*M.G.H. SS.*, XVIII), Hanover, 1863.
Annales Monastici, ed. H. R. Luard, 5 vols, Rolls Series, London, 1864-69.
Annales Stadenses, ed. I. M. Lappenberg (*M.G.H. SS.*, XVI), Hanover, 1859.
Aquinas, St. Thomas, *Quaestiones Quodlibetales*, ed. R. Spazzi, 8th edition, revised, Rome, 1949.

——, *Summa Contra Gentiles*, ed. Leonina Manualis, Rome, 1934.

——, *Summa Theologiae*, ed. De Rubeis, Billuart, P. Faucher, O.P., *et al.*, cum textu ex recensione Leonina, Rome, 1948.

Arnoldus, Frater, O.P., *De correctione ecclesiae epistola et Anonymi de Innocentio IV P.M Antichristo libellus*, ed. E. Winkelmann, Berlin, 1865.

Austorc d'Aurillac, see Jeanroy.

Beaumanoir, Philippe de, *Les coutumes du Beauvoisis*, ed. Le Comte Beugnot, 2 vols (Société de l'histoire de France), Paris, 1842.

Bernard, St., *The Letters of St. Bernard of Clairvaux*, newly translated by Bruno Scott James, London, 1953.

Bonaventure, St., *Opera Omnia*, Quaracchi edition, 10 vols, Florence, 1882-1902, Vol. IV, *In Quartum Librum Sententiarum Magistri Petri Lombardi*.

Bracton, Henry de, *Legibus et consuetudinibus Angliae*, ed. Sir T. Twiss, 6 vols, Rolls Series, London, 1878-83.

Bonomel, Ricaut, *Poems*, see *Poezie Provenzali*.

Bruno of Olmütz, *Analecten zur Geschichte Deutschlands und Italiens*, No. I, ed. C. Höfler, in *Abhandlungen der historischen classe der Königlich Bayerischen Akademie der Wissenschaften*, No. IV, Munich, 1846.

Burchardus de Monte Sion, in *Peregrinatores Medii Aevi Quatuor*, ed. J. C. M. Laurent, Leipzig, 1864.

Caesarius of Heisterbach, *Dialogus Miraculorum*, ed. J. Strange, 2 vols, Brussels, 1851.

Cantilupe, Thomas de, *Registrum Thome de Cantilupo, Episcopi Herefordensis 1275-1282*, ed. R. G. Griffiths (Canterbury & York Series, Vol. II), London, 1907.

Catherine of Siena, St., *Epistolario di Santa Caterina da Siena*, ed. E. Dupré Theseider, Vol. I (Fonti per la Storia d'Italia), Rome, 1940.

Charles of Anjou, *Codice diplomatico del regno di Carlo I e II d'Angiò dal 1265 al 1309*, ed. G. del Giudice, 2 vols, Naples, 1863-9.

——, "Lettre des Chrétiens de Terre-Sainte à Charles d'Anjou, 22 avril 1260", ed. H.-F. Delaborde, *Revue de L'Orient latin*, II, 1894, pp. 206-215.

Chronicle of Morea, *Crusaders as Conquerors*, trans. H. E. Lurier (Records of Civilisation, No. LXIX), New York, 1964.

Chronicle of Novgorod, 1016-1471, translated by R. M. Michell & N. Forbes (Camden Society, Third Series, Vol. XXV), London, 1914.

Chroniques, *Les Grandes Chroniques de France*, ed. J. Viard, 10 vols (Société de l'histoire de France), Paris, 1920-53.

Clement IV, *Les Registres de Clément IV*, ed. E. Jordan (Bibliothèque des Ecoles françaises d'Athènes et de Rome), Paris, 1893-1945.

Constitutiones pro zelo fidei, see Finke, below.

Continuatio Sansblasiensis, ed. R. Wilmans (*M.G.H. SS*, XX), Hanover, 1868.

Desclot, Bernat, *Chronicle of the Reign of King Pedro III of Aragon*, translated by F. L. Critchlow, 2 vols, Part I, 1134-1275, Part II, 1276-1285, Princeton, N.J., 1928-34.

Finke, H., *Konzilienstudien zur Geschichte des 13 Jahrhunderts*, Ergänzungen und Berichtigungen zu Hefele-Knöpfler "Conciliengeschichte", Band V and VI, Münster, 1891.

Frederick II, *Historia diplomatica Friderici II*, ed. A. Huillard-Bréholles, 12 parts in 7 vols, Paris, 1852-61.

Gerhoh de Reichersberg, *De investigatione antichristi*, ed. E. Sackur (*M.G.H. SS*, *Libelli de Lite*, III), Hanover, 1897.

Giffard, Walter, *The Register of Walter Giffard, Lord Archbishop of York*, 1266-1279 (Surtees Society, Vol. CIX), London, 1904.

Gilbert of Tournai, *Collectio de scandalis ecclesiae*, ed. A. Stroick in *Archivum Franciscanum Historicum*, XXIV, 1931, pp. 33-62.

Gray, Walter, *The Register of Walter Gray, Lord Archbishop of York* (Surtees Society, Vol. LVI), London, 1870.

Gregory IX, *Les Registres de Grégoire IX*, ed. L. Auvray, 4 vols (Bibliothèque des Ecoles françaises d'Athènes et de Rome), Paris, 1899-1955.

Gregory X, *Les Registres de Grégoire X*, 1272-1276, (*et de Jean XXI*, 1276-1277) ed. J. Guiraud (& E. Cadier), (Bibliothèque des Ecoles françaises d'Athènes et de Rome), Paris, 1892-1960.

Grosseteste, Robert, bishop of Lincoln, *Epistolae*, ed. H. R. Luard, Rolls Series, London, 1861.

Henry III, *Royal and other historical letters illustrative of the reign of Henry III*, ed. W. W. Shirley, 2 vols, Rolls Series, London, 1862-66.

Honorius IV, *Les Registres d'Honorius IV*, ed. M. Prou (Bibliothèque des Ecoles françaises d'Athènes et de Rome), Paris, 1886-88.

Hostiensis, *Summa Aurea*, Lyons, 1588.

Humbert de Romans, *Opus Tripartitum*, in E. Brown, *Appendix ad Fascicularum Rerum Expetendarum & Fugiendarum*, London, 1690.

——, *A Treatise on Preaching*, ed. W. M. Conlon, London, 1955.

Innocent IV, *In Quinque Libros Decretalium*, Venice, 1578.

——, "Lettere 'Secretae' d'Innocenzo IV", ed. G. Abate, in *Miscellanea Franciscana* Vol. LV, 1955, pp. 317-373.

——, *Les Registres d'Innocent IV*, ed. E. Berger, 4 vols (Bibliothèque des Ecoles françaises d'Athènes et de Rome), Paris, 1884-1921.

Innocent V, *Documenta*, see Laurent.

Irish Penitentials, ed. L. Bieler, with Appendix by D. A. Binchy (Scriptores Latini Hiberniae, Vol. V), Dublin, 1963.

Jacques de Vitry, *Historia Iherosolimitana*, in *Gesta Dei per Francos*, ed. Bongars.

——, *Lettres de Jacques de Vitry*, ed. R. B. C. Huygens (édition critique), Leiden, 1960.

James I, King of Aragon, *The Chronicle of James I, king of Aragon, surnamed the Conqueror, written by himself*, trans. J. Forster, 2 vols, London, 1883.

John XXI, see Gregory X.

Joinville, Jean de, *Histoire de Saint Louis*, texte original, ed. N. de Wailly, ninth edition, Paris, 1921.

Le Romeyn, John, *The Register of John Le Romeyn, Lord Archbishop of York, 1286-1296*, 2 vols (Surtees Society, Vols CXXIII and CXXVIII), London, 1913, 1916.

Louis, St., *Les Etablissements de Saint Louis*, ed. P. Viollet, 4 vols (Société de l'histoire de France), Paris, 1881-6.

Martin IV, *Les Registres de Martin IV*, *1281-1285*, ed. les membres de l'Ecole française de Rome et F. Olivier-Martin (Bibliothèque des Ecoles françaises d'Athènes et de Rome), Paris, 1901-35.

Malaspina, Saba, *Sallae sive Rerum Sicularum, Liber VI ab anno Christi MCCL usque ad annum MCCLXXVI*, ed. L. A. Muratori (Rerum Italicarum Scriptores, Vol. VIII), Milan, 1726.

Menko, *Chronicon Werumensium*, ed. L. Weiland (*M.G.H.*, *SS*, XXIII), Hanover, 1874.

Minstrel of Rheims, *Récits d'un Ménestrel de Reims au treisième siècle*, ed. N. de Wailly, Paris, 1876.

Muntaner, Ramon, *Chronicle of Muntaner*, 2 vols (Hakluyt Society, Vols 47 and 50), London, 1920-21.

Nicholas III, *Les Registres de Nicholas III, 1277-1280*, ed. J. Gay (Bibliothèque des Ecoles françaises d'Athènes et de Rome), Paris, 1898-1938.
Nicholas IV, *Les Registres de Nicholas IV*, ed. E. Langlois (Bibliothèque des Ecoles françaises d'Athènes et de Rome), Paris, 1886-1893.

Oliver Scholasticus, *Die Schriften des Kölner Domscholasters, späteren Bischofs von Paderborn und Kardinal-Bischofs von S. Sabina*, ed. H. Hoogeweg (Bibliothek des Litterarischen Vereins in Stuttgart, Vol. CCII), Tübingen, 1894.
Osbernus, *De Expugnatione Lyxbonensi*, ed. W. Stubbs, in *Chronicles and Memorials of the Reign of Richard I*, Vol. I, Rolls Series, London, 1864, pp. cxlii-clxxxii.
Otto of Freising, *Ottonis et Rahewini, Gesta Friderici I Imperatoris*, ed. G. Waitz (Scriptores Rerum Germanicarum in usum scholarum, ex *M.G.H.*), Hanover, 1884.
Ottoboni, Cardinal, "The letters of Cardinal Ottoboni", ed. R. Graham, *English Historical Review*, XV, 1900, pp. 87-120.

Paris, Matthew, *Chronica majora*, ed. H. R. Luard, 7 vols, Rolls Series, London, 1872-1883.
Peckham, John, *Registrum Epistolarum Fratris Johannis Peckham, Archiepiscopi Cantuariensis*, ed. C. T. Martin, 3 vols, Rolls Series, London, 1882-1885.
Pontissara, John of, *Registrum Johannis de Pontissara, Episcopi Wyntoniensis, 1282-1304*, ed. C. Deedes, 2 vols (Canterbury & York Series, Vols XIX, XXX), London, 1915-1924.

Raymund of Pennafort, *Summa Sancti Raymundi de Peniafort Barcinonensis, O.P., De Poenitentia et Matrimonio (cum glossis Joannis de Friburgo)*, Rome, 1603.
Raynaldus-Baronius, Vols XIII-XX of *Annales Ecclesiastici*, Rome, 1646-1663.
Revel, Hugh, Letter of Hugh Revel to Guy de Dampierre, Count of Flanders, in "Six lettres relatives aux croisades", ed. P. Riant, in *Archives de l'Orient latin*, Vol. I, pp. 383-392.
Ricoldo de Monte Croce, ed. R. Röhricht, in *Archives de l'Orient latin*, Vol. II, Documents II, pp. 258-296, Paris, 1884.
Rigaud, Eude, *Journal des visites pastorales d'Eude Rigaud, archevêque de Rouen*, 1248-1269, ed. T. Bonnin, Rouen, 1852.
Robert de Clari, *La Conquête de Constantinople*, ed. P. Lauer (Les classiques français du moyen âge), Paris, 1924.
Roland of Padua, *Chronica Rolandini Patavini*, ed. P. Jaffé (*M.G.H. SS.*, XIX), Hanover, 1866.
Rothelin, *Manuscrit de Rothelin* (Continuation of William of Tyre) (*Recueil des historiens des croisades, Historiens occidentaux*, Vol. II) Paris, 1859.
Rutebeuf, *Oeuvres complètes de Rutebeuf, Trouvère du XIIIe siècle*, ed. A. Jubinal, Paris, 1839.
——, *Onze poèmes de Rutebeuf concernant la croisade*, ed. J. Bastin & E. Faral (Documents relatifs à l'histoire des croisades publiées par l'Academie des Inscriptions et Belles-Lettres), Paris, 1946.

Saga of Hacon and a fragment of the Saga of Magnus, trans. Sir G. W. Dasent in *Icelandic Sagas*, Vol. IV, Rolls Series, London, 1894.
Salimbene de Adam, *Chronica*, ed. O. Holder-Egger, (*M.G.H. SS*, XXXII), Hanover, 1905-13.

Sanudo, Marino, *Liber secretorum fidelium crucis*, in *Bongars*, Part II.
——, *Secreta fidelium crucis*, Bodley MS Tanner 190.

Thomas de Cantimpré, *Le Bien universel ou les abeilles mystiques*, trans. V. Willart, Brussels, 1650.

Triennis et biennis decima ab anno MCCXLVII collecta, ed. MM. Guigniant et de Wailly (*Recueil des historiens des Galles et de la France*, XXI), Paris, 1855.

Urban IV, *Les Registres d'Urbain IV*, 1261-1264, ed. L. Dorez & J. Guirand, 4 vols (Bibliothèque des Ecoles françaises d'Athènes et de Rome), Paris, 1899-1958.

Villehardouin, G. de, *La Conquête de Constantinople de Geffroi de Ville-Hardouin avec la Continuation de Henri de Valenciennes*, ed. N. de Wailly, Paris, 1872.

Vincent of Prague, *Annales*, ed. W. Wattenbach, (*M.G.H. SS*, XVII), Hanover, 1861.

Wickwane, William, *The Register of William Wickwane, Lord Archbishop of York, 1279-1285* (Surtees Society, Vol. CXIV), London, 1907.

William of Auxerre, *Summa Aurea in quattuor libros sententiarum: a subtilissimo doctore Magistro Guillermo altissiodorensi edita*, ed. Magister Guillermus de Quercu, Paris, 1500.

William of Beaulieu, *Vita Ludovici noni*, ed. MM. Daunou et Naudet (*Recueil des historiens des Galles et de la France*, XX), Paris, 1840.

William of Chartres, *De vita et actibus regis Francorum Ludovici*, ed. MM. Daunou et Naudet (*Recueil des historiens des Galles et de la France*, XX), Paris, 1840.

William of Nangis, *Chronicon*, ed. MM. Daunou et Naudet (*Recueil des historiens des Galles et de la France*, XX), Paris, 1840.

——, *Gesta sanctae memoriae Ludovici regis Franciae*, ed. MM. Daunou et Naudet (*Recueil des historiens des Galles et de la France*, XX), Paris, 1840.

William of St. Pathus, *Vie de Saint Louis*, ed. H-F. Delaborde (Collection de Textes pour servir à l'étude et à l'enseignement de l'histoire), Paris, 1899.

(iii) SECONDARY

Alphandéry, P., *La Chrétienté et l'idée de croisade* (texte établi par A. Dupront), 2 vols. Vol. I, *Les premières croisades*, Paris, 1954, Vol. II, *Recommencements nécessaires*, Paris, 1959.

Anciaux, P., *Le Sacrement de la Pénitence*, Louvain, Paris, 1957.

——, *La théologie du sacrement de pénitence au XIIe siecle*, Louvain, 1949.

——, "La théologie de la pénitence chez quelques maîtres parisiens de la première moitié du XIIIe siècle", *Ephemerides theologicae Lovanienses*, Vol. XXIV, 1948, pp. 24-58.

Atiya, A. S., *The Crusade, historiography and bibliography*, Bloomington, Indiana, 1962.

Auer, J., *Studien zu den Reformschriften für das zweite Lyoner Konzil*, Freiburg, 1910.

Backes, N., *Kardinal Simon de Brion (Papst Martin IV)*, Berlin, 1910.

Berger, E., *Histoire de Blanche de Castille, reine de France*, Paris, 1895.

——, *Saint Louis et Innocent IV, Etude sur les rapports de la France et du Saint-Siège*, Paris, 1887.

——, *Thomae Cantipratensis bonum universale de apibus, quid illustrandis saeculi Decimi Tertii Moribus Conferat*, Paris, 1895.

Blochet, E., *Les relations diplomatiques des Hohenstaufen avec les sultans d'Egypte*, *Revue historique*, Vol. 80, 1902, pp. 51-64.

Bréhier, L., *L'Eglise et L'Orient au moyen âge: Les croisades*, Paris, 1907.

Bridrey, E., *La condition juridique des croisés et le privilège de Croix*, Paris, 1900.

Brundage, J. A., *The Crusades, a documentary survey*, Milwaukee, Wis., 1962.

——, *Medieval Canon Law and the Crusader*, Madison, Milwaukee and London, 1969.

Buisson, L., *König Ludwig IX, der Heilige, und das Recht*, Freiburg, 1954.

Burns, R. I., *The Crusader Kingdom of Valencia, Reconstruction on a Thirteenth Century Frontier*, 2 vols, Cambridge, Mass., 1967.
——, "Christian-Islamic Confrontation in the West: The Thirteenth-Century Dream of Conversion", *The American Historical Review*, 76, 1971, pp. 1386-1434.
——, "Journey from Islam, Incipient Cultural Transition in the Conquered Kingdom of Valencia, 1240-1280", *Speculum*, XXXV, 1960, pp. 337-356.
Byrne, E. H., *Genoese Shipping in the Twelfth and Thirteenth Centuries* (Monographs of the Mediaeval Academy of America, No. 1), Cambridge, Mass., 1930.

Cahen, C., *La Syrie du nord à l'époque des Croisades et la principauté franque d'Antioche*, Paris, 1940.
——, "Notes sur l'histoire des croisades et de l'orient latin", *Bulletin de la Faculté des lettres de Strasbourg*, 28-29, 1949-51, pp. 118-125, 286-310, 328-346.
Campbell, G. J., "The Attitude of the Monarchy towards the use of ecclesiastical censures in the reign of Saint Louis", *Speculum*, XXXV, 1960, pp. 535-555.
——, "The protest of Saint Louis", *Traditio*, XV, 1959, pp. 405-418.
Cauwenbergh, E. van, *Les Pèlerinages expiatoires et judiciaires dans le droit communal de la Belgique au moyen âge* (University of Louvain, Recueil de Travaux, 48e fasc.), 1922.
Cohn, N., *The Pursuit of the Millenium*, London, 1957.
Courtney, F., "New explanations of indulgences", *Clergy Review*, 44, 1959, pp. 464-79.
Crone, G. R., "New Light on the Hereford Map", *Geographical Journal*, 131, 1965.
——, *The Hereford World Map*, London, 1948.
——, *The World Map of Richard of Haldingham in Hereford Cathedral*, London, 1954.
Denholm-Young, N., *Richard of Cornwall*, Oxford, 1947.
Devic, C. & Vaissète, J., *Histoire Générale de Languedoc*, 16 vols in 18, Toulouse 1872-1904.
Digard, G., *Philippe le Bel et le Saint-Siège*, 2 vols, Paris, 1936.
Dodu, G., *Histoire des institutions monarchiques dans le royaume latin de Jérusalem 1099-1291*, Paris, 1894.

Falanga, A. J., *Charity the Form of the Virtues according to St.Thomas*, Washington, 1948.
Fliche, A. & Martin, V., *Histoire de l'Eglise depuis les origines jusqu'à nos jours*, Vols 1- , Paris, 1934- .
Forest, A., Steenberghen, F. van & Gandillac, M., *Le movement doctrinal du XIe au XIVe siècle* (Vol. 13 of Fliche et Martin, *Histoire de l'Eglise*), Paris, 1956.

Galtier, P., "Les indulgences: origine et nature, à propos d'un ouvrage recent", *Gregorianum*, 31, 1950, pp. 258-274.
Garrigou-Lagrange, R., *De Eucharistia. Accedunt De Paenitentia quaestiones dogmaticae Commentarius in Summam theologicam S. Thomae*, Rome, 1946.
Gatto, L., *Il Pontificato di Gregorio X, 1272-1276*, Rome, 1959.
Geanakoplos, D. J., *Emperor Michael Palaeologus and the West, 1258-1282*, Cambridge, Mass., 1959.
Gottlob, A., *Kreuzablass und Almosenablass* (Kirchenrechtliche Abhandlungen, Heft 31/32), Stuttgart, 1906.
——, *Die Päpstlichen Kreuzzugs-Steuern des 13 Jahrhunderts*, Heiligenstadt, 1892.
Gretser, J., *De Cruce Christi*, 3 vols, Ingolstadt, 1600-05.
Grousset, R., *Histoire des Croisades et du Royaume franc de Jérusalem*, 3 vols, Paris, 1934-36.
Guidi, P., *Rationes decimarum Italiae nei secoli XIII e XIV*, Vatican, 1932.

Ham, E. B., *Rutebeuf and Louis IX* (University of North Carolina Studies in Romance Language and Literature, No. 42), Chapel Hill, 1962.

Hampe, K., *Urban IV und Manfred, 1261-1264* (Heidelberger Abhandlungen zur mittleren und neueren Geschichte, Heft II), Heidelburg, 1905.

Harnack, A., *Dogmengeschichte*, 4th edition, Tübingen, 1905.

Hefele-Leclercq, *Histoire des Conciles, d'après les documents originaux*, 1- vols, Paris, 1907- .

Heidemann, J., *Papst Clemens IV* (Kirchengeschichtliche Studien, VI, 4), Münster, 1903.

Heintke, F., *Humbert von Romans der fünfte Ordensmeister der Dominikaner* (Historische Studien, No. 222), Berlin, 1933.

Herde, P., *Beiträge zum päpstlichen Kanzlei- und Urkundenwesen im dreizehnten Jahrhundert*, Kallmünz, 1961.

Heyd, W., *Histoire du Commerce du Levant au Moyen-Age*, 2 vols, Amsterdam, 1959 (reprint).

Hill, G., *A History of Cyprus*, 4 vols, Cambridge, 1940-52.

Holdsworth, W. S., *A History of English Law*, 16 vols, London, 1922-66.

Jeanroy, A., "Le troubadour Austorc d'Aurillac et son sirventés sur la septième Croisade", *Mélanges Chabaneau*, Festschrift Camille Chabaneau, Erlangen, 1907, pp. 81-87.

John, E., "Papalism ancient and modern", *New Blackfriars*, 49, 1967-68, pp. 117-120, 199-208, 244-250.

Jordan, E., *L'Allemagne et l'Italie aux XIIe et XIIIe siècles*, Paris, 1939.

——, *De Mercatoribus Camerae Apostolicae Saeculo XIII* (published thesis, faculty of letters, University of Paris), Rennes, 1909.

——, *Les origines de la domination angevine en Italie*, Paris, 1909.

Jungmann, J. A., *Die Lateinischen Bussriten in ihrer geschichtlichen Entwicklung*, Innsbruck, 1932.

Kantorowicz, E., *Frederick the Second, 1194-1250*, translated by E. O. Lorimer, London, 1957 (reprint).

Kurzawa, B., *De effectibus sacramentorum relate ad Corpus Christi Mysticum apud S. Albertum Magnum*, Friberg, Switzerland, 1950.

Lagarde, G. de, *La naissance de l'esprit laïque au declin du moyen âge*, 4 vols (in 6), Vienna and Paris, 1934-1946.

Lecoy de la Marche, A., "La prédication de la croisade au treizième siècle", *Revue des questions historiques*, 25th year, new series, Vol. IV, XLVIIIe de la collection, Paris, July, 1890.

La Monte, J., *Feudal Monarchy in the Latin Kingdom of Jerusalem, 1100-1291*, Cambridge, Mass., 1932.

Laurent, M. H., *Beatus Innocentius PP V*, *Studia et Documenta*, Rome, 1943.

Le Bras, G., *Institutions ecclésiastiques de la Chrétienté médiévale* (Vol. 12 of Fliche et Martin, *Histoire de l'Eglise*), Tournai, 1959-64.

Lewent, K., "Das altprovenzalische Kreuzlied", *Romanische Forschungen*, XXI, 1905 (1907).

Lottin, O., *Psychologie et morale aux XIIe et XIIIe siècles*, 6 vols in 7, Gembloux, 1948-1960.

Luchaire, A., *Innocent III, le Concile de Latran et la réforme de l'église*, Paris, 1908.

——, *Innocent III: La question d'Orient*, 2nd edition, Paris, 1911.

Lunt, W. E., *Financial Relations of the Papacy with England to 1327*, Cambridge, Mass., 1939.

——, *Papal Revenues in the Middle Ages* (Columbia University Records of Civilisation, XIX), 2 vols, New York, 1934.

——, *The Valuation of Norwich*, Oxford, 1926.

Lynch, K. F., "The doctrine of Alexander of Hales on the nature of Sacramental Grace", *Franciscan Studies*, 19, 1959, pp. 334-383.

Marc-Bonnet, H., "Le Saint-Siège et Charles d'Anjou sous Innocent IV et Alexandre IV", *Revue historique*, 199-200, 1948, pp. 38-65.

Mas Latrie, L. de, *Traités de paix et de commerce et documents divers concernant les relations des Chrétiens avec les Arabes de l'Afrique septentrionale*, Paris, 1866.

Mayer, H. E., *Bibliographie zur Geschichte der Kreuzzüge*, Hanover, 1960. Supplement up to 1967 in *Historische Zeitschrift*, Sonderheft, 3, 1969.

Michel, K., *Das Opus Tripartitum des Humbertus de Romanis*, Graz, 1926.

Mitchell, R. J., *The Spring Voyage, the Jerusalem pilgrimage in 1458*, London, 1964.

Natalini, V., *De Natura Gratiae Sacramentalis iuxta S. Bonaventuram* (Studia Antoniana, 17), Rome, 1961.

Norden, W., *Das Papsttum und Byzanz*, Berlin, 1903.

Oakley, T. P., "Alleviations of penance in the continental penitentials", *Speculum*, XI, 1937, pp. 488-502.

Ohlmann, R., "St. Bonaventure and the Power of the Keys", *Franciscan Studies*, 6, 1946, pp. 293-315 and 437-465.

Paulus, N., *Geschichte des Ablasses im Mittelalter vom Ursprunge bis zur Mitte des 14 Jahrhunderts*, Paderborn, 1922-23.

Poschmann, B., *Die abendländische Kirchenbusse im frühen Mittelalter* (Breslauer Studien zur historischen Theologie, Band XVI), Breslau, 1930.

——, *Der Ablass im Licht der Bussgeschichte* (Theophaneia, Band IV), Bonn, 1948.

——, *Busse und Letzte Ölung* (Handbuch der Dogmengeschichte, IV, 3), Freiburg, 1951.

Powicke, F. M., *King Henry III and the Lord Edward*, 2 vols, Oxford, 1947.

Prawer, J., "Colonisation activities in the Latin Kingdom of Jerusalem", *Revue belge de philologie et d'histoire*, XXIX, 1951, pp. 1063-1118.

——, "Etude préliminarie sur les sources et la composition du 'Livre des Assises des Bourgeois' ", *Revue historique de droit français et étranger*, 4th series, 32nd year, 1954, pp. 198-227.

——, *Histoire du royaume latin de Jérusalem*, 2 vols, Paris, 1969-70.

——, *The Latin Kingdom of Jerusalem*: European Colonialism in the Middle Ages, London, 1972.

——, "La noblesse et le régime féodal du royaume latin de Jérusalem", *Le Moyen Age*, LXV, 1959, pp. 41-74.

——, "The settlement of the Latins in Jerusalem", *Speculum*, XXVII, 1952, pp. 490-503.

Puttkamer, G. von, *Papst Innocenz IV*, Münster, 1930.

Queller, D. E., "Thirteenth century Diplomatic Envoys, Nuncii and Procuratores", *Speculum*, XXXV, 1960, pp. 196-213.

Rahner, K., Review of B. Poschmann, *Der Ablass im Licht der Bussgeschichte*, in *Zeitschrift für Katholische Theologie*, 71, 1949, pp. 481-490.

Regout, R. H. W., *La doctrine de la guerre juste de St. Augustin à nos jours d'après les théologiens et les canonistes catholiques*, Paris, 1934.

Rey, E., *Les colonies franques de Syrie au XIIe et XIIIe siècles*, Paris, 1883.

Riant, P., *Expéditions et pèlerinages des Scandinaves en Terre Sainte au temps des croisades*, Paris, 1865 (with Tables, 1869).

Richard, J., *Le Royaume latin de Jérusalem*, Paris, 1953.
Riley-Smith, J., *The Knights of St. John in Jerusalem and Cyprus, c.1050-1310*. A history of the Order of the Hospital of St. John of Jerusalem, Vol. I, London, 1967.
——, *The Feudal Nobility and the Kingdom of Jerusalem 1174-1277*, London and Basingstoke, 1973.
Rodenberg, C., *Innocenz IV und das Königreich Sicilien 1245-1254*, Halle, 1892.
Röhricht, R., "Etudes sur les derniers temps du royaume de Jérusalem", in *Archives de l'Orient latin*, Paris, Vol. I, 1881, pp. 617-652, Vol. II, 1884, pp. 365-409.
——, *Geschichte des Königreichs Jerusalem (1100-1291)*, Innsbruck, 1898.
——, "Das Kreuzpredigten gegen den Islam", *Zeitschrift für Kirchengeschichte*, Heft 4, Vol. VI, 1884.
——, "Die Pastorellen 1251", *Zeitschrift für Kirchengeschichte*, Heft 2, Vol. VI, 1884.
Runciman, Sir Stephen, *A History of the Crusades*, 3 vols, Cambridge 1951-4.
——, *The Sicilian Vespers*, Cambridge, 1958.

Sambin, P., *Problemi Politici Attraverso Lettere Inedite de Innocenzo IV* (Istituto Veneto de Scienze, Memorie Classe, Vol. XXXI), Venice, 1955.
Schwerin, U., *Die Aufrufe der Päpste zur Befreiung des Heiligen Landes von den Anfängen bis zum Ausgang Innozenz IV* (Historische Studien, Vol. 301), Berlin, 1937.
Steinherz, S., *Die Einhebung des Lyoner Zehnten im Erz Salzburg 1282-84* (Mittheilungen des Instituts für österreichische Geschichtsforschung, XIV, pp. 1-86).
Sternfeld, R., *Der Kardinal Johann Gaëtan Orsini (Papst Nikolaus III) 1244-1277* (Historische Studien, Vol. 52), Berlin, 1905.
——, *Ludwigs des Heiligen Kreuzzug nach Tunis 1270 und die Politik Karls I von Sizilien* (Historische Studien, Vol. 4), Berlin, 1896.
Stévaux, A., "La doctrine de la charité dans les commentaires des sentences de St. Albert, de St. Bonaventure et de St. Thomas", *Ephemerides theologicae Lovanienses*, XXIV, 1948, pp. 59-97.
Strayer, J. R., "The Crusades of Louis IX", in *The Later Crusades 1189-1311*, ed. R. W. Wolff & H. W. Hazard, Philadelphia, 1962, pp. 487-518.
——, "The Laicization of French and English Society in the thirteenth century", *Speculum*, XV, 1940, pp. 76-86.
Stroick, A., "Verfasser und Quellen der Collectio de Scandalis Ecclesiae Reformschrift des Fr. Gilbert von Tournay", *Archivum Franciscanum Historicum*, XXIII, 1930, pp. 3-41, 273-299, 433-466.

Tardif, J., "Le procès d'Enguerran de Coucy", *Bibliothèque de l'Ecole des Chartes*, LXXIX, 1918, pp. 5-44, 414-454.
Teetaert, A. S. T., "La Doctrine pénitentielle de St. Raymond de Penyafort, O.P.", *Analecta Sacra Tarraconensia*, IV, 1928, pp. 120-182 (1-62).
——, "La 'Summa de poenitentia' de S. Raymond de Penyafort", *Ephemerides Theologicae Lovanienses*, V, 1928, pp. 49-72.
Tenckhoff, F., *Papst Alexander IV*, Paderborn, 1907.
Tillemont, L.S. Le Nain de, *Vie de Saint Louis*, ed. J. de Gaulle, 6 vols (Société de l'histoire de France), Paris 1847-51.
Throop, P. A., *Criticism of the Crusades*, Amsterdam, 1940.
Trabut-Cussac, J-P., "Le financement de la croisade anglaise de 1270", *Bibliothèque de l'Ecole des Chartes*, CXIX, Paris, 1962 (année '61), pp. 113-140.

Ullmann, W., *The Growth of Papal Government in the Middle Ages*, London 1955.
——, *Mediaeval Papalism. The Political Theories of the Medieval Canonists*, London, 1949.

Van Cleve, T.C., *The Emperor Frederick II of Hohenstaufen*, Immutator Mundi, Oxford, 1972.
Vanderpol, A. M., *La doctrine scholastique du droit de guerre*, Paris, 1919.
Vanneste, A., "Le sacrament de pénitence chez Guillaume d'Auvergne", *Ephemerides Theologicae Lovanienses*, XXVIII, 1952, pp. 98-118.
Villey, M., *La croisade, Essai sur la formation d'une théorie juridique*, Paris, 1942.
——, "L'idee de la croisade chez les juristes du moyen-âge", *Relazioni* de X Congresso internazionale di scienze storiche, Rome, 4-11 September, 1955, Vol. III, *Storia del Medioevo*, Florence, 1955, pp. 565-594.
Volk, O., *Die Abendländische-Hierarchische Kreuzzugidee*, Halle, 1911.

Wallon, H., *Saint Louis et son temps*, 2 vols, Paris, 1875.
Walter, F., *Die Politik der Kurie unter Gregor X*, Berlin, 1894.
Webb, C. C. J., "Roger Bacon on Alphonse of Poitiers", in *Essays in History Presented to R. Lane Poole*, ed. H. W. C. Davis, Oxford, 1927, pp. 290-300.
Wolff, R. L. & Hazard, H. W., *The Later Crusades, 1189-1311* (Vol II of *A History of the Crusades*, general ed. K. Setton), Philadelphia, 1962.
Wright, J. K., *The Geographical Lore of the time of the Crusades*, New York, 1925.

INDEX

The following symbols will be used:
[1] *crucesignatus*, [2] *crucesignatus* and crusader to the Holy Land, [3] crusading official, [4] crusading official and crusader to the Holy Land, [5] area of crusading business, [6] area of crusade, [7] person(s) against whom crusade was preached or waged

17, 20, 21, 65-6, 71-2, 183-6 and *passim*; as expression of feudal ideals, 9, 10, 29; (First) as archetypal, 7, 10; as fitting endeavour for plenary indulgence, 26, 35-51, 52-98 and *passim*; as penance, 21, 29, 35-51, 81, 100, 102, 114-118, 183; as pilgrimage, 10, 100, 102 and *passim*; reactions to defeat, 78-9, 81; separated from plenary indulgence, 66 and *passim*; as subsuming all forms of penance, 41; as synonymous with indulgence, 88 n. 179; as tied to plenary indulgence, 35-51, 52-62, 66, 88 n. 179, 97 and *passim*; traditional, 3, 10, 11-13, 21, 64, 66, 96, 183-6; as of unique spiritual value, 21, 64, 65, 183 and *passim*; vow as integral to, 137, 183; (non-papal), Angevin, against Aragon, 72, 88, 94-8; against Corfu, 94-5; against Michael I Palaeologus, 86-87; Aragonese, against Tunis, 67, 87-88; Children's, 78 n. 125; French, against Aragon, 72, 95-8, 141 n. 34, 154, 155, 174; Hohenstaufen, against the papacy, 20-1 (see also under Anti-crusade); *Pastoureaux*, 78; (papal); First, 10, 11, 14, 17, 20, 56, 66; Second, 10 n.11, 12 n.14, 70 n. 79, 103; Fourth, 86; Fifth, 109; twelfth century, 4; thirteenth century, 3, 19, 21, 22, 23-31, 86, 135, 174, 183-6 and *passim*; (English), 107, 111, 145 n. 65; (see also under Edward, Henry, Richard of Cornwall, William of Longespée); (French), of Alphonse of Poitiers (see under Alphonse of France, crusade in aid of Louis IX); of Louis IX (see under Louis IX); against Albigenses, 18, 69; against allies of the Hohenstaufen, 71-2, 80-1, 175; against Baibars, 60; against Cathars (see under Albigenses); against Christians, 16-21, 70-2, 81, 94; against the Colonna family, 20; against Conrad, 76, 78, 88; against Conradin, 88; against the duke of Bavaria, 175; against enemies of the papacy, 19-20, 174; against the English barons, 20, 64, 82, 83-4; against excommunicates, 19, 87 n. 178; against external enemies of the Church, 14-6, 66-9 and *passim*; against Ezzelino di Romano, 71-2, 80, 92; against Frederick II, 19, 20 n. 27, 69-86, 107-10, 176 and *passim*; against the Greeks, 17, 86-8, 91, 179 n. 315; against heretics 16-19, 69-74, 80-1, 91, 92-4; against heretics (relapsed) 18; against the Hohenstaufen, 5, 19, 69-86, 92, 113, 155, 184 (see also under Conrad, Conradin, Frederick, Manfred); against the infidel (see under Crusade (papal) against Saracens); against internal enemies of the Church, 16-19, 69-94 and *passim*; against Manfred, 80-2, 85; against the Moors, 14, 66-7, 155; against pagans, 15-16, 88-91, 93, 94, 155, 179 n. 315; against pagans (relapsed), 18, 91, 93; against the Saracens, 3-15, 23-31, 82, 88, 92, 107, 112 n. 62, 179 and *passim* (see also under Crusade (papal), geographical goal, Holy Land, Jerusalem); against schismatics, 16, 69, 91 (see also under Crusade (papal), against the Greeks); against the Slavs, 4, 14, 15-16, 18, 70 n. 79, 88-91, 93, 103, 184; against the Tartars, 15, 67-9, 88-91; against the Wends, 103 (see also under Crusade (papal), against the Slavs); geographical goal, Dacia, 16 (see also under geographical goal, Eastern and Northern frontiers of Europe); diverted from the Holy Land, 4 n. 2, 5, 13, 14, 64, 66-98, 104, 107, 112, 113, 114, 165, 184 and *passim*; Eastern and Northern frontiers of Europe, 4, 14, 15-16, 18, 67-9, 88-91, 93, 155, 156; Holy Land, 3-15, 23-31, 35-51, 54, 55, 60, 61, 64, 66, 67, 68, 71, 74, 76, 83, 86, 103, 104, 105, 106, 108, 109, 112, 113, 114, 117, 127, 128, 129 n. 162, 136, 142, 151, 154, 165, 175, 179, 183, 185, 187-99 (see also under Holy Land); Holy Places (see under geographical goal, Holy Land, Jerusalem); Hungary, 68, 106; Jerusalem, 9, 13-14, 23, 56, 66, 94, 110 and *passim* (see also under geographical goal, Holy Land); Latin Kingdom of Constantinople, 5 n. 3, 17, 76, 86-7, 139, 150-1, 162 n. 184; Lithuania, 16, 93 (see also under Crusade (papal), geographical goal, Eastern and Northern frontiers of Europe); Livonia, 89, 90 (see also under geographical goal, Eastern and Northern frontiers of Europe); Northern Africa, 87, 92, 103 n. 18, 111, 112 (see also under Crusade (non-papal), Aragonese, against

heretical legislation of, 19, 92; anti-papal propaganda of, 20-21, 73; central object of papal crusading efforts, 70-76; claims supremacy, 23; and council of Lyons, 23, 73; crusade against (see under Crusade (papal), against Frederick); death of, 76; deposition of, 23, 74; as heretic, 19, 68, 69-73; and Holy Land, 23, 75-6; letter of to Louis IX, 74; to Richard of Cornwall, 20 n. 26; sees self as saviour, 20; support of a reserved crime, 115

[1]Frederick II, duke of Austria, *crucesignatus*, 72, 89
[2]Freising, bishop of. See under Otto
Friars Minor, 93, 109, 123. See also under Franciscans
Friars Preachers, 75, 108-9, 126. See also under Dominicans
[5]Frisia, 109, 111
[2]Frisians, *crucesignati* and crusaders, 108-9, 123-4

[1]G. rector of Hayes, Kent, *crucesignatus*, 159
[5]Gascony, 165
Gautier de Reynel, 161 n. 179
General passage to Outremer, 52, 53, 96, 108 n. 46, 109, 131, 151, 168, 179, 180 and *passim*
Genoese, 180 n. 320. See also under Italian city states
[2]Geoffrey IV, viscount of Châteaudun, *crucesignatus* and crusader, 146, 166
[2]Geoffrey of Sargines, crusader, 155 n. 138
[1]Gerard de Marbais-Marbisoux, lord of Bruco, *crucesignatus*, 131, 142
[3]Gerard of Modena, collector, 177
Geraudus. See under Gibaud de Saint Verain
Gerhoh of Reichersberg, *de investigatione antichristi*, 10 n. 11, 204
[6][5]Germany, 50, 75, 107, 109, 123, 154, 176, 199 and *passim*. See also under Holy Roman Emperor, Holy Roman Empire, Romans, king of the
[6]Gerona, 98 n. 226
[1]Gibaud de Saint Verain, *crucesignatus*, 52-3 n. 3, 143
[1]Giffard, Richard, *crucesignatus*, 52 n. 3, 146
Giffard, Walter, archbishop of York, 63; *Register*, 102, n. 17, 115, 116, 162 n. 186 175, 204
[1]Gilbert de Clare, earl of Gloucester, *crucesignatus*, 145 n. 65
Gilbert of Tournai, o.f.m., *Collectio de Scandalis Ecclesiae*, 120 n. 107, 123, 132 n. 179, 169, 205
[1]Gloucester, earl of. See under Gilbert
[3]Godfrey de Fontaines (Guy de Laudino?), bishop of Cambrai, collector, 129 n. 162
[5]Gran, patriarchate of, 85
Gray, Walter, archbishop of York, *Register*, 56 n. 16, 139 n. 19, 205
[6]Greece, 17, 86-8, 94. See also under Achaia, Constantinople, Latin Empire, of, Corfu
[7]Greek Emperors. See under John Vatatzes, Michael I Palaeologus
[7]Greeks, 8, 17, 86-8, 91, 95. See also under Crusade (papal) against, the Greeks; Crusade (papal) motives for, aid to the Latin Empire of Constantinople, John Vatatzes, Michael I Palaeologus, Schism, Eastern
Gregory VII, Hildebrand, pope, 6, 8, 19
Gregory IX, pope, 19 n. 25, 25, 73, 128 n. 154, 142 n. 39, 144, 171, 197; *Register*, 129, 205
[2]Gregory X, pope, *crucesignatus* and crusader, 23-31, 58, 61, 68, 86, 87, 94, 137 n. 4, 152, 155, 163; *Constitutiones*, ix, 23-31, 137, 143 n. 49, 144, 152, 170, 187, 204; text of, 196-9; *Register*, 58, 64, 103 n. 21, 114, 120, 121, 125, 130, 131, 137, 139, 142, 148 n. 89, 149 n. 96, 152, 156, 168, 170, 171, 176 n. 299, 177 n. 305, 205. See also under Crusading decrees
Gregory XI, pope, 4 n. 1

[3]John of Pontissara, bishop of Winchester, *Register*, 65, 206
John von Nassau, bishop-elect of Utrecht, 98, 153
[3]John de Dist, chaplain to William of Holland, 76
John de Plano Carpine, o.f.m., *Ystoria Mongalorum*, 15 n. 18, 88-9, 91 n. 197, 203
[1]John de Selleston, vicar of Rothwell, *crucesignatus*, 162 n.186, 163
[1]John de Charolais, count of Burgundy, *crucesignatus*, 130, 148 n. 89
John I, count of Dreux, 146 n. 72
[1]John de Fagecourt, *crucesignatus* (penance enjoined), 116
[2]John d'Ibelin, lord of Arsuf, *bailli* of Jerusalem, crusader, 158 n. 158
[2]John d'Ibelin, lord of Caesarea, crusader, 127 n. 148
[2]John de Montfort, lord of Tyre, crusader, 142 n. 44, 146 n. 72, 148 n. 90, 158
[2]John (?), count of Sarrebruck, lord of Aspremont, *crucesignatus* and crusader, 55 n. 13
John de Wooton, 102-3 n. 17
[2]Joigny, count of. See under William
[2]Joinville, Jean, sieur de, *crucesignatus* and crusader, 52 nn. 2, 3, 53 nn. 4, 7, 64 n. 58, 161, 170 n. 260; *Histoire de Saint Louis*, 26 n. 11, 52 nn. 1, 2, 3, 55 n. 13, 77, 101 n. 7, 102, 111, 121, 144 n. 61, 160, 161, 205
Judaism, 13. See also under Jews

[7]Khwarismians, 23
[5]Kulm, 89 n. 188

[2]La Marche, count of. See under Hugh
Lambert the Teuton, o.f.m., Inquisitor, 93
[1]Lancaster, duke of. See under Edmund
[1]Landry de Fleury, *crucesignatus*, 146
Laon, 83
[6]Las Nevas, battle of, 67
Lateran, Council of. See under Council, Fourth Lateran
Lay protections, of *crucesignati*, 169; by paid advocates, 169
Lay subsidies, granted to *crucesignati*, 52-3, 145, 148; as loan, 145 n. 65, 148
Leicester, earl of. See under Simon
Leicester, count of. See under Amaury
Leon, king of. See under Alfonso, Ferdinand
Le Romeyn, John, archbishop of York, *Register*, 56 n.16, 103 n. 17, 162-3, 205
[5]Liège, 123
[1]Liège, bishop of. See under Henry
Lincoln, bishop of. See under Grosseteste
[6]Lisbon, 103
[3]Lismore, bishop of. See under Thomas
[6]Lithuania, 88 n. 180, 93
[1]Lithuania, king of. See under Mindowe
[6]Livonia, 89, 90
Llewellyn ap Griffith, prince of Wales, 117
Lombard, Peter 37
[5]Lombardy, 75
[1]Lopez, o.f.m., bishop of Morocco, *crucesignatus*, 91-2
Louis VIII, king of France, 26 n. 12
[2]Louis IX, king of France, *crucesignatus* and crusader, 24, 26, 31, 91 n. 197, 116, 128, 161, 165; first crusade of, 24, 52 n. 2, 53 n. 7, 55 n. 13, 62, 74-5, 76, 89, 107, 108, 109, 111, 118, 122, 123 n. 131, 127, 130, 141, 155, 180 and *passim*; second crusade of, 60, 68, 84, 86, 101 n. 7, 112, 113, 114, 121 n. 119, 124, 141

Muntaner, Ramon, *Chronicle*, 67 n. 68, 72, 88 n. 179, 97, 154, 205; idea of crusade of, 88 n. 179, 97

Naples, queen of. See under Joanna
Narbonne, archbishop of. See under William
Navarre, 95
Navarre, king of. See under Thibault
Nesle, seigneur de. See under Simon
Nesle, dame de. See under Alix
Nestorian Christians, 91. See also under Tartars
⁵Neufmarché, priory of, 162
Nicholas III, pope, 154, 163; *Register*, 61 nn. 44, 45, 87 n. 176, 94, 95, 96, 143, 147, 148 n. 89, 153, 154, 157, 161, 168, 177, 178, 206
Nicholas IV, pope, o.f.m., 56 n. 16, 103 n. 17; *Register*, 101, 102, 206
³Nicholas, o.praem., archbishop of Prussia, 108
³Nicholas de Brie, bishop of Troyes, collector, 124, 131
Nicholas de Fontanis, bishop of Cambrai, 166
¹Nicholas d'Offin, *crucesignatus*, 142 n. 44
⁶Norway, crusade in, 16, 89. See also under *Crucesignati* (Norwegian), Hakon
Norway, king of, 16, 115, 156-7. See also under Hakon
Norwegians. See under *crucesignati* (Norwegian)
Norwich, bishop of. See under Walter
³Nostell, St. Oswald's, prior of, collector, 152
Novgorod, *The Chronicle of*, 88, 204
Nur-ed-Din, 135

Oaths, 100, 102
¹Odo de Corpelay, *crucesignatus*, 142-3
¹Offin. See under Nicholas, Robert
²Oliver, bishop of Paderborn. See under Oliver Scholasticus
²Oliver Scholasticus (Thomas Oliverius, cardinal bishop of Sabina), crusader, *Historia Damiatina*, 109 n. 50, 206; *Letters*, 153 n. 120, 206
Olmütz, bishop of. See under Bruno
Oporto, bishop of. See under Peter
¹Orange, count of. See under Barral
Orléans, bishop of. See under William
Osbernus, *de expugnatione Lyxbonensi*, 14 n. 17, 103 n. 19, 121 n. 118, 206
²Otto, o.cist., bishop of Freising, crusader, *Gesta Friderici I Imperatoris*, 12 n. 14, 206
⁷Otto II, duke of Bavaria, 175
Otto II, count of Guelders, 144 n. 56
Ottokar, king of Bohemia, 94
⁶Outremer, 12 n. 14, 15, 20, 23, 78, 109. See also under Crusader States, General passage, Holy Land, Holy Places, Jerusalem

Pagans. See under Conversion, Crusade (papal), against, pagans, relapsed pagans; Crusade (papal), motives for, conversion, reconversion
Palmer, Helwysa, 102-3 n. 17
Palmer, Isabella, 102-3 n. 17
Papal crusading policy, abdication of control of, by popes, 90-1, 185; abuses of, 112, 131-2, 184-5 and *passim*; aimed at material advantage of *crucesignati*, 30-1, 135-6, 137-181, 183-6 and *passim*; aimed at spiritual advantage of *crucesignati*, 30-1, 35-132, 183-6 and *passim*; ambiguities in, 47-8, 123, 124 n. 140, 183-6 and *passim*; criticism of (see under Crusades, critics of); chief instruments of (see under Ecclesiastical sanctions, Indulgences, Papal privileges, Papal

how funds calculated, 148, 149; organisational problems encountered, failure to fulfil conditions, 130-1, 147; grants of overlapping areas, 152-3; infringements of feudal rights, 146-7, 152; infringement of prior rights, 146-7, 166; payment of arrears, 149 (see also under Amalric de Montfort and Richard of Cornwall); unworthy objects of, 145; territorial allocation, 146-7; when made, 147-8; means of enforcing payment, 150, 171-8 *passim*; negligence in collecting monies, 152; obstacles to collection of monies, 149-54, 156-7, 177 (see also under Crusading officials, obstruction placed in way of); period of collection, 28, 95, 141; relationship of to feudal structures, 141, 146, 152; reluctance to undertake guardianship of monies, 153; sources, crusading tax, as almsdeed, 150; attempted extensions of, 141; categories of, 149; differing papal contributions, 25-6, 190, 197; hundredth, 150-1; poll tax, 27-8, 197-8; tenth, 26, 27, 28, 60, 115, 122 n. 128, 130, 137, 140, 141, 146, 147, 197; as basic unit of, 141; defaults in payment of, 115, 177, extended; 141; hereditary, 146; immunity from payment of, 27, 151-2, 170 (see also under *Crucesignati*, immunities, granted to); effect of such immunities on crusade, 151-3; of Lyons, 28, 141, 150, 156, 197; objections of clerics to paying, 69, 141, 149-51, 152-3; relief from payment of promised, 150; twelfth, 150; twentieth, 26, 60, 115, 137, 140, 141-2, 191; thirtieth, 142; fines for blasphemy, 27, 144, 196; ill-gotten gains, 144; legacies, 28, 142-3, 152; legacies unspecified, 142-3 (see also under Vows, crusading, inherited, Vows, crusading, redemption by legacy); monetary contributions to funds, 27-8, 55-6, 62, 82-3 (see also under Indulgences, plenary, crusading, granted to contributors of money); redemptions, 122, 125, 152 (see also under Vows, crusading, redemptions). See also under Lay subsidies granted to *crucesignati*

Papal supremacy, 23. See also under Crusade (papal) motives for, assertion of papal supremacy

Pardoners, 96; false, 153

Paris, 63, 150

Paris, University of, 92

Paris, Matthew, o.s.b., 25 n. 6, 28, 77, 120 n. 107, 125; *Chronica majora*, ix, 19 n. 25, 23 n. 2, 69, 73-4 n. 98, 77, 79, 80, 81, 88, 89, 101 n. 7, 110, 111, 127-9, 143, 148, 159, 165-6, 187(-95), 206

Pastoureaux, 78

³Paulus, bishop of Hamar, *crucesignatus*, 140

²Payn de Chaourse, *crucesignatus* and crusader, 149 n. 96

Peckham, John, o.f.m., archbishop of Canterbury, *Register*, ix, 53-4 n. 9, 65, 117, 153 n. 120, 156, 158, 176, 177, 206

Pedro III, king of Aragon, 67, 72, 87-88, 97, 157, 172 n. 266

Pelagius, 99

²Pembroke, earl of. See under William

Penance, ecclesiastical *(poena injuncta)*, 36-51 *passim*; commutation of, 40, 99-100, 102; by crusade, 114-18 (see also under Vows, crusading, as *poena imjuncta*); list of reserved crimes commuted by taking cross, 115; by pilgrimage, 99, 100, 102; redemption of, 99, 104-5; as almsdeeds, 104-5; by substitution, 99, 104-5; vicariously performed, 104-5; voluntary, 100; sacramental imposition of supersedes solemn penance, 99-100; sacrament of, 35-51, *passim*

Persona ficta, 172

³Peter Capoccius, cardinal deacon of S. Georgio, legate (wrongly styled in text bishop-elect of Ferrara), 50, 108

Peter, bishop of Angoulême, objects to paying crusade tax, 150

Peter, bishop of Oporto, 14 n.17

Peter (Hugh?), bishop of Saintes, objects to paying crusade tax, 150

Equilibrium

THOMAS BURNS